Francis of Assisi

Also available from
Sophia Institute Press®
by Michael de la Bedoyere:

SaintMaker:
The Remarkable Life of Francis de Sales,
Shepherd of Kings and Commoners,
Sinners and Saints

Michael de la Bedoye

Francis of Assisi

The Man Who Found Perfect Joy

SOPHIA INSTITUTE PRESS®

Manchester, New Hampshire /99

Francis of Assisi: The Man Who Found Perfect Joy was originally published in 1962 by Harper and Row under the title *Francis: A Biography of
the Saint of Assisi*. This 1999 edition by Sophia Institute Press contains
minor editorial revisions throughout the text.

Copyright © 1962, 1999 Charlotte de la Bedoyere

All rights reserved

Printed in the United States of America

Jacket design by Lorraine Bilodeau

The cover artwork is a detail of Domenico Ghirlandaio's
Miracle of the Child, S. Trinita, Florence, Italy (photo
Copyright © 1997 Art Resource, New York).

Sophia Institute Press®
Box 5284, Manchester, NH 03108
1-800-888-9344
www.sophiainstitute.com

Library of Congress Cataloging-in-Publication Data

De la Bedoyere, Michael, 1900-
    [Francis]
    Francis of Assisi : the man who found perfect joy / Michael
de la Bedoyere.
       p. cm.
    Originally published: Francis. New York : Harper & Row, 1962.
    Includes bibliographical references.
    ISBN 0-918477-89-1 (pbk. : alk. paper)
    1. Francis, of Assisi, Saint, 1182-1226. 2. Christian saints —
Italy — Biography. I. Title.
BX4700.F6D38 1999
271'.302 — dc21
[B]   98-52838 CIP

99 00 01 02 03 10 9 8 7 6 5 4 3 2 1

To L.,
nearest and
dearest

Contents

Chronology

1182
Francis is born in Assisi.

1202
Francis joins in the battle of Collestrada
or Ponte San Giovanni, and is taken prisoner.

1203
Francis is released from the Perugian prison.

1205
Francis embraces the leper.

1206
The Crucifix speaks to Francis in San Damiano.

1206-1207
Francis is tried and renounces his father.

1209
Francis hears the Gospel words at the
Portiuncula (February 24); Giles joins Francis (April 23).

1210
Innocent III approves the first rule.

1212
Clare joins Francis (Palm Sunday).

May 9, 1213
The Lord Orlando gives La Verna to Francis and his followers.

1216
Honorius III approves Portiuncula Indulgence.

1217-1218
Francis sends out missionaries to foreign lands, befriends Cardinal
Ugolino, and appoints Peter Catanei as minister general.

1219
Francis embarks on a missionary journey
to Egypt and the Holy Land.

1220
Francis visits Rome, where Cardinal Ugolino
is appointed cardinal protector of the order.

March 10, 1221
Peter Catanei dies, and Elias
succeeds him as minister general.

1221-1223
Francis drafts later rules; Pope Honorius III
approves the Rule of 1223 (November 20).

1222
The Chapter of Mats convenes.

1224
Francis receives the
Stigmata on Mount La Verna.

1225
Francis composes the "Canticle of the Sun."

October 3, 1226
Francis dies at the Portiuncula.

Introduction

Few years go by without the appearance of a new life or study of Giovanni di Bernardone, universally known as Saint Francis of Assisi. Such is the measure of his popularity, not only with Christians generally, but with many others who would hardly think of interesting themselves in the life of any other saint of the Church's calendar.

There is, however, a further explanation of this popularity and the need felt by so many writers to study the life and character of Francis. It springs from the contrast between the relatively little we know for certain about him as a man among men, who lived between the years 1182 and 1226, and the immense amount we know about his formative influence on posterity. He was one of those key figures in Western history who cast a spell on the world.

As Renan said, "An anecdotal and legendary history can be truer than truth itself, for the glory of the legend belongs to the man who has known how to inspire his humble admirers with the values that, without him, they would never have discovered." And Remy de Gourmont (anything but an orthodox Christian) wrote, "No man since Saint Paul has had an equal influence on the orientation of the human spirit as the founder of the Friars Minor: a new poetry, a new art, a renewed religion have radiated from the humble Portiuncula convent through the Christian world."

This unlearned, humble little poor man of Assisi has in some way touched men and women of every generation. In him they have found a neighbor, a friend, an inspiration that has transcended the accidents of space and time and even of ideological outlook.

His own disciples did not hesitate to try to shape the actual incidents of his life in such a way as to establish a conformity between that unpresuming life and the life of Jesus Christ. This may seem to us today to be an act of daring, not far removed from blasphemy; yet it remains true that posterity has found in him an authority, a sureness, an attraction, a dedication, a simplicity, a rightness, a fearlessness, an inner joy, a love, a judgment, an understanding, a common sense, an insight into God's love and bounty, that we can only think of as a spiritual and psychological stamp, impressed by Christ, in a manner that parallels the bodily impression of the wounds of Christ in his flesh. As von Hügel expressed it: "Thus could Dante find — surely, most rightly — in the *Poverello* ['little poor one'] of Assisi — so supremely detached, so expansively attached, so heroic without rigorism, so loving without softness — perhaps the nearest reproduction of the divine paradox of the life of Jesus Himself."[1]

But to be able to say so much is very different from being able to retell the life of Saint Francis in such a way as to show

---

[1] Baron Friedrich von Hügel, *Essays and Addresses on the Philosophy of Religion* (London: J. M. Dent and Sons Ltd., 1921), 127.

and illustrate just where and why and how Francis succeeded in somehow irradiating — and also judging — not only his contemporaries and immediate followers, but also posterity. He left but a few pages of writing which can for certain be attributed to him, although they happen to include the first great poem written in the common tongue of his time. The chronology and incidents of his life have for generations been subject to higher textual criticism which requires a scientific training for proper judgment and appreciation. And as for the vast number of reported sayings and stories of his "legend," these can only be judged and used with the help of some "sixth sense" which enables the biographer to sift authenticity from part-authenticity or the fairy tale that the uncritical writers of those times judged to be edifying.

The contemporaries of Francis of Assisi had very little idea of what we call the empirical or critical spirit which for us is the necessary basis of our judgment of a man's record. They lived in a fixed world of Divine Revelation, known through faith as certain, and a closed universe whose center was the earth and whose boundary was the visible blue vault of heaven. Their primary aim was to work out the logical implications of the truths of Revelation within that closed universe, the understanding of which they had inherited from classical antiquity. They did this with consummate skill where the fundamental truths about human destiny and conduct were concerned, and it is only in matters of science and its enormously important application to the temporal ways of human living that we have to adapt what they taught. God, Revelation, and the human spirit were the only matters supremely important to them. Therefore, they were only moderately interested in mere, apparently unrelated, facts and in biographical and historical accuracy.

Yet we should not exaggerate this relative disinterest in accurate record, nor suspect all that they had to say about a saint like Francis of Assisi. In fact, it is surprising how well the record stands up to scholarly criticism. But it is significant that the story of his life was first told in *legenda*. Legend did not then mean fairy tale or made-up story — the invention of its author. It meant exactly what it said: "something to be read." Its first purpose was edification, but it was edification based on truth. But where edification is the first object, the most impressive of the various accounts was likely to win the day — and nothing was more impressive than any "legend" of God's direct and miraculous intervention in the life of a holy man.

It seems to me that against this background it is justifiable and indeed inevitable that the modern biographer, who makes no pretense to the scholarship required for the scientific assessment of the conflicting sources, should rely in the main on his own insight and flair to present his hero as a living and credible man whose behavior and character we in this age can understand — a man whose personality and actions provide a clue to the profound influence he still exerts on us in this day and age.

But in case the reader misunderstands me, let me assure him that I have taken the trouble to study the judgment and findings of scholars, such as Arnaldo Fortini, who, in his six volumes recently published,[2] has amassed vast quantities of

[2] Arnaldo Fortini, *Nova Vita di San Francesco* (Tipografia Porziuncola at Santa Maria degli Angeli, 1959). In 1981, an English translation by Helen Moak was published by Crossroad in New York under the title *Francis of Assisi*. — ED.

new information, especially where the historical background is concerned. In this country, the recent findings of Miss Rosalind B. Brooke[3] which suggests considerable changes in the traditional chronology, and the critical assessment made by Dr. Moorman,[4] recently made Bishop of Ripon, have been invaluable. But it would be pretentious of me to list the many lives and works which I have read or consulted. I have done so, not primarily with scholarship in mind, but to ensure, so far as I am able, that this attempt to re-see Francis with contemporary eyes and for the benefit of us who live in this particular age is as accurately based as is in my power.

The personality and teaching of Francis have served every generation since his death, but it is not an accident that it is in modern times that his world influence has been greatest. The reason is not difficult to discover. Francis, in his own day, challenged, with the supernatural strength which he, in his faith and simplicity, derived from the words of the Crucifix in San Damiano — "Repair my Church" — the "establishment," whether of Church or state. He did not do this in the spirit of the many would-be reformers of those times who, in seeking reform, thought it necessary also to destroy. He did it with the salute of the chivalry he adored and with the strength of his humility — a humility that derived from his love and imitation of Christ; hence his absolute belief in and devotion to the Church which represented and, indeed, was Christ on earth.

---

[3] Rosalind B. Brooke, *Early Franciscan Government: Elias to Bonaventure* (Cambridge, 1959).

[4] J. R. H. Moorman, *The Sources for the Life of St. Francis of Assisi* (Manchester, 1940).

He was no philosopher or theorist. The man who could instinctively appreciate and express the beauty of God's creation all around him equally appreciated every outward sign of inward grace.

Not the Church only, but the churches, the priests, and the least important shrine were seen by him as God's work and sign. But with an astonishing clarity of mind, he always clearly distinguished between the authenticity of the sign and the human weakness of those who carried and served the sign. Hence, whether it was a question of Church, state, or society, he could indict with a rare wisdom and rigor the false, and indeed (as he thought) the self-destroying, values and ambitions of the men who served Church, state, and society.

There was something almost savage in the "root and crop" nature of his indictment, for that indictment was literally based on Christ's words in the Gospels. For Francis, there could be no theoretical compromise, even though as a person he was the kindest, gentlest, most lovable and attractive of men. It was the unique marriage of this rigid, uncompromising standard of judgment where the great issues of Christian and human life were concerned, with his personal vision and courtesy, with his love of weak, fallible humanity, living in a world whose every sight and sound sang to him of God's goodness, which gave birth to and explains his special genius.

Francis's times were, as will be told in this book, bad times, both in Church and in social behavior and values, but at any rate, the "establishment" was far less rigid than it has grown to be in ours. Today, men are bound, more strongly than they ever were before, to social groups and fashions, to conventions, to ambitions, and to notions of the "good life," which would have utterly horrified Francis. They would have horrified him not only because in them he could have found no trace or glimmer of Christ and the Gospels, but also because he would have understood at once their intrinsically self-defeating nature.

The wonderful attraction of Francis as a man lay in the fact that he really did love happiness; he really did want men to enjoy and appreciate living. God and the world that God created sang to him of joy and beauty. There was absolutely nothing in him of the moral trickery which seeks to persuade men that they will inevitably be happy because they are trying to live up to high standards. Francis *was* happy — born happy, a gift of God like any other, and his life seems uniquely to have expressed the paradox that detachment, penance, and suffering, accepted in the right way, *can* and *do* bring sublime joy and happiness. In his case, this could be so because of his absolute and tremendous love of Christ, who so intensely suffered for mankind. But I think we should not underrate the fact that the simple, clear logic of Francis's mind and personality, combined with his natural appreciation of beauty in sight and sound and of the unspoiled human being, was a vital factor in causing him to speak quite literally when he said he found such joy even in the greatest suffering undergone for the right intention. His supernatural dedication was tremendous; but his nature, also, was one of rare natural joy and love.

Nor is the application of the moral so very obscure for us. Who has not felt a desire to be relieved of the burdens and responsibilities of life as it is lived today — life which seems to be driven on, not by our own free choice of satisfactory human living, but by the force of appetites and ambitions, by having to live up to conventions and worldly standards and what the neighbors will say? Far worse and even more enslaving are the responsibilities and anxieties which so-called good citizenship imposes on us in a world ever threatened by social, economic, and even military competition and strife. Does any of this make for true happiness?

What Francis would have told us to do in our world may well be an idle and unanswerable question. But that the free, uninhibited, sane spirit of Francis — individualist, God-centered, and therefore eccentric to our own accepted and so often self-destroying social values — is even more relevant to our own times than to his can hardly be doubted.

In telling the story of Saint Francis, with contemporary values and worries in mind, I have followed the events and crises of Francis's life in a roughly chronological fashion, but I have sought to deal with them as episodes whose significance in Francis's own development and in their moral for us has to be explained and evaluated. I am aware that this has involved a certain amount of repetition, since the moral of Saint Francis remains fundamentally the same throughout. It may be, too, that if we are to get to know Saint Francis in a deeper sense than just to know the events of his life, the repetition of essentially the same lesson will not come amiss. It is one which we badly need to understand today and to apply to ourselves, as well as may be within our powers.

I should perhaps mention here that the story of Saint Francis, as it has come down to us, abounds with the miraculous and the preternatural. Much of this will in any case be repellent to the many today who believe that miracles cannot happen, with a dogmatic certainty, comparable with, but surely much less well founded than, Christian dogmatic beliefs. For my part, I would adopt a scholastic tag and say that miracles need not be multiplied without necessity. The legend of Saint Francis certainly multiplies them. The greatest miracle in the story of Saint Francis is that of the Stigmata on Mount La Verna, and I cannot see how this miracle can be doubted without accusing Francis himself, only a few months before his death, as well as his immediate followers, of bad faith. It was the spiritual climax of his life, the gateway to his death literally with a song in his heart. I have recounted other miracles that may be harder to believe, yet which vividly illustrate his character. But I have sought to convey the character and teaching of Saint Francis through its own common sense and reasonableness rather than through the confirmatory miracles which so evidently helped and edified those who first reported them.

I would like to thank my wife for her constant interest and her unstinted help in typing; my publishers for having suggested the subject; and the fathers of the Capuchin Friary in Crawley for the loan of books from their library, books which I have kept so long as to tax their patience and their kindness.

Francis of Assisi

Chapter One

❧

Francis Overcomes His Greatest Fear

"I had rather commit thirty mortal sins than contract leprosy," the pious de Joinville said to Saint Louis.[5] He could hardly have put it more strongly, for he was saying that he would prefer to take his chance of burning in Hell for all eternity — and in the Middle Ages, men took the fire of Hell very literally — than be touched by the loathsome disease that was the terror of the times.

Housed in the lazarettos dotted all over Europe, these miserable relics of men could only walk abroad dressed in a long tunic, their hands gloved, and holding a clicker or rattle perpetually warning the passerby to keep his distance. Forbidden to talk to others, the leper had to place himself to windward when someone wished to talk to him. The Church Herself, despite Her great work for the sick, could only pray for the leper's salvation in a world beyond the miseries of this one. The leper, dire symbol of sin, was excluded from the pity for the downtrodden and the suffering, sympathy for whom was part of the medieval ideal of chivalry then in the ascendant. The leper's

---

[5] Jean de Joinville (c. 1224-1317), French chronicler; Louis IX (1214-1270), King of France from 1226-1270.

3

single hope once his leprosy had been noted and reported was the Lazar's hope, for the Church saw in the parable of Lazarus "covered with sores" who was "carried to Heaven by the angels" the spiritual symbol of the leper.[6] Hence, when the bells rang to announce the banning of a leper, people came, silently and morbidly curious to watch, as the touching ceremony which cut the leper off from sound mankind was ready to begin.

"My brother, God's dear *poverello*," said the priest, vested in cassock and cotta,[7] "through sadness and tribulation, through illness, desolation, leprosy, and so many earthly miseries lies the road to the heavenly kingdom where misery and infirmity are no more, where all are pure and clean, without shadow of beastliness, more resplendent than the sun. . . . My brother, this separation only touches your body, for in your spirit, which is so much more important, you may still be one with us. Keep hidden, and be patient. God be with you." Then the priest, taking up a handful of black earth from the cemetery, scattered it over the leper's head, saying, "Die to the world, and be born again to God."

This rite, while giving consolation and supreme hope to the spirit, could not alter the gradual thickening of the skin, the lumpy excrescences, the open sores, the falling away of the eyebrows, the grotesque enlarging of the ears and nose, the eventual dropping off of the fingers and toes, and the fetid smell. It was a man condemned to be a diseased deformity who

---

[6] Luke 16:19-31.

[7] A cassock is a closely fitting, ankle-length robe. A cotta, a type of surplice, is a short, loose, white vestment worn over a cassock.

walked away from the Church and the world to be born again of suffering and isolation.

"Click, click, click." The sound drove healthy people to one side of the road as they held their noses and looked the other way. It was a sound only too familiar to the men, women, and children of thirteenth-century Assisi as they trudged their way down the steep, dusty slopes from their little fortress city through the thick woods on to the great Umbrian plain, once floor of a vast lake. There, sealed within the delicate green of the great valley and its vast amphitheater of rosy hills and blue mountain ranges — the "Galilee of Italy," as Renan was one day to call it — stood Assisi's *ospidale*, San Lazzaro dell'Arce, the town's lazaretto. It was not so very far distant, as it happened, from a desolate little rectangular chapel, destined one day to become a flaming basilica in the gold of the setting sun. Within range of this hospice of living death, the good countrymen would be on the lookout for the lepers, the kindlier among them murmuring a prayer, the rougher a curse, but all intent, if possible, on avoiding the *miselli*, the miserable ones.

All except one: a young man in his middle twenties. A young man who was then far indeed from dreaming, dreamer though he was, that his life would be commemorated in the golden frame housing that little chapel which would in years to come catch the eye of numberless visitors as of an evening they looked down over the town across the great valley.

His clothes, rather than his face, caught the eye as he rode that day. He had neither the time nor the inclination to look around him, but anyone could tell that only the best quality and dye in the cloth, only the most fashionable cut in cloak and hose, were good enough for him.

Courteously, the rider would smile back a greeting from a passerby, and with a special love and tenderness, he would lean over to give a coin to a passing beggar; but his smile was now an inner smile, his charity almost a ritual, as though a distant habitual reflection of the laughter and the glad largesse of the person whom all the people of Assisi knew as the born leader of the fashionable younger set of the town. Even though his clothes were the best a man could buy, they were unusually sober and hardly warm enough for this time of the year. He had, in fact, hastily put them on that morning with hardly a thought for personal comfort. His large eyes, "black and candid," had an apprehensive and almost frightened look, and those who recognized him may have wondered once again how it had come about that this "*beau-laid*," less than average in height, slender and delicate in build, with his thin, unmanly beard, had ever gained ascendancy over the swaggering young toughs and bullies of a town of very doubtful moral reputation.

"Click, click, click." The dreaded sound could now be heard in an empty countryside and it was growing louder. It filled the rider with a fascinated dread, for he alone of those who passed by that day was being driven toward it by an inner compulsion.

It was not by any means the first time that this compulsion had led him near the lazaretto. He had long been haunted by the despair and misery that lay behind those thick stone walls, yet unable, prodigal as he had been to the beggars and the sick, to feel anything but stark horror when he saw one of those outcasts. Those *miselli*, ritually cut off from the fellowship of mankind, were still, his conscience told him, his brothers — his brothers in Christ our Lord, aching for "the crumbs that fell from the rich man's table."[8] They were as much his brothers as the beggars of Assisi and of Rome itself, where he had once changed clothes with a beggar to show his chivalrous sympathy with the oppressed. And he was a rich man with indulgent parents who had never denied him anything he wanted so long as it helped to advertise his family's increasing prosperity. But it was an even deeper compulsion that had brought him again and again to the spot, and sent him galloping away as the sight and smell of these repulsive creatures turned nightmare into hideous and unbearable reality.

But at last he had come to realize with absolute clarity and certainty that to gallop away from the lepers was also to gallop away from his deepest self, from that mysterious, unanalyzed, indeed incomprehensible feeling that called him to the greatness — to the sanctity even — which he knew he had it in him to fulfill.

Years earlier, when he had been captured and made prisoner, in the clash between the Assisians and the Perugians, he had boasted to his fellow prisoners: "You'll see, one day I shall be worshiped by the whole world." Another time, as in full armor he had ridden south to the wars, seeking the honors of knighthood, he had exclaimed — once again, surely, to the mocking delight of those around him — "I know that one day I shall become a great prince." Was this the adolescent exhibitionism of a dreamer, who all the time knew in his heart that he would spend his life dully trading fine cloth at his father's counter and one day inherit his share of the *nouveau riche* business? Everyone thought so.

[8] Luke 16:21.

But this was to be the thousandth, even the millionth, indeed the unique exception. Within that frail, unprepossessing body, behind that showman's gesture, were the seeds of a greatness far beyond any exhibitionist's rosiest dream. But whether they were ever to grow and fulfill themselves must depend, as always, on that mystery of human nature, the free act of response and decision.

On this particular day, the young man's hour of testing had come — he knew it. Already he had failed — perhaps once, twice, three times.

The appalling struggle in the nature of a person so unfitted (it seemed) for the heroic had already led to strange and morbid fancies.

He had been haunted by the vision of that old woman in the marketplace, an ugly, pious hunchback whom he passed every day, kindly dropping in her apron a shower of little coins, for he was known to be the most recklessly generous man in town. Was he trying to buy the cure for this compulsion by the natural generosity within him and with the grand showy gesture which made him so popular? Was he simply acting — as it seemed he had been when, on that pilgrimage to Rome, he had scattered his gold on the altar and steps of Saint Peter's in disgust at the parsimony of his fellow pilgrims and then gone out into the sunshine to change clothes with a beggar and play the part of a beggar himself? Now, as he rode on to meet the test which would show whether he was a mere play-actor and dreamer or someone who could truly realize in himself a princely destiny, he shuddered again as he thought of the old woman and her frightening hump, obsessed by the fear that he, so lately the most popular fop of Assisi, would grow a deformity like hers. Was it, as we are told, a temptation of the Devil threatening this calamity if he pursued his quixotic purpose with the lepers? Or was it not rather an expression of his deep-seated fear that if he touched one of these deformities, he, too, would soon find himself cut off from his fellows and be condemned to shuffle along the roads as he clicked his dreaded warning?

But if his whole over-refined being seemed to turn over within him so as to conjure up phantasms and phobias warning him against the terrible deed that, as he well knew, could alone save him for his true destiny, he also felt himself not to be without powerful help, for had he not heard deep within his soul a voice urgently calling to him? As he recalled it, he repeated it again and again to himself that morning. It had said, "Francis, you want, do you not, to do my will? Well, then, the first thing you have to do is to despise and loathe everything for which your senses are crying out. You must, instead, love and long for those very things you have been despising and loathing. Do this, and you will find out that what once seemed to you to be attractive and pleasing will seem bitter and beyond bearing, while all that you have hitherto loathed will be transformed into something joyous and infinitely attractive."

"Click, click, click." The sore-covered deformity of what had once been a young man like Francis met Francis's terrified eyes. The moment had come. It was now or never.

Jumping off his horse, Francis ran forward to meet Lazarus. Did his failing flesh and blood once again hesitate and shrink back as, plunging his hands into his purse, Francis pulled out a handful of gold to pour onto the poor wretch? Too often he had paid himself off by paying others. No, not this time. He gave the gold and himself; closing his eyes maybe — and who would not? — he held out his long, thin arms and grasped the leper's cold, emaciated, ulcerated hand, raised it to his lips, and kissed it with a recklessness and native courtesy which were ever to be characteristic of his dedicated life.

The deed was done. The test was over. Henceforth he was to be a free man, enjoying as few mortals have enjoyed the freedom and spontaneity of the sons of God.[9]

Twenty years later, Francesco di Bernardone, virtually blind, recalled in that short, solemn, pleading document of his — his last will and testament to the world — that this was the moment when he first achieved freedom. "In my worldly days," he dictated to Brother Leo, "I could not bear even to look a leper in the face, but the Lord led me to them, and I showed mercy to them. It was like a somersault. Things that I had thought utterly contrary to my nature suddenly became delightful to me — as delightful to my senses as to my spirit. Soon after that, I left the world."

Evidently he had never forgotten either the horror or the bliss of that moment. Decisive in his own life, it is decisive, too, for those who want to know the secret of Saint Francis of Assisi.

Only if we can feel in ourselves something of the horror which leprosy aroused in a healthy, vain, exhibitionist, and rather snobbish young man shall we be able to measure the magnitude of this single act of self-conquest. This response to what he knew in his heart to be God's will for him, impossible as it seemed to his fastidious nature, was to afford him the

[9] Cf. Rom. 8:21.

power to assess, with deadly accuracy and yet unprecedented balance and love, the paltry worth of life on earth and its vanities as all but a chosen few are content to live it. From now on, he was to walk his own way — a way that seemed crazy to the world, but a way which has ever since haunted the world.

Many there are who condemn the vanities and illusions of worldly life, but do so without sympathy and understanding, do so as a matter of principle or with a "holier than thou" attitude. But Francis had shared, and would always share. He had in his moment of self-conquest "known himself," and known all other men in their weakness. He would not need to condemn the man when condemning his stupidity and his sin. He would lure him to better things, as God had lured Francis himself. Having achieved this freedom, he could live before his fellows and before posterity the free life which inevitably follows the dedication of the whole self — the supreme freedom of the supreme goodness. He would live the detached, utterly selfless, Godward life which so mysteriously breaks the hearts of sinners and worldlings, as well as the hearts of saints. Allow this young man of Assisi to have been vain and snobbish and silly, as in all honesty he seems to have been, and you still have to allow that these weaknesses were the raw material with which, in conquering himself, he conquered the world, as no one else has done save his Master, Christ, the Son of God.[10]

[10] Cf. John 16:33.

Chapter Two

Francis Searches for Worldly Joy

In hearing the story of Francis and the leper, the reader may
have been left with a false impression. The incident marked
the climax of a long and painful period of self-conquest, not a
sudden and spectacular conversion. Such sudden conversions,
although they manifest the power of God, do not easily fit into
our humdrum lives. Nor do they fit into the very human life
and character of Francesco di Bernardone. He started like us,
and his search for the meaning and secret of human life took
him, like us, a long time. His success story in its end differs rad-
ically from our failure stories, but in its beginnings we can all
feel very much at home.

What sort of a person was this boy who one day was to find
freedom in kissing a leper and, by doing so, was to turn the
world we know (and too much love) upside down, so that anyone who cares to follow him may see it for the first time right
side up? In what kind of world did he live? What had been his
hopes, his ambitions, his ideas of a successful life?

Born in 1182, he was the son of Pietro di Bernardone, a
very well-to-do cloth merchant of Assisi, who lived, it is now
believed, in a house situated above the family business near
the site of the present Assisi post office. This tall house, to

which access was probably gained by an external staircase, was then sandwiched between the Benedictine church of Saint Paul and the church of Saint Nicholas at the western end of the town's marketplace, the present Piazza Vittorio Emmanuele, near the Roman temple of Minerva now converted into a church.

Quite literally, Francis was born a bourgeois, a member of the citizenry, one of the merchant class. At that time, the class was rapidly growing in wealth and social importance at the expense of the feudal aristocracy, especially in the self-governing Italian towns in which petty wars were endemic, giving opportunity for rapid enrichment against the background of increased international trading due especially to the Crusades and the recent sack of Constantinople. It was part of the picture of social change which was affecting all of western Europe.

His mother, whose name was Pica, may have been a French woman from Picardy (hence the name), where her merchant husband, Pietro, could have met her while on one of his frequent journeys to the great cloth markets of Europe.

Possibly the youngest son (we know for certain of another brother, Angelo), since we are told that his mother loved him "more than her other sons," the baby came into the world while his father was on one of these business journeys to France. The baby was baptized in the present cathedral of San Ruffino (then uncompleted) and christened Giovanni (John).

This child was born with a gift for being different, and by no means the least remarkable example of this gift was that we hear no more of his baptismal name. Sooner or later, he came to be called "the Frenchman," Francesco, and by doing so, he not only became the only saint canonized with a nickname, but he also initiated the army of saints, popes, kings, princes, and common-or-garden folk who, in seven hundred years of Christendom, have been called Francis.

The nickname, according to one explanation, was given to him because of his father's absence in France at the time of his birth, although it may also be a confirmation of his mother's French origin. But the most likely explanation is to be sought in his own rapturous delight as a boy with the French troubadours and jongleurs who roamed about Italy composing and singing their love songs and instilling a new code of courtesy and chivalry toward women. It may be that his father took him more than once as a child to France on his expeditions. This would have helped to make him familiar with the French Provençal tongue. These trade journeys, examples of a fever for profit, were highly organized affairs, the merchants traveling caravan-fashion to the French and Flemish markets. Because of this, the undertaking of such long journeys involved no special danger for wife and family.

From the start, one must realize that Francis, both before and after his conversion, was to be a rebel and an eccentric — a crank, as the serious, self-important men of the world would see him. In one sense, at least, he was never to take himself or his life seriously, as men understand the word *seriously*, namely, succeeding in the conventional forms of career-making and good citizenship. He would be playboy outside the conventions of respectable behavior, or saint outside the conventions of sanctity. It was this which was to make him so original and, consequently, a man who, undreamed by himself, would profoundly affect posterity, revolutionizing the then-accepted standards in art, literature, social conventions, and social values.

He went, but with little pedagogic profit, to the episcopal school attached to the church of Saint George, situated on the site of the present church of Santa Chiara, as lovely a spot as any in that city hung over the plain. He certainly learned to read and write — the latter badly, but with a firm hand, so that in the days to come, he would always dictate. Inevitably he picked up a smattering of Latin, which comes easily to the Italian ear.

Francis's father wanted no scholar son, but a practical one who could be apprenticed from his earliest years to the all-important business of money-making. The boy, it seems, was ready enough to do his father's bidding, but it was clear from the earliest years that his was an altogether different character with traits that probably derived from his mother.

The church of Saint George was the center of the cult of chivalry, and the boy's lifelong devotion to its ideals must have been rooted in the traditions of that church-school. His passion for the knightly code developed into something like a mania as he grew up. The freakish, extroverted idealism of the troubadours, in which poetry and song about joy and sadness and a longing for the unattainable, the heroic, the perfect fulfillment of love, exciting the hearts of rough men used to a squalid and ribald code, took Francis right out of the bourgeois, conventional Christian world of the grasping, ambitious, and tough Bernardones. His later relations with his father and brothers strongly suggest from the start an only half-suppressed dislike of everything for which his father stood. This fact may well provide the best clue to the problem which preoccupied early biographers when dealing with the early years of so unique a saint.

The morals of Assisi were notorious even in the tough Italy of those days and not only where the subject of sex was concerned. "A New Babylon" was the title given to the little town by the early chroniclers.

Fortini gives a detailed account of the debauchery which annually took place in Francis's own parish church of Saint Nicholas when on that saint's feast day the boy-bishop was installed. It was a kind of saturnalia, lasting through Christmas and the feast of the Holy Innocents, during which the common people were allowed a temporary compensation for the harsh life which they led under the feudal, communal, and religious authorities. The boy-bishop, in effect, symbolized, during this period of the year, the upsetting of the normal social order. This annual psychological détente or safety valve was set against a background of murders, beatings, thuggery, robbery of every kind, oppression, cheating, and all forms of turpitude. The few powerful or rich, whether nobles or *nouveaux riches*, lorded it over the common people, most of these desperately poor and too often a prey to the many diseases of the time, thus creating, then as always, a habitual climate of crime and debauchery.

Thomas of Celano,[11] Francis's first and most reliable biographer, tells us that the boy was no different from the youth of the day who had been taught from their earliest years, "by signs and sounds, certain very shameful and detestable things." With such a start, "when the children are a little older, they always fall into worse conduct still of their own impulse. . . .

---

[11] Thomas of Celano (c. 1190-1260), who joined Francis's band of friars around 1214, wrote two biographies of the saint.

When they have begun to enter the gates of youth, what manner of persons do you think they become? Then indeed, plunging into every kind of debauchery, since they are free to fulfill their pleasure, they give themselves over with all their might to the service of wickedness."

He speaks, too, of Francis sheltering under the name of Christianity until his twenty-fifth year, drawing others into sin, dressing up in women's clothes, and leading many into evil and crime. A later Franciscan tradition sought to soften Celano's unedifying testimony. The breviary hymn to Saint Francis was even changed. The original words, "*Plus suis nutritoribus se gessit insolenter*," were changed to "*Divinis charismatibus preventus est clementer.*" In other words: "He behaved worse than his elders" became "He was saved by divine grace."

This pious softening of the realities proved unfortunate, for the later story of Francis's life only becomes intelligible when we realize the true causes and the real nature of his renunciation of the world in terms more total than in the case of any other of the well-known Christian saints — and yet in terms which possess a delicacy, attraction, and humanity from the fact that, tainted by the ways of an exceedingly wicked world, Francis had nevertheless instinctively grown up to seize, from the perversions of love, social interchange, gallantry, ambition, and human kinship, that which was basically good and fruitful in them.

We know for certain that Francis was not spared carnal temptations in later life, and he had a way of dealing with them that was not wholly traditional. Celano himself, in the second life which he wrote, tells the wonderful story of the occasion when Francis suffered "a grievous temptation of lust."

Every normal means of ridding himself of the temptation failed, so he went out of the cell and "plunged naked into deep snow. Then, collecting the snow in handfuls, he made seven snowmen and began to address his body thus: 'See, this large one is your wife; those four are your two sons and daughters; and those other two are the servant and the maid needed to wait on them. Hurry up and find enough clothes for them all, for they are all dying of cold. If, however, you are beginning to feel that all this trouble is a little too much for you, then remember that it is better to serve God only.' "

If Francis's early life left him a prey to this humble and natural temptation, at least he kept his sense of humor over it and found a very sensible way of dealing with it. In the end, he must have thoroughly enjoyed his own joke.

The proximate occasions of sins, as the theologians put it, not only attracted the young Francis, but surrounded him wherever he went and whatever he did. He was, in fact, the center around which they circled, for he was the born leader of his age group. Fortini argues that he became one of the most prominent figures in the Company of San Vittorino and the Bastone (meaning "staff"), a society of young folk of both sexes — singers, dancers, and merrymakers — who, on certain feast days and other holidays, danced and feasted night and day as they made their way through the streets, singing love songs in a kind of bacchanalian revelry which too often led to quarrels and even murder. Bullfighting was another manifestation of the high spirits of Assisi youth at the time. One may hope that the boy who possessed an unusual power over the animals he loved disapproved from the beginning of this particular sport.

Yet two factors suggest that all this dissipation went with a naturally good disposition of temperament. The first — on Celano's own witness — was the natural generosity of his nature. "Extremely rich, he was more interested in spending all he had than in accumulating money." However much it might harm him, he gave freely to friends and to the poor.

The second was that, from early life, he was to find in the idealism of chivalry, itself also expressed in song and music, the antidote to these baser pleasures. In this new idealism, he would find his mind turning away from the self-centered, arrogant viciousness, so typical in all times of the young when given too much money and the chance of irresponsible independence.

Knighthood itself, to which Francis (since he was not nobly born) could not aspire, save through some deed of valor on the battlefield, was then seen as a kind of lay religious order, a quasi-sacrament. It was not that Italian knights and knightly warriors troubled very much to live up to the highest ideals of their profession — or rather, they easily passed from a mood of idealistic fervor to one of crudity and savagery. But at this period, they were at least beginning to be affected by the wider concept of chivalry which was sweeping over Italy from the north. Many of the great troubadours of France, such as William of Poitiers, Bernard de Ventadour, Macabru, Peter of Auvergne of Toulouse, Vidal, and Rambaut of Orange, visited Italy, and in the songs they made up as they traveled, they recalled the ancient and better times when bravery and courtesy went hand in hand under the inspiration of Christian traditions and legends.

Although the Church had always exalted the place of woman — how could it have been otherwise, given the rank accorded to the Virgin Mary? — other factors, which may have included Arab and Albigensian[12] influences, helped to create an ideal of love as a pursuit and passion for its own romantic self. Woman as such embodied the ideal which men worthy of the name sang of and fought for. It was becoming fashionable to fall in love with a code of love rather than with women in the flesh. This kind of romanticism, although not without its own dangers for a generation in which personal lives too often remained crude, was exactly fitted to inspire a first idealism in a young man like Francesco di Bernardone, poet, dreamer, swaggerer, man of the world, and determined to be different in every way from the duller, grosser fellows around him — and with the opportunity to accomplish his purpose. He would become different one day especially in his capacity to rise above mere carnal passion and place woman herself on a throne to be worshiped with all knightly honor and courtesy in song, music, and dance. One may reasonably deduce that as he grew older, his dissipation became more of an outward show, a cover to hide the deeper feelings that were making themselves felt within him.

Francis, then, victim to some extent of a degrading early environment, made a very bad start, but he must in time have overcome that handicap to find in the picturesque figure of troubadour and knight a providential stage along his destined way and one which throughout his life would notably affect

---

[12] Albigensianism was a dualist heresy begun in southern France in the eleventh century that regarded the flesh and material creation as evil and rejected the sacraments, Church authority, and the doctrines of Hell, Purgatory, and the resurrection of the body.

the special, individualist character of his life, his way of seeing things, and his work.

In those days when life was not confined by the conventions of respectability, a boy, living, under the blue skies, the cheerful social life of a small Italian town within whose walls every man was a neighbor, gossip, friend, or only too often deadly enemy, very quickly grew into a man. With his highly prosperous and influential merchant father to back him and perhaps shrewdly to discern in him no bad advertisement for the family's name, Francis, dressed in the finest wool and silks, according to the standards of the international fashions, had the means, even in his early teens, of outshining everyone of his class in Assisi.

His hard-fisted father, however, must have often ground his teeth and clenched his fists with annoyance at the prodigality and profligacy of his strange son; but the shrewdness and experience of the parvenu trader made him believe that his boy was also a likely person, when tamed by life and experience, to take advantage of the inflationary times and carry the name of Bernardone to further prosperity in money-making, as well as to the higher social ranges of power and nobility. Such successful commoners, just recently freed from service to the feudal lords, spiritual and temporal, had at this time the world at their feet, if only they made the best use of their opportunities.

All this is surely implied in Pietro di Bernardone's words, as reported by the faithful chronicle of *The Three Companions:*[13]

---

[13] That is, *Legenda Trium Sociorum*, writings about Saint Francis based on the two biographies by Thomas of Celano and other sources.

"The way you pour out your money, one would think you were the son of a great prince, not of a simple merchant." The smirk of satisfaction on his face is not hard to imagine; and the ebullient boy, whose personality and lively imagination compensated for his small size and unprepossessing appearance, his delicacy of build and delicate, shining eyes, had no shame about nursing hopes that one day he would indeed be a great and noble knight — and why not, indeed, a prince?

Of Francis's religious life as a boy and young man, we hear practically nothing. Yet when very young, he must have been deeply impressed by the universal mourning caused by the fall of Jerusalem, a tragedy that shocked all Christendom.[14] We cannot but see him as an observant although hardly fervent Catholic, readily, but tactfully, showing his disapproval, not only of the irreverence and blasphemy then only too common, but of the novel, reformist views of the many who in those days imagined that religious standards could be improved by questioning the principles and practices on which the Church rested.

The outward, visible signs of inward power would always be most important to Francis, whether as a holy man, a poet, a friend, or a nature lover. Naturally well-balanced in his spiritual outlook through life, Francis, as a young man, would have found little difficulty in combining a light-hearted and even sinful life with respect and love for religion and, as we know, with a genuine delight in acts of generosity toward all worse off, in spirit or body, than himself. The picturesque religious

---

[14] In 1187, Jerusalem was taken by Moslem forces led by Saladin (1137-1193), sultan of Egypt and Syria.

ceremonies and pageants — for many, the only compensation for the miseries of the dark, daily grind — must also have delighted him for their color, beauty, and symbolic significance.

A mixed-up young fellow, as most imaginative and restless people tend to be? Certainly — but all the ingredients were at least sincere expressions of a personality capable of impressing and leading all with whom he came into contact, despite the lack of judgment and application to which parents and schoolmasters, then as today, look for indications of a young person's successful future.

Knowing what was to come, one wonders whether Francis, even then, on some beautiful moonlit evening, would take a few of his more poetic friends to wander down the wooded paths or out to the wild isolation of the rugged hills above the town to sing of the beauty of creation and the wonder of that world of dark, shadowy masses beneath the silver light, in such contrast with the cruelties, passions, and ambitions of unregenerate man. One wonders, too, whether even then Francis possessed that rare power over animal creation so that the cats and the dogs, the horses and the donkeys (too often maltreated and neglected by those around him), the birds and the rabbits would instinctively come nearer to him, knowing that this boy was their special friend. One can certainly imagine him, especially when still very young, exercising his power over the creatures of the countryside to the surprise and wonder of other children. Alas, all this has been overlooked by the chroniclers of his earliest days.

Chapter Three

※

Francis Ventures Off to Battle

Daydreams, dissipations, dressing up: such things alone do not, alas, make knights. It was the other side of Francis's character which prompted him to seize the opportunity that came his way to tread the harder road toward the fulfillment of his great ambitions. In order to become a knight, one had to be ready to take the discipline and knocks of a soldiering career, for which, in those days, a city like Assisi would offer opportunities in plenty.

The town stands nobly on a spur of Monte Subasio, and the endless rolling mountain ranges cover strategic positions over the roads that lead south from Florence, Arezzo, and Perugia to Spoleto, Rieti, Rome, and the distant south, the gateway toward the lands of the Saracens[15] waiting to be conquered for Christ — and the rich loot which lay within the grasp of their conquerors.

The end of the twelfth century was a period of political and social change between the weakening feudal age, represented by the Imperial Germanic cause of the Ghibellines, and the rise of the civic communes under the protection of the papacy in the party called, for outdated reasons, the Guelphs.

---

[15] The Moslem opponents of the Crusaders.

Only a few years before the birth of Francis, the consul-governed Commune of Assisi had been involved in fierce struggles between the feudal lords, whose massive, heavily defended castles dotted the heights of the countryside, and the burghers, who had risen from the artisan and laboring classes as commercial opportunities increased. The latter were claiming and maintaining the rights to which they felt entitled through their rapidly growing wealth and industry. It was a phase in the long struggle between the *Majores* and the *Minores*, the latter to become a keyword in Franciscan history.

The *Minores* had felt that it was now or never. Unless they were prepared to fight the lords who stood above them in every sense and defeat them once and for all, they would be reduced forever to the servile status imposed upon them by the emperor's representative in Assisi, Conrad von Lutzenfeld, Count of Assisi, who morally and physically stood over the town in his ancient *rocca*, or fortified castle.

These were years of famine and misery for the common people and a time of political dread for the merchants like Pietro di Bernardone. They were times symbolized in Assisian history by the voice of an unknown man who, foreseeing the clash to come, went about the streets chanting the words "*Pax et bonum*" ("Peace and goodness") — words which were to make a very deep impression on the boy Francesco, yet words whose significance would not be felt by him for many years. To rid themselves of Conrad and establish forever their communal independence was the ambition of the proud people of Assisi.

When Francis was sixteen years old, Conrad decided to change sides and journey to Rome to do homage to the new young Pope, Innocent III.[16] It was the people's opportunity, and they rose against the Imperial soldiers in the *rocca* and destroyed it. In order to ensure their future security against all the feudal lords in the fortresses above the town, they built stout walls and defendable gates around the city, parts of which, like the ruins of the *rocca* itself, have endured until this day.

The victory over the despots which finally established the independence of the burghers was followed by a tempestuous attack against the menacing lords who surrounded the town. Sassorosso — on the eastern flank of Monte Subasio and near the Benedictine monastery so familiar to Francis because of his family's association with the Benedictine church near his house — Montemoro, Poggio San Damiano, and many others were attacked.

We know nothing of the young Francis's role during those years of civic feud, but we can hardly doubt that the young dreamer of knightly prowess wanted to play as active a part in the struggle as in the reckless dissipation which an atmosphere of war engenders. Later, as we shall see, he was to prove himself an expert builder of walls which have also endured to this day. Can we doubt that he learned the art as one of the volunteers who labored so effectively and rapidly in securing themselves behind impregnable ramparts?

It was only five years later that Francis the soldier took his place in the certain records of history. This time, the issue was very different and much more dangerous. The defeated lords of Sassorosso and the other feudal fortresses decided to obtain

[16] Innocent III (1160-1216), Pope from 1198.

redress by a carefully calculated ruse. They asked for citizen-ship of the neighboring papal city of Perugia, whose size and splendor far outmatched Assisi, promising in return to put un-der Perugian overlordship Assisi lands, situated at Collestrada near the Ponte San Giovanni, which crosses the Tiber half-way between the two towns. Naturally, the rivalry between the two towns was of long standing.

To submit to this high-handed action on the part of the feudal lords would involve Assisi in a humiliation that was not to be borne, even though Assisi could hardly hope to overcome Perugia, especially at a time when it was trying to consolidate its threatened victory over its own lords. "Losing face" was as unforgivable a sin in those days as it is today. Both sides real-ized that it meant war, and both feverishly prepared for it — a war which would really settle whether the commune or the lords, the *Minores* or the *Majores*, would in future hold and rule Assisi.

In November 1202, when Francis was twenty, Assisi de-cided that its men must go forth and challenge the men of Perugia. In medieval fashion, the bells ringing and the trum-pets sounding, the available menfolk of Assisi, organized ac-cording to parishes and professional guilds and followed by the great bullock-drawn carriage with its cross and altar draped with the red and blue colors of Assisi, set out from the heart of the town. With them went the archers and the cavalry, to which latter company Francis belonged, since he was a rich man able to afford chargers and equipment. The womenfolk, proud of their handsome, excited men, yet anxious for their fate, applauded the splendid pageant even though they knew only too well what might happen. We can see Francis among the company — a picturesque, richly accoutered figure, even though so small and frail for the shirt-mail, the cone-shaped helmet, and the heavy lance.

Alas, like so many of those who issued forth from the gates of Assisi that morning, he was to ride, not to glory, but to defeat and humiliation and nearly to his death.

The Assisian army marched to take up defensive positions on the hill (*colle*) and road (*strada*) in front of the bend in the Tiber where the bridge crossed it. The Perugians, infuriated by the audacity of their enemies, hurried down to give battle. The struggle was soon over. The splendid military procession that had so proudly made its way through the bare winter countryside was cut to pieces by the Perugians, and Francis himself was lucky to be taken prisoner.

It was a day which was to remain vividly in his mind all through his life. Years later, he seemed to relive the dire scene when, preaching in Perugia, he rebuked Perugian soldiers who were mocking him and saying, "We will not listen to him, for he comes from Assisi." In answer, Francis prophesied dire consequences for them. But far deeper was the impression made on him by the useless slaughter and the fatuity of men who chose the fatal lottery of war to determine who should gain power and who should lose it. The voice of the preacher, "*Pax et bonum, pax et bonum,*" echoed in his heart from then on, and he would never be able to still it.

The battle of Collestrada or Ponte San Giovanni was in fact but one incident in an undecided war that lasted some years and played an important part in the nature and meaning of Francis's conversion. That now he should be clamped into a Perugian jail was providential. Because of his status as the son of the rich Pietro di Bernardone and as a cavalryman, he was imprisoned with other men of birth in conditions at least a little better than the horrors reserved for the common soldier.

Francis was unaware that, among the nobles who had gone over from Assisi to Perugia, there was a young daughter of the patrician Offreducci family called Clare. Might not she, although still so young, have accompanied her mother to visit the sick prisoners and recognized among them the pale, drawn, suffering face of the young man whose name was on everyone's lips in Assisi — the rakish son of Bernardone?

At first, Francis must have remained fairly cheerful in prison despite disappointment, the bitter cold, and the rough food, not to mention the teasing which the stronger and tougher men reserved for him in particular. For it was now that he retorted to a fellow prisoner who could not understand why he remained light-hearted in such dreadful conditions: "Who do you think I am? One fine day, the whole world will bow to me." It was the same courageous prisoner who instinctively took the side of "a very proud and unbearable man," as Celano describes him. So unpleasant was this fellow that the others agreed to boycott him. Somehow Francis's genius for friendship accomplished the impossible, and his companions were at length induced to bear with the unbearable man.

These two prison stories taken together tell us a good deal about Francis in his early twenties; native goodness and understanding were always to be found behind the flashy facade.

But to imprison a lively, volatile nature like that of Francis — extroverted in behavior, yet inwardly imaginative; a dreamer, a lover, a person who could not do without the beauties of God's creation now cut off from him by thick prison walls — was inevitably to drive him sooner rather than later to melancholy introspection. His very being needed, as it always would, the fresh, invigorating air of freedom, both mental and physical; the wide horizon; the hills; the little odd corners where, at his leisure, he could concentrate on the delicacy of a flower, the close-up beauty of an insect, the strength of a jutting rock. Deprived of all this, he soon fell very sick — sickness of a gravity sufficient to end his days. According to the custom of the times, often merciful under the outward harshness, he was released.

Celano seems to go out of his way to account for this illness as the penalty of "sin in youthful heat." This was a commonplace diagnosis of the times, especially where the observer was a man of religion. But unless Francis was already the victim of some wasting disease, like tuberculosis (which has been suggested), he would have had to be corrupt indeed to have been weakened through such a cause. We may safely dismiss the suggestion, and find in the confinement of a medieval prison acting on a person delicate in every sense of the word, a sufficiently obvious cause of grave illness. Celano himself, in fact, unconsciously admits as much when he says that Francis's first desire on leaving prison and thus recovering a little was "to look curiously on the landscape around . . . at the beauty of the fields, the pleasantness of the vineyards, on anything that is fair to see." The disease, in other words, was the blindness, deafness, and numbness imposed on a person of such exceptional sensitivity.

But a year's imprisonment had done its work and, as Celano insists, Francis found to his dismay that the things in which he had previously delighted now seemed to have lost their old magic. It was not only the body and its sense impressions which, he discovered as he hobbled about with a stick, had been affected, but he had lost that spirit within him which had given to his body its *joie de vivre* and to his senses the spiritual power to interpret and enjoy the color and shape and feel of the world around him. In other words, instead of rediscovering the world he had so loved, he felt he had lost all savor in living. As so many others have done after a long illness, he found himself intolerably depressed. This depression not only made it impossible for him to enjoy sheer living, as of old; it made him wonder whether, after all, there was so much to be said for the parties, the songs, the dances, and the universal acclaim, all of which used to be so tremendously stimulating.

This kind of reaction is common enough among ordinary mortals, especially in a youthful crisis. In fact, the illness and the subsequent depression seemed slowly to work their way out of his system and to leave him, as he thought, as keen as ever to enjoy fresh exploits and more good times in the lordly manner to which he had accustomed the town. At the back of his mind, even while he was resuming the old way of living, there was, however, a strange and novel sense of deep dissatisfaction to which he could hardly give a name — some underlying positive yearning which he could not explain, even to himself. Looking back later, he would be able to give it its proper name: an obscure awareness of Divine Love calling deep down within him.

Francis was as yet far from understanding this and, insofar as he felt any need to do anything different, from acting on it. We have to think of him during this period of illness and recovery as a person still largely unconscious of anything so very unsatisfactory in his record. By all his standards, he had done very well indeed. A success in Assisi, immensely popular, a true soldier still treated as a hero, even though he had suffered the ill-fortune of being dismounted and taken prisoner, and — so far as we know — giving satisfaction to his parents, at least as a good advertisement for the House of Bernardone, he saw no reason why his passing sense of dissatisfaction with the progress of the future prince should not be cured by embarking on the next step in his promising career.

The perfect opportunity soon presented itself. In it, religious and romantic idealism were conveniently wedded, together with the chance of real distinction as a soldier to make up for the misfortunes of the past.

He had made friends with a young Count Gentile. This may have been his real name or an invention of the chroniclers to suggest the man's gentlemanly status. This nobleman evidently discussed at length with Francis certain plans to go to Apulia, Italy's heel, to fight under the already legendary knight and hero Walter de Brienne, to defend the boy King of Sicily, later to be the Emperor Frederick II, and his widowed mother. She had put herself under the protection of the powerful, young Pope Innocent. It was another version of the old theme: the longstanding struggle between empire and papacy, Germany and Italy, feudalism and the rising bourgeoisie. But the glamour that attracted Francis was the protection of an endangered boy and his mother. Even more exciting in Francis's mind was the thought that beyond Apulia lay, across the seas, the lands of the infidels, the conquest of whom, in the name of the Cross, called to every decent young Italian with opportunity, ambition, and hunger for glory.

Francis was fascinated by the call and the vision. The old days had returned. They had, indeed, become vastly better days.

The outcome suggests that he also saw in the adventure not only a chance of attaining at last to true knighthood, but a chance of escape — escape from his father and the avaricious profit-making and power-seeking values which dominated Pietro and Brother Angelo. Already he must have been asking himself, as many a man born with a silver spoon in his mouth has done, what sense there was in the competitive struggle for power and wealth. Far greater was the satisfaction of becoming a companion of Arthur and Roland.

Francis's passion for dress and display was given full scope, and although, as the chronicler has to confess, he could not equal the count, he spared no pains to set himself up as the finest non-noble knight Assisi had ever seen.

So excited was he that one night he dreamed that he had been called to the palace of a beautiful bride, a palace chock-a-block with shields and glittering armor, all in readiness for the accouterment of a company of knights. These were all for him and his fellow knights, he was told. It was on the next day that Francis assured his friends that he was indeed certain now to become a great prince one day.

In this euphoric mood, which had followed so rapidly on his depression, he managed to combine with his preparations for the great adventure a very difficult act of typical generosity. Meeting some impecunious knight in Assisi, ruined by the wars, he got off his horse and presented him with the sumptuous cloak he was wearing. Then he took him to his home to give him the rest of his armor.

The date was 1205. Francis therefore was twenty-three years old, when, in his second-best suit, he trotted down from Assisi with his noble friend along the road leading to Foligno and Spoleto, with the whole world — spiritual and temporal — at his feet, as it seemed.

All of Assisi must have cheered them and their servants as they trotted away, their armor flashing in the sun. Once again we can hardly escape believing that the girl Clare, now eleven years of age, had been taken from the cathedral square, where her family lived, to the town's marketplace to witness this strange exodus about which everyone was talking. Her gaze, doubtless, was not so much on the noble Gentile, but rather on the little, bearded Francesco di Bernardone, so brave, so high-spirited, so unforgettable with his dark, piercing eyes.

Poor, dreaming, simple Francesco! Spoleto, despite its duke, its great *rocca*, and its fine cathedral, was only a paltry thirty miles from Assisi, while Apulia was getting on for three hundred, and Palestine, goodness knows how far. But Francis never got beyond the reality of Spoleto in his inexhaustible imaginative vision of glory.

Some suggest that at Spoleto, he fell sick again and during his sickness had his famous dream described by all the earliest sources. In this dream, he heard a voice asking him whether the master or the servant would be more likely to help him to success in his life. He naturally answered that it would be the master.

"Why, then," the voice asked, "do you run away from the master who is God and follow the mere servant?"

"Lord, what do you wish me to do?" he answered.

"Return to your native city, and you will discover where your future lies."[17]

It has been suggested that this dream came after some experience or adventure in Spoleto which threw Francis once again into deep depression and sent his castle in Spain toppling to the ground. But may it not have been that Francis, whose mind was so easily excited by grandiose ideas, had already had time to recall Collestrada and the Perugian prison and the shambles that lay on the banks of the Tiber? *"Pax et bonum"* may once again have rung in his ears, and the thought of the preacher's words may have stimulated the dream, in which he was bidden to return home to find his true vocation — a vocation which one day would cause him to interpret the glory of chivalry and the Crusades in a very different light from that of Count Gentile.

But one cannot forbear mentioning Paul Sabatier's explanation, unfounded as it may be, because it fits in so well with the moodiness and inconsistency of the unconverted Francis. The suggestion is that Gentile, a great lord far above the status of any Bernardone, had all the time been taking the little upstart bourgeois "for a ride." Thirty miles to Spoleto was long enough for the joke to be played out. "Better go home now, you silly little fellow," the great man might have said with a roar of laughter as he galloped on with his people, leaving Francis in tears. One is inclined to weep oneself at the thought of this terrible rebuff, if something of the sort took place.

---

[17] This theme of "Why serve some lowly person when you have a chance of serving a prince or lord?" recurs again and again in Francis's mind during his life.

Francis Ventures Off to Battle

It is best, perhaps, to see in the dream evidence of the truth, so obvious ever since his release from prison. Francis, always the focus of two contending moods within him — *joie de vivre* and a deep-down, gnawing conscience which expressed itself in his idealism and generosity of heart and hand — was becoming more aware of this call of conscience, this sense of unfulfillment, this growing impatience with the values of the world around him. Did he realize at Spoleto that this adventure was no more than a psychological as well as a physical escape from his real destiny?

Never was there a slower or more reluctant process of conversion in a person of real goodwill and unlimited potentialities, and one so evidently called by God to a unique destiny. Back again in Assisi and feeling, surely, rather ashamed of himself, Francis could only make another attempt to prop up his shattered illusions.

No doubt, when he sadly and shamefacedly returned home, the wiser for his experience, his armor dusty and his colors faded, he made such plausible excuses as he could find: his health had broken down again . . . the effects of prison . . . that year's illness . . . new and better ideas in his head.

His noble friend was now well on his way south, and the true story, whatever it was, had never got back to Assisi. Anyway, now he felt much better. Why not gather together the old friends of the Company of San Vittorino and the Bastone and have fun together? Thus he could drown for a little longer the voice of conscience which made itself so very vividly felt in Spoleto.

It is not easy to believe that Francis acted in this way, but he must have done so, for we know what he did.

As one of the richest men in town, he was, as Celano narrates in detail, asked to be master of a great feast that was being arranged. As such, he would hold the *bastone*, or staff, which indicated his presidency for the night of feasting, dancing, and singing. Celano says that the request was made because he was so rich and therefore well able to foot the bill — the master's privilege. He could not refuse, lest he be called a miser.

Once again, his natural generosity went with his renewed determination to seek escape through the excitement of preparing a sumptuous banquet to be held in some leafy garden, as the golden light on the horizon turned gradually into soft darkness, in which the lamps and lanterns flickered. At such a banquet, the young men, quickly excited by the first cups of wine, would sit between the prettiest and most popular girls. At the head of the table was Francis, crowned with a garland of flowers. To him the *bastone* was solemnly presented, to the delight of all the cheering company.

When the meal was finished and the wine drunk, it was time for the music and the love songs. Francis, with his attractive voice and skill on the lute, was expected to sing and lead the company — most of them the worse for drink — through the narrow ways of the hilly town, climbing the frequent steps or gaily running down them, boys and girls together, their singing and shouting growing ever more inharmonious.

For a time, all went with a swing, with the protests from sober citizens from their windows, and, doubtless, many a shower of unsavory liquid neatly evaded or gloriously hitting its mark, adding to the company's hilariousness. But wine is heady, and the party grew ragged, some going one way and some another.

"What's happened to Francesco?" someone shouted. Here was a new game: a midnight hide-and-seek. At last the shout was heard: "Here he is!" And they all rushed to where the call came from.

To their amazement, their madcap Francesco was standing alone with an inexplicably serious look on his face. He described himself later as having been pricked all over with knives and feeling unable to move from the spot. The *bastone* had dropped from his hand. It was as though he did not hear or see his friends as they came to persuade him that it was still early and there was still plenty of time for more fun. There was only one explanation, they thought. Francesco had at last fallen in love. Perhaps he had been smitten by one of the girls near him at the banquet.

"What on earth are you thinking about?" someone shouted to him. "Why didn't you come with us? Is this a new brainwave of yours? Or have you fallen in love? Are you thinking of getting married?"

Whoever he was, the man who asked him this last question, soberly reported by the early biographers, elicited the famous reply: "You have hit the nail on the head. Yes, I am thinking of getting married. I shall marry the noblest, richest, and most beautiful girl you can possibly imagine."

They all roared with laughter. It was just the kind of remark they expected from Francesco. But Francis for once did not join in the laughter.

How the night ended we do not know. But something had happened which they certainly did not understand. Francis never again acted the playboy, although he did his best for a time not to show outwardly that something — something which even he himself did not yet understand — had changed within him.

That extraordinary evening was to prove the real turn of the tide in the long process of Francis's conversion. But just as it is difficult for a long time to know whether a tide has really started turning, so Francis himself had to wait still longer before he himself could say — and prove — that a new life had really begun.

Chapter Four

Francis Wrestles with His Conversion

It is important to stress once again this curious slowness and this mystery in Francis's so gradual realization that life was meant to be something other than having a good time, seeing himself as a knight or prince, or dreaming of worldly success. It is as though the depth and uniqueness of his final conviction had to be measured by the time he took to face up to them.

Francis would always be a poet and a rebel against man-made conventions, a man who grasped realities intuitively by feel, vision, and an inner realization of what was before him or in him. He could never analyze or put two and two together and calculate the tidy sum. During this period, one realizes it so clearly. Francis's early biographers made it all sound so simple. Each experience — the illness, the turning back from Spoleto, the sudden sickening at the futility of the social scene, the first obscure vision of a better way — these were all classic examples of God's call.

The only difficulty is that if it was all so simple, why did the future saint, whose natural generosity of heart and depth of spiritual convictions were later to be made so clear, take so long to see the obvious? The answer is surely that with his exceptional sensitivity and honesty, he was aware of change and distress deep down within him, yet he could not see the pattern and express it either to himself or to others by living it. And corresponding with this subconscious awareness of a deeper reality was his keen perception of the fun and beauty of just being and just living and dreaming of intoxicating possibilities in life and the world around him. We shall see that Francis was never to lose this dualism of perception, although he had yet to learn through heroism, sacrifice, and the harshest of disciplines how to relate the one to the other.

Now at last there were real signs that the inner perception was growing, although without destroying the flesh-and-blood delight in the richness and beauty of life. In his refusal ever to turn his back on anything which God has given to man to be rightly enjoyed was to lie his special charm and unique influence. But Assisi is a town which, in one direction, seems to greet the softness and peace of the Umbrian lowland, while, in others, whether to the arid, deserted north or to the steep, rock-strewn contours of Monte Subasio in the east, it springs from nature at its toughest. The elements of both aspects of his native city were in Francis's makeup. From now on, the second was to gain mastery over the first, yet without destroying it.

After that last nighttime revel, he was rarely seen by his old friends. He lived quietly, presumably still helping his father in the cloth business, for we have no reason to suppose that he had stopped working at the trade in which he had been brought up, and one can hardly imagine his father tolerating a wholly idle son.

When free, he liked to ride out to the barren, rocky country, where he could be alone to pray and meditate on the future. He would always have a passion for the fresher, cooler air of highlands and mountains, for wildernesses untouched by man. There he could find free, God-praising creatures of the earth and sky. There innocent nature seemed to wash away the complexities and sins of men, his own worries and conscience-pangs not least. Dotted about were caves and old, rough shelters and ruins from much earlier days. Caves in the great wooded fissure on the slopes of Monte Subasio must have been a place of retreat for him, for in them, he would one day establish his dwelling with his brothers, and they have become known to posterity as the Carceri (literally, prisons).

We are told by Celano that Francis went about with a friend of his own age. To this friend Francis would mysteriously talk of a great and precious treasure that he had found. They would wander together, often to a favorite grotto, which some have sought to identify as a hiding place of early Christians. Francis would stay a long time in it while his friend waited outside. This friend has never been identified, but it has been suggested that it may have been his future secretary, Leo, while others have said that it was the future Brother Elias, who would one day gain notoriety through failing to conform with the gentleness and humility of his spiritual leader.

At any event, despite the great difference between the gentle Leo and the tumultuous Elias, both men were always to enjoy in a special way Francis's friendship. Francis's love for Elias and trust in him has always been a little puzzling, and it may well have been due to the fact that their intimacy started in these early days. Only this friend was allowed to know what was going on in Francis's mind and heart at this time.

"He was glad that no one knew what he was doing," wrote Celano. "He was praying that the Lord would show him a clear way ahead and teach him how to do His will. This was for him a time of inner torture, and he could find no peace so long as he could not bring himself to take a real step forward. Madly his mind seemed to toss to and fro. He seemed to feel a fire within him, and he found it hard not to betray his feelings to others. He realized how gravely he had sinned and thwarted God's plans for him, and he was bitterly sorry. Even now he could not repress the same old silly fancies, but the pleasure they had once given him did not return. He felt no guarantee or certainty that he would not drift back to his old ways. The worry which all this was causing him was so acute that his very appearance seemed to alter."

It was at this time, too, that this young man with an unusual gift for objectifying the phantasms of his strong imagination felt himself haunted by the scenes of Christ's Passion, with their lesson of total forgiving and total sharing. These vivid evocations would deeply affect him and leave him weeping copiously. Celano's description, freely translated above into a modern idiom, vividly expresses something we can all recognize in any attempt at self-reform. If, in reading lives of holy people, we sometimes feel that their conversion was a *coup de foudre* with little seeming reference to our own cases, at least we cannot say the same of the way along which Francesco di Bernardone had to tread.

Although we are told that this desolation and perhaps rather morbid and emotional concentration on the image of suffering gradually turned to consolation, as he redoubled his prayers and meditations, Francis, it seems, had to move forward to firmer spiritual ground by a kind of stratagem very typical of his nature.

He was beginning to realize the true meaning for him of those strange words he uttered to his amused companions on that last night out: "I shall marry the noblest, richest, and most beautiful girl you can possibly imagine."

Then it was only a vague, unformulated ideal, automatically expressed in the terminology of the romantic language of chivalry and the *chanson de geste*. It was the lady of his better dreams. Now he found himself interpreting the ideal in terms of an aspect of his character which was to prove decisive.

As we have mentioned, everyone agrees that, whatever his other faults, he had been generous and even prodigal all his life. The till to which his father appears to have given him access — in a certain measure, at any rate, so that he could advertise his family's trading success — enabled him not only to shine among his friends, but also to express a sense of brotherhood where the beggars, the poor, the lame, and the unfortunate were concerned. He was a sharer.

We may be sure that in his giving there was no touch of pity or condescension. He was not going about "doing good"[18] — still less thinking, "What a good fellow I am." Insofar as there was a spiritual or moral motive, it was one of humility. *Per amore di Dio* ("for the love of God") meant for him precisely what it said and implied. Before God all men were equal and equally in debt. In sharing even one's coat with a beggar or a poor knight, one was simply accepting the basic facts of life, supernatural and natural.

He could not understand and never would understand the notion that a man might build up around himself walls of

[18] Acts 10:38.

division and separation, made of gold or property, in order to establish his own self-sufficiency and security against the world and his neighbor. It was a sin against God's fatherhood and bounty, and a perversion of the nature of man and human society. In his pilgrimage to Rome, to which we have referred and which he was now to make, there was something of contempt in his reaction to the avarice of the pilgrims and in his gesture of actually changing clothes and taking the place of a beggar, a beggar whom he knew to be fully equal to himself before God, whatever the respectable pilgrims might think and do.

All this explains the mood of this present first stage in his conversion. His natural generosity and desire to share were becoming the fundamental principle of his ideal of chivalry, and "the noblest, richest, and most beautiful girl you can imagine" was becoming alive before him as the "Lady Poverty," whom he would marry and defend all through his life. In seeing himself before God as the least of men, he was inevitably falling in love with her and courting her.

"If any of the poor people asked for his help as he walked along the streets, he gave them money or, if short of it, his hat or his belt, rather than leave them with nothing. He would go so far as to take off his shirt in some dark corner and ask the poor man to take it for the love of God. When his father and his brother were away, he saw to it there was as much food as if the whole family were at home. When his mother asked why he insisted upon this, he explained that the extra was for his brothers the poor." Such is Celano's account.

No one, of course, would dare to try to explain what went on deep in his heart during this slow period of deepened insight and conversion in 1205 and 1206, when Francis was twenty-three and twenty-four. One can only follow the external clues and hint as best one may at the inner processes they suggest: the illness and depression after his imprisonment; the attempt to resume the old life; the strange words after the banquet; the unknown friend; the love of prayer in places far from men; the discovery of Lady Poverty; the dramatic pilgrimage to Rome.

But all this was not yet enough. Something held him back from the total giving of self. Such total giving he slowly realized to be the real all-important test, God's full requirement of the once-playboy dreamer. He had to make a plunge from the potentialities of his charming and chivalrous nature into the ice-cold waters of existential reality. God's will, however terrifying it seemed, had to be embraced. His own dreams and tastes must count for nothing.

We have described at the beginning of this book how he faced up to this dramatic test and found freedom of soul and mind in undergoing it. Poverty he could always instinctively and naturally love. Ugliness, corruption, and disease still horrified his fastidious nature. Of all ugliness and disease, the most hideous and symbolic to him were what lay behind and near the walls of the lazaretto which called on all sane men to keep as far away as possible.

But Francis at last was not to be fobbed off with the line that lepers were not his brothers in the flesh as well as in the spirit. Lepers were as much God's children as he was, and their needs were far, far greater than his. If he was to be true to himself and to the mission which, as he realized ever more clearly, God was asking him to live and preach, he must put that

Francis of Assisi

chivalry of his to a final trial and include the lepers within the
bands of his own brothers through the days to come.

Could he do it? Could he prove himself authentic and no
sham, as he felt himself so long to have been? We have seen
that Francis could.

Having thus conquered himself, Francis would always seek
out the lazaretto and minister to its sorry inmates — led to
them by his certainty that when he was walking with a leper,
he was walking with Christ, who then, and forever after,
turned his bitterness and disgust, his fear of the painful and
ugly, into sweetness. After he had kissed the leper, he prayed
for light. *The Three Companions* tells us that he consulted
Guido, Bishop of Assisi, who had no doubt at all about the
goodness and the serious intentions of this unexpected penitent, but great doubts as to what would become of him in the
future.

This in its way is another very surprising thing, for Guido
was someone rather different from any modern bishop. He was
a proud and immensely rich feudal lord, owning half the city
and great properties outside it. For his feudal rights he was prepared to fight to the bitter end. His episcopate, writes Fortini,
was full of lawsuits and legal actions, libel cases, arbitrations,
declarations, and sentences. When there was cause, he would
in fury go down in person into the streets and not hesitate to
lay hands on those who tried to cross him. Francis was the rich
son of a powerful father battling with any lords, ecclesiastical
or secular, for the newly won rights of his class. Yet here he
was, humbly consulting this frightening personage and so successfully that Guido was in time to play a decisive part in shap-
ing the saint's future.

There was nothing that Francis liked better at this time than solitary prayer in some old half-abandoned chapel, of which there were a number near Assisi.

Francis was always visual and concrete in his approach to problems, and his devotion expressed itself instinctively in the simplest and homeliest ways. A church or chapel, even more than the great sweeps of sunlit country or the rocks and caves of mountainsides, was the place where God dwelled. The altar, the sacred vessels, the priest ritually set apart for the service of the altar: these meant a tremendous amount to him. While he would wish them all to be the best and most worthy of the sacred role which they served, it never occurred to him that the reformation of the priests or the beautifying of the outward service of God were more important than the authenticity of the consecrated instrument.

Just as later in his life, he was to have a special reverence for the Hebrew letter *Thau*,[19] the significance of which he was to hear expounded one day by Pope Innocent III, just as he was to use it as his special sign, so he always saw in the living and material human symbol the sign of the inward grace, of the power of God so infinitely more important than the effort of man.

This Catholic realism was to prove decisive for Francis in an age when reformers of behavior and morals abounded, most of them to incur condemnation for patent excesses and dangerous doctrinal deviations. In spite of the low standards of the clergy, even in Assisi, and the attraction of a host of reformers, outwardly so like himself, it is extraordinary that there was

[19] See Chapter 14.

never a shadow of heretical tendency, still less purpose, in his outlook.

He knew of priests living in concubinage and amassing riches by dishonest means, as well as of priests reduced to penury through episcopal exactions. He knew of churches neglected because no one seemed to care. Trafficking in holy things was the result of a clerical cupidity especially galling to a man who loved Christ's poverty and wished to imitate it. He saw high offices in the Church obtained through trickery and favoritism, and he saw their holders bleeding the people to enrich themselves. It was against all this scandalous state of affairs, too often to be met with, that the reformers were protesting.

Peter Valdes had had an experience curiously similar to the one on which Francis was meditating. A rich merchant of Lyons, he had sold all his goods or given them to the poor because of the woman he loved. Thus was founded the sect of the *Vaudois* or *Waldenses* or poor men of Lyons, who had been blessed by Alexander III[20] and had spread all over France and Italy. But theirs was the road to heresy and denial of the validity of any exclusive priestly office and power, and so they incurred papal condemnation, even though a section continued to live orthodox Catholic lives. More widely spread in Italy were the *humiliati* of Milan, forerunners, it seems, of the Quakers. Much more dangerous were the Cathars or Albigensians, called in Italy *Paterini*, whose Manichean heresy[21] produced

---

[20] Alexander III (died 1181), Pope from 1159.

[21] Manicheism maintains that a cosmic conflict exists between a good realm of light and an evil realm of darkness, and that

fruits of virtue and self-denial that shamed the orthodox and endangered the foundation of Church and state.

These reforming movements and their zealous disciples were well known in Assisi, whose statutes regulated for their condemnation. How significant it is, then, that Francis, whose mind was clearly working along similar lines of evangelical reform, and who knew little of theology and Scripture, was not tempted to make contact with them.

In a marked way, his was an *anima naturaliter catolica* ("a soul by nature Catholic"), one which instinctively shunned the exaggeration of reform while holding firm to its intuitions about the terrible and foolish wrongness of the accepted values of the world and the people among whom he lived. We shall see how this Catholic "literalness" of an eccentric mind in dispute with the values of the world around him guided him forward toward a way of sanctity unique in its personal quality, yet always orthodox.

matter and flesh are in the realm of darkness. Thus, man's body is regarded as evil, and man's duty is to aid the forces of good by practicing extreme asceticism.

Chapter Five

The Crucifix Speaks to Francis

Particularly dear to Francis at this time was an ancient chapel long allowed virtually to fall into ruins, dedicated to San Damiano, which hung on a steep hillside to the south of Assisi. Its legend, "*domus mea*" ("my house"), seemed a mockery with its neglect, broken-down walls, and faded frescoes. In it hung a Byzantine wooden crucifix, painted in red, gold, and blue. It did not represent the tortured Christ of later art; but the large, open, dark eyes of the Crucified looked down with a haunting vividness. It was a striking example of the early painted crucifixes, and it is strange that it should have survived the neglect of the chapel.[22]

Before it, Francis loved to pray for the light which would shine through the darkness of his mind. As he looked up one day, he saw the lips of the Christ move, and he heard the words, "Francis, you see that my house is falling down; go and repair it for me." And Francis answered simply, "Willingly, Lord."

This experience was no invention of the chroniclers, but whether it was an actual miracle or an intensely vivid subjective experience of a person who instinctively objectified in

[22] The restored original is now in the church of Santa Chiara.

time and space what he heard and felt within him, is a question to be answered by each person for himself. Nor is the question of the first importance, for the significance of the experience reflected without any doubt the ever-closer communion between God and Francis.

How far Francis was from any notion of purifying or reforming the Church is clear from his reaction. His literal mind understood the words in their most literal sense. He was in a crumbling church, and God was simply asking him to repair it. His thoughts must have flashed back to his boyhood when he had learned — or at least watched — the technique of building walls around his hometown.

The overpowering thing for him at that moment was that Christ — above all, the majestic, yet so human, figure of the Crucified in brilliant colors surrounded by saints — had spoken to him. He had obscurely known and heard God's voice within him before, and it had given him the strength to kiss the leper, but in Francis's mind, there was a whole world of difference between inner promptings, however certain, and what in daylight one could see, hear, and touch. Here at last was the authentic confirmation that God was with him, instructing him about what here and now he should do. Others of different makeup might not need this outward sign. Francis, of all people, did.

We can imagine him bounding out of the little church — the church with jagged gashes in its ocher stone walls, and parts of the roof open to the rain — to run to the lonely priest in whose care it was. He took all the money he had on him and tried to thrust it into the astonished priest's hands. "Please buy oil with it," Francis cried, "and place a lamp for me to burn forever before the Crucifix. I'll bring you plenty more to keep the lamp lit."

Francis's mind leapt at once to the outward sign which would symbolize the personal experience of God's spoken word. Then he rushed to Assisi, entered his father's shop, and took out of the stores a great piece of scarlet cloth, the finest available, fit for kings and princes. He jumped onto his horse, made the Sign of the Cross, and galloped off to the market of Foligno, the nearest trading center, for he could scarcely have sold it in Assisi without his father hearing of it. His road, he must have remembered, perhaps with a smile, was the same as that which had led him to his fruitless journey to Spoleto. Now it was the true knight's quest.

There, in the always-busy marketplace and cloth fair, he quickly sold the cloth, and, mindful for a fleeting moment perhaps that the cloth was not really his to sell, he sold his horse as well. No doubt he at once regretted having done so, for now it would take him three or four hours to get back to San Damiano. Anyway, it was too late for regrets. The money he had acquired was sacred. It had paid for a royal cloth fit for the decoration of a church. He must be content to tramp back as fast as his legs would carry him.

The old priest was still there as the strange young man returned, sweating and covered with dust, his pockets bulging with money. Francis dropped down to his knees, his cupped hands filled with gold and silver coins.

"Now we can repair the church as God Himself would want it to be repaired," he must have said as he explained how he had got the money. It is doubtful if the poor priest managed to get a word in, as Francis poured out his heart, his story, and a good deal of his life's history, with perhaps a little treatise on economics as he understood them. Whatever the rights of private property, they manifestly could not weigh in the balance against God's rights. Before the priest could interrupt, Francis begged that he might stay forever at San Damiano to serve God in God's way.

The sight of so much money, if nothing else, put the priest on his guard. He must have known something of Francesco's reputation for irresponsibility and wild behavior. If this young man, beside himself and tired, was not dangerous, his father, the powerful merchant, most certainly was. But Francesco was welcome to stay the night, or, for that matter, as long as he wished.

Then Francis, perhaps only to get rid of the coins, some of them in his pockets, some lying about, collected them together and dropped them contemptuously on a windowsill.

This passing and instinctive gesture was to symbolize and govern the rest of his life. Money, coin, was the symbol of human servitude, the factor which, above all, separated man from man, destroying the love and brotherhood of men in Christ. As he was to tell his followers in one of those seemingly simple, but devastatingly pregnant, observations: "If we have money, we shall also have to have armed men to guard it." The tragedies of civilized man are expressed in those few words.

At this moment, Francis's father, Pietro di Bernardone, for the first and last time in his life, enters upon the scene as an actor with a major part to play in the drama which was, unknown to him, to be acted out before the eyes of all future generations.

The Crucifix Speaks to Francis

Up until now, what we indirectly know of him suggests that he was a traveled man of some education; a very successful trader in the harsh, competitive bargaining of a small but growing city; a bit of a snob, but with enough imagination to appreciate the business value of the ostentation which made the Bernardone name constantly talked about; and an indulgent father with rather lax standards of parental authority when all was going well. At the same time, he was the type of self-made man who could be ingratiating and generous at one moment, then, losing for some reason his sense of security, suddenly become nasty and suspicious.

Then, as so often happens with parents and their children, the first delighted recognition of oneself in the child turns to a kind of frustrated fury when the child seems to have abused and indulged the oddnesses and weaknesses which the parent believes he has learned to control in the school of life. There is nothing to be done about it, for it is the parents' double weakness: weakness in themselves and weakness in not having had the will to control the child in good time. There is nothing to be done — except impotently to storm and rage, inevitably making matters worse.

Bernardone, it appears, was on his travels during this time. When he returned home to be told how his son, suddenly suffering from some kind of religious mania, had taken the richest cloth in his shop and sold it to get funds in order to repair an old country church, he completely lost his temper. Extravagance in a young man who is expected to settle down in due course to the money-making business of life was one thing. Running away from home and business, stealing from the shop, and imagining himself to be some kind of crazy hermit were quite another. Where was the boy anyway? Bernardone was told that Francis was living with the chaplain at San Damiano.

Only the strongest measures, in Bernardone's opinion, would knock some sense into the young fellow's head. We think of Pietro as an old man, but he may well have been still under fifty — with plenty of energy left and a youthful enough determination to save his son and the family's good name from scandal and ruin.

Gathering together a party of friends, Bernardone set out for San Damiano to bring his son back through main force if necessary. A diet of bread and water under lock and key in the little prison-like strongroom of the house would put an end to all this nonsense.

But when the party reached the church, they found no Francis. Doubtless the frightened chaplain explained in detail all that had happened. The full truth was even worse than the rumors, but the father must have got some satisfaction from the thought that his son at least understood that he meant business. Clearly, terror had driven poor Francis away. Pietro, who knew his medieval rights as a father, could afford to bide his time.

Up to a point, Bernardone had judged well. Francis, the knight of poverty and of the crucified Christ, the man who had kissed the leper (which not another soul in Assisi would have had the courage to do) had indeed fled in terror. "Francis, who after all had only just become a knight of Christ, heard the threatening shouts of the party coming to find him. He held his ground until he could see them, and then ran away as fast as his legs could carry him, to hide in a cave he had prepared for the occasion. There he hid for a month." So *The Three Companions* delightfully reports.

There is something particularly endearing in the reflection that Francis, who had "only just become a knight of Christ," could not really be expected to stand up to his own father. Capable of solitude and the sublimely heroic, able to string himself up to the impossibility of kissing a leper, the impact of his own family could still turn his bones to jelly, as though he was still a child. In fact, he would need a month of solitude and prayer to nerve himself for a fresh test to which, no doubt, he was bound to stand up, but only after heavy repairs to that spiritual castle in the air which could still melt when his past became too real to him. His friend, no doubt, shared the secret of his hiding place and brought him food.

At length, so we are told, "relying entirely on the Lord and with an inner glow and with the clearest understanding of what he ought to do, he left his hole and hastened, steadfastly and joyfully, to Assisi."

The crazy behavior of Francesco di Bernardone had slowly become the gossip of Assisi. Suddenly this generous, high-spirited, fashionable young man had become the butt of every tongue. The whole thing had become absurd and humiliating. The young fop had let everyone down. His old friends turned against him. Those who had envied him his success gloried in his humiliation. He had gone completely mad, or a devil had taken possession of him.

His friend must have told him of the feelings of the people of Assisi. Once more, Francesco passed from weakness to strength. It was a challenge. He must be ready to fight for his cause, for his Master, Jesus Christ, and for his fair lady, Poverty.

He must return to Assisi to fight the battle of the Lord as a true knight.

Suddenly, at the corner of a street in the town, someone saw him. For weeks now, he had been living on virtually nothing. Always thin and spare, the figure passing through the town was more like a scarecrow with its soiled clothes hanging around it. Could it be Francesco? The sun caught his face as he looked up. Yes, that was Francesco's smile, although drawn now on a skeleton-like mask with an unkempt beard. It had the quality of the macabre.

Yes, it was Francesco. Francesco had indeed gone mad. *Pazzo!* ("Madman!") The ugly word passed from mouth to mouth, and soon Francis was followed by a crowd of jeering Italians, crossing themselves or warding off the evil eye to avert the curse that had evidently fallen on him. The poor and the beggars were loudest in their jeering at this figure of fun, now more pitiable than themselves. If Clare was at her window, perhaps she alone in Assisi half-understood.

Outwardly untroubled by the reception he got, Francis walked on to find his father — his father, the proud merchant and notability, whose enemies at last felt they had got their revenge, and in what unexpected measure!

Bernardone, hearing the dreadful news that his son had actually returned to the town, a madman with the crowds mocking him, rushed out, seized his son, and dragged him into the privacy of his house. This was beyond all measure. Mad or not, the answer was a good flogging there and then. Then, making use of the legal rights of those times when a son "misused his substance," he threw him into the cell in his house, banged the heavy door, and drew the bolts. Let the boy cool his heels until the father, who was going off again on business, returned. Chains on his son's hands and feet could further guard against an escape that would be a final disaster for the Bernardone family.

It is hard to forgive Bernardone his brutality and stupidity, even though he was acting within his rights, but his behavior helps us to realize that the real Francis was a far odder and more difficult person than the pious streamlining traditions of hagiography allow. The fear that his son might escape and start another mob chase of the Bernardone lunatic must have been overwhelming for a respectable merchant. Let us hope, too, that he was not sorry to leave further responsibility to Pica, his wife. Pica, like any other good mother when faced with a desperate quarrel between father and son, went to plead with her son. We need not improve the story by romantically supposing that Pica understood everything. No one could understand, not even Francis himself.

But having doubtless tried to explain his father's sheer frustration and asked her son to bear with him and try to behave a little more reasonably — one must remember, she had had to put up with Francis's earlier extravagances in an opposite sense — she found herself listening to the whole story of what had been happening to her son during those last months. It did not take her long to realize that this was no play-acting, no new mad fancy of her boy's unstable brain. Good Christian as she was, she understood that this was the real thing — a call from God, strangely as it seemed to be expressed in her son's behavior. Perhaps she shook her head and wondered what would become of it all, what dangers would beset her son. Even religion, as all wise mothers know, is best followed along the beaten, conventional track. If he wanted to become a monk or hermit, there were simpler ways. In this view, she would have had, did she but know it, the wholehearted assent of the Bishop of Assisi. To be "drunk with the love of God," as the chroniclers put it, sounds well enough in theory; it is another matter when it is happening to one's own strange child.

Anyway, she left the door of the prison open for Francis discreetly to escape from home for the last time in his life and, unseen by the people, to return to San Damiano. If only Pietro had had so much common sense.

Francis, living with the priest at San Damiano a life akin to that of a religious oblate — this was shortly to prove important — hoped to be left alone until God showed him the way forward more clearly.

But Pietro di Bernardone was not the kind of man who could let bygones be bygones. Had he been so, he would probably not have become so rich. The affair had rankled while he was away. Now, when he heard that his son had fled, this time with his wife's connivance, his rage became greater than ever.

One may charitably hope that part of his concern was a genuine anxiety about his son's future. Could he look after himself? Was he to be trusted not to bring further disgrace on the Bernardone family and business? Brooding over this, he began to realize that his son had behaved no better than a common thief. True, Pietro had been liberal with pocket money for Francis when his popularity had been a business asset. But there was all the difference in the world between his son's enjoying himself at his father's expense and his taking, without any permission, his best cloth, for the ridiculous purpose of repairing an old church in which apparently no one else — even the bishop — was interested. This was throwing good money away — and stolen money at that.

Chapter Six

※

Francis Gives Up All for God

Was Francis a thief? Technically, he may well have been, for a man can steal from his parents as well as from a stranger, and in those days, the authority of father over son was safeguarded by stringent laws. But it requires little imagination to understand what was in Francis's mind. So unusual a son must have delighted a father whose growing wealth gave him hope of rising in the social scale. Francis's natural generosity may well have been inherited from a similar generosity in his father, despite the differences of motive. That difference showed plainly enough now.

The father's natural generosity was in his own interests. Money given away was also power and influence for himself and his family. Francis gave away because he had no interest whatever in the idea of accumulating wealth, and recently he had come to realize that accumulating wealth was the most powerful way of separating man from man. Lady Poverty, who made all men brothers in Christ, was his present ideal.

What could be more natural or obvious than for him to take it for granted that if God Himself wanted money for the repair of His church, then the money which he himself no longer required for having a good time, should be used — and a thousand times more appropriately — for the service of God. This view would have been so instinctive in him that he would hardly have had to pause to think it out.

Bernardone in his rage saw things in the opposite way. The cloth was his, not his son's, and it was for him to decide how it should be used. Let his son return the money, and then they could all go into the question of Francis's future.

Francis, naturally, was all willingness to repay, seeing how his father felt about it. But how? The money, in his view, was no longer his. It had been donated to God, who had asked that the church be repaired.

Francis was never a good moral theologian. One cannot but suspect that he was already conceiving the dramatic gesture which would bring the whole sorry business to an end, with himself freed at last from the shackles of convention and slavery to the false gods of human acquisitiveness. If there were matter for legitimate dispute, God would decide it in His own way.

Bernardone, on the other hand, intended to appeal to the consuls. He knew that they must uphold the cheated father, particularly now that his son's mind seemed hardly on this side of sanity. The punishment, according to the statutes of Assisi, would be nothing less than banishment. Thus the city magistrates, members of Pietro's own class and his friends, readily agreed to send a messenger to San Damiano requesting the defaulting young man's presence before them on a certain day at a certain time. Following the legal custom, the herald called upon the accused to appear before the consuls.

Francis, however, answered in a most unexpected way. As though a lawyer born, he challenged the jurisdiction of the court and turned the tables on his father. He claimed to be no longer a layman, but a religious, serving God and the little church. Consequently he was responsible only to the spiritual power whose judge was Bishop Guido.

The claim was legally valid, and the consuls had to inform Pietro di Bernardone that the case could not be tried by them. They must have done this with considerable relief, since the last thing they wanted was any quarrel with the formidable bishop. We hear of no consultation by Francis himself, although he may have been advised by his friend, the priest at San Damiano. In any case, it was all common sense — a gift that Francis had in full measure. It had, after all, been common sense about the self-defeating conventions of the world which had brought him to where he now stood.

Soon a fresh herald appeared — the bishop's. To his order that the young man should appear at the episcopal palace for judgment, Francis assented with alacrity. "The bishop is the father and lord of all souls," he said.

The bishop's court was held in the afternoon in the large forecourt of the episcopal palace which, then as now, gave on to the Piazza of Santa Maria Maggiore. The palace in those days, however, was virtually a feudal fortress guarding one of the main entries to the fortified town.

Naturally, the town was buzzing with rumors and gossip about this extraordinary family quarrel and the fate of the unbelievable Francesco di Bernardone. It was as good as a holiday, and the people of Assisi, despite the bitter cold of this cold winter, crowded into the court to get the best view of the proceedings. They were not mistaken in thinking that this was to be an occasion — although not a soul among them could have dreamed that they were to be spectators of one of the immortal scenes of Christian history.

Francis that morning, well-dressed for once — he had a special reason — made his way up the snow-covered hill from San Damiano. With him he brought a purse containing the money in dispute. He was, of course, completely ready to accept the bishop's verdict. The bishop had no inkling of how this good, but fanciful, man was going to conduct his defense.

We cannot doubt that Francis was elated and excited, if only because here was a theater in which public recognition could be given to the fact that he had at last left the world behind him and been formally attached to the company of men and women officially dedicated to the service of God.

As the bells rang out, the mighty bishop in miter and magnificent blue cape, surrounded by his canons and advisers, took his seat on the steps of the palace in full view of the packed piazza.

After the preliminaries, Francis, kneeling before the bishop in the presence of the silent crowd, listened to the discussion of the case, his father stating with ample detail his seemingly so well-founded grievances.

"Your father," said the bishop, "is very angry with you and deeply offended. You tell me you wish to be a religious. Well, then, you must give him back the money you have taken, since you may not have legally acquired it. God does not wish you to use this money for the works of the Church, tainted as it also is by the sin of your father, whose anger must cease once the money is restored to him. Have faith in God, my son. Be a man; do not be afraid. God will help you and shower on you whatever you may need for the restoration of His church."

The moment had come for Francis's immortal gesture.

He rose from his knees, and, standing before the bishop, he said, "Not the money only, my Lord, for that belongs to him. All my clothes also I wish to return to him with a full heart." Francis then handed over the purse and, after slipping through a door, returned carrying the clothes he had been wearing. He laid them at his father's feet. Celano makes no bones about the fact that he stood there before the bishop, the officials, and the people, stark naked.

Standing thus, he said, "I want you all to know and understand that up until now, it is Pietro di Bernardone whom I have called my father. But now that I have undertaken to serve God, I give him back the money about which he has made such a fuss, together with all the clothes he has given me. Now at last I can say in all honesty, 'Our Father who art in Heaven' and no longer, 'my father Pietro di Bernardone.' "

It was unnecessary for formal judgment to be given. Guido, the possessor himself of many worldly goods, realized that he was faced with something bigger than himself, something bigger than the ways of human justice. He rose, went down the steps, and taking off his great cape, he wrapped it around the spare body of the naked Francis.

The last we see or hear of Pietro di Bernardone in this story is the angry muttering by the crowd, hostile toward him now, as he bent down to pick up what legally belonged to him and disappeared. Where was Pica, and how did she feel? We do not know.

The famous trial brings the fully formed Francis before us for the first time, and it is necessary to pause and study the meaning of this strange drama.

What strikes us most about it today is the uninhibited, almost passionate, nature of Francis's behavior. There was no compromise in it, no regard for the conventions, no interest in anyone's feelings. As with kissing the leper, Francis could only conquer himself by going far beyond what common sense would judge to be sufficient.

Two aspects of the scene may well shock us today: Francis's appearing naked and his throwing his very clothes in his father's face as though saying, "Well, if you're going to be so mean, take the lot, and I hope you're satisfied."

As for the taking off of all his clothes, one has to remember that this would have been far less of a shock in the thirteenth century than in the twentieth. Men and women in those days slept without clothes and swam without them. The naked as such did not shock in its right time and place. It was this that made it possible for Francis always to see in literal nakedness a graphic symbol of complete denudation of all worldly goods and possessions. The crowd, we are told, took his side. They were indignant with the father — and, according to *The Three Companions*, for the very sensible reason that Bernardone took the clothes, content to leave his son naked before the crowd.

For Francis, at whom they had been so recently leering as a madman, they were now filled with compassion, even to "weeping bitterly." The tables had certainly been turned. Even so, Francis's literal gesture of total deprivation before the world was meant primarily to be symbolic of where he knew himself now to stand. After all the months of attempts at self-conquest, of failure utterly to destroy the person he had been, he needed to reassure himself by a public act — dramatic, positive, and uncompromising.

In him, the act, the deed, was what really counted and really had significance. He had always been an actor in the literal sense of one who *acts*, and if he was to be true to himself and his new life, it must still be a life of acts — acts inspired by a totally fresh understanding of true values as he saw them, but still characteristic of his own nature and psychological makeup.

Total deprivation, as the only true human freedom and consequently the only way of being linked with Christ, was the new and authentic version of the Francis who had once sought that freedom in a world of distraction and endless romantic dreams. He had found at last, and publicly expressed, his Holy Grail, his Lady Poverty.

Still inspired by the naked, crucified Christ who had spoken to him in San Damiano, his present nakedness was also a literal following of the naked Christ on the Cross. His intense devotion to the Passion, which had resulted from the miracle of San Damiano, would never be far from the center of his consciousness, although, being the many-sided person he was, Francis was to become a man who wanted to laugh with joy at his freedom in God's beautiful world and weep with compassion and love at the sufferings of his Lord, and he never seemed to know which to do.

There was never anything petty or mean about Francis's nature, so we have to take it that the repudiation of his father and the returning to him of his clothes were no more than the logical completion of the act of total deprivation in imitation of Christ and in service to his key to human happiness, the Lady Poverty.

Dismissing him, Bishop Guido must, however, have shaken his head, wondering what on earth would become of this strange new recruit to the clergy who seemed to be a law unto himself. These were, he knew, the days when Christendom seemed to be full of people not unlike Francis — reformers and holy men who claimed to be literal followers of Christ, although taking sometimes not a little pride in the thought that their lives of devotional poverty were in such glaring contrast with those of worldly and often immoral bishops and priests.

It says much for Bishop Guido — and for Francis — that he could see no new *Waldenses*, no budding *Paterini*, in his protégé. We must suppose that the bishop had the opportunity of long talks with Francis during this period, and, if he could not fail to notice the extravagances of his conduct and views, he could find no germ of heresy. On the contrary, Francis was in every way deeply submissive to the Church, with a special veneration for the priesthood even in unworthy hands.

Today, of course, he would not have got away with it. He would have had to study for the priesthood or be accepted as a brother in a properly constituted religious order. But in those days, Guido evidently saw no harm in, as it were, letting Francis loose to find his true vocation. He was satisfied that Francis's basic good sense and solid orthodoxy would in time soften the edges of his seemingly extreme antisocial views about which at the moment there was no arguing, since, on Francis's premises, they were wholly uncontrovertible. Soon, the Pope himself would have to admit as much. Guido, a good and just man at heart, knew only too well how the arrogance of his own nature, sharpened by the grandeur of his position, the cares of office, and the responsibilities for his own properties and those of the Church, limited his freedom to be himself and to serve God with the uncompromising fervor so evident in this young man. Anyway, a period of what we would call a retreat would be a good prescription for this singular addition to the massive ranks of churchmen.

Francis, therefore, with his bishop's blessing, set off with immense joy to pray and, through prayer and fasting, to find his way as a religious toward the full vocation to which God was calling him.

Chapter Seven

Francis Discovers His True Calling

It was springtime in 1207, and Francis about twenty-five years old, when, as so many writers have put it, the bird at last escaped from the cage — the cage of family ties, of the trading at the cloth counter, of the distractions and dissipations in which he had tried to find fulfillment. Above all, it was the cage of his old self, which had fought so long against inspiration and inner urges that would destroy that old self and yet, in the very act of destroying it, enable it to rise again, purified, enlightened, and close to God, instead of to the conventions and corruptions of the world.

Inevitably, the new Francis, yet somehow very much the old Francis still, dressed like a poor man in cheap and tattered clothes, tramped northward through the harsh, rocky, and utterly deserted country down which ran the flooded River Tescio.

Nothing is easier to imagine than the happy little man, free at last, and singing the songs of the troubadours at the top of his voice to the birds, to the high-riding clouds, to the young spring green, and to the shadowed masses of larch and fir. Equally full of intensity for him, as with great gulps he breathed in God's pure air, was the miracle at his feet as he saw the delicate structure of the smallest dried-up autumn leaf, the endless configurations of the massive limestone rocks, the pools of flood water, the tenderness of the little scuttling rabbits, even the despised worm over which he carefully stepped, for a worm, too, is a living creature of God. Up and down he climbed, to wonder and to praise God for the endless configuration of land and water, of rock and cave, so welcoming in the heat of the noonday sun, or to rest his eyes on the cool shadows and the patches of snow which the winter had left behind in a sheltered corner.

All this was a proclamation and confirmation of the infinite variety of God's works and blessings. Francis's obscure sense of God's presence deep in his heart was married to the visible, tangible handiwork of God all around him.

Has any man ever been happier than Francis on those first days of emancipation and liberty, as he trudged on and on over the hills and valleys in the direction of Gubbio? He had achieved his first ambition. He had become a jongleur of Christ, leaping and laughing at the beauty of God's valleys and God's hills.

Nothing could daunt him in that mood. At a crossroads, he met with a party of toughs, possibly Perugian soldiers scouting between the frontiers of the two cities. They challenged the madman filling the air with his song. Delighted, Francis shouted, "I am the herald of the great King." Madder and madder!

One of them egged on the others to have a bit of fun at his expense. They fell on him, tore off his coat, and threw him into a snow-filled hole. "So much for the herald," they cried as they went their way.

Francis was transported, as usual, with joy at the thought of how much worse Christ had been treated, and he wept in compassion, forgetting about his own bruises. He picked himself up, shook the snow off his face and hands, and went on, pensive for a while, then singing again as gaily as ever. It had all been a part of a herald's service to his Prince.

As he made his way forward, the spring floods seemed to spread across the land. He must find shelter. Soon he came to the ancient Benedictine monastery of Santa Maria di Val Fabrica, ruled by Prior Hugo. It would have been better called a military fortress than a religious house, for it guarded Assisian territory to the north. Short of provisions, due to the floods, the monks reluctantly took in the suspicious-looking traveler, setting him to work in the kitchen for a hunk of bread and a bowl of thin soup. If these men of God did not seem to be imitating their Master, Christ, Francis could congratulate himself with a smile on having no choice but to do so.

In due course, there stood before him, at the foot of a great fantastically shaped mountain, the ancient town of Gubbio, its stone walls, its many towers, its squares, its palaces and houses, under the protection of San Ubaldo buried three thousand feet above.

Gubbio, beautiful as it was and still is, would live in history not for its beauty, but for a wolf which Francis would one day tame. But on this first visit, he met a friend, not a wolf — a friend believed to have been called Frederick of the Long Sword (*Spada Lunga*), probably a comrade-in-arms at Collestrada in the Perugian prison. From this friend, he obtained his first religious habit — a hermit's tunic, a leather belt, sandals, and a stout stick.

Francis the solitary hermit? All his life he would ask himself whether this was not his true vocation.

It is clear that as yet he had no conception of how, in fact, he would lead his new life and exercise his new function as herald of the great King. For the moment, he was content to be his new self, and, in course of time, he made his way back to Assisi where, according to *The Three Companions*, he devoted himself again to the care of the lepers.

But he had never forgotten the words of the crucifix, "Repair my Church," and having, if we may so put it, thoroughly enjoyed his long spiritual holiday, he returned to begin the one definite job he had to do.

Gone now forever was the time when he thought he could repair San Damiano by acquiring money and buying the stones and mortar and tools. On the other hand, he certainly could not repair the church without these things and without eating. The answer was obvious to him.

First, there was the lamp which no longer burned, for the oil that had been bought was long used up. So he climbed up to Assisi to ask for a gift of some oil. Francis, once the most fashionable man in town, then considered a madcap, now had to be a genuine beggar. Even if he had defied conventions by practicing the part in Rome, the real thing in his hometown did not come easily to him.

The reality, as perhaps he caught sight of some of his old friends, frightened him and made him ashamed. He hastily retreated, wishing himself back on his spiritual holiday. He turned away from the town, and then, gaining courage as usual with his second wind, he quickly recovered his senses. All he needed was a little trick with which to cheer himself up and cheer up the source of supply. He sang his plea for oil and for stones for the repairing of God's church in a little rhythmic chant: "One stone, one reward; two stones, two rewards; three stones, three rewards." Doggerel is always fun. Many laughed at Bernardone's dotty son. But some laughed with him, and many gave.

Soon San Damiano became quite a busy place. If one had to walk up the steep hill to beg, at least one could roll the stones down it. Francis knew his mason's job, and others, delighting in the sense of common work under a happy, singing, skilled foreman, were glad to work with him.

It was a happy time with a delightful sense of solid achievement. Was it too happy? Francis, thinking of his Savior's Passion, began to have scruples.

Was his new life of denudation and imitation of his Master going to prove one long jolly holiday? True, the work in the summer heat day after day was exhausting. He had never been physically strong, and he had certainly not been brought up to be a laborer. But the delighted chaplain was only too happy to look after his benefactor's health and to prepare for him specially succulent and nourishing food. Whatever Francis did, life seemed to be made too easy for his spiritual health. Besides, as he shrewdly noted, he would not always have such a kindly priest to look after him. No, he must go a-begging again, and he must shift for himself, trusting in God alone.

"Get up, you lazy hound, and beg your food from door to door," as Celano makes him say. What this meant in practice is brought home to us by Celano's further observation that the food which the people of Assisi put into his begging platter "filled him with horror" — a timely reminder that this was no game that the delicately nurtured Francis was playing. Harder to swallow than the food were the hatred and mockery of his father and brothers at the sight of a Bernardone brought down to the lowest social level of the town.

His father, unreconciled, cursed him so vigorously that Francis, broken-hearted and literal as usual, hired a beggar to take his father's place and he blessed the beggar instead. His brother Angelo, during the following winter, passed him one day, so *The Three Companions* tells us, and turning to a passerby, sarcastically said, "You ask Francis to sell you a pennyworth of his sweat," as though to underline his brother's fall from the prosperity of the past to his present abjection. Francis had his answer: "Not to you, but to God, do I do my selling, for He will give me better money." All this, given his special sensitivity, must have deeply hurt a loving nature like his with the usual Italian family affection and so much more.

"Repair my Church!" Spring had changed to summer and summer to autumn, and the work continued. At length, San Damiano was new and fresh once again. The year 1207 was turning to 1208 when Francis, indefatigably obedient, undertook to repair a second little tumbledown church, San Pietro della Spina, a mile or two south of San Damiano, near some Bernardone property. This work was completed sometime during the course of 1208.

Francis then took his well-used tools and made his way along the Via Antica to the west, through the forest of oaks, to stop near a crossroads with the way to Bettona.

Both San Pietro and this fresh chapel he was seeking were well known to him, for he was close to his beloved San Lazzaro dell'Arce. In a little clearing within the oak forest was an ancient, long-neglected, rectangular chapel with a rounded roof, dedicated to Our Lady of the Angels, and commonly called the Portiuncula, or "little portion," because, so people said, Saint Benedict[23] himself was given a little parcel, or portion, of land near the chapel. Certainly it had from time immemorial belonged to the Benedictines on Monte Subasio high above, and consequently was closely associated with Francis and his family through the Benedictine church so near his own home.

Evidently it had not, up until now, attracted his special attention, or else he would have earlier set to repair it. But now, as he was looking at its crumbling masonry and its roof open to the wind and rain, year by year causing the fresco of the Assumption to fade and disintegrate, he must surely have had a feeling that he had found home at last. Perhaps because the Portiuncula, so far from the town, so deeply buried in the woods, seemed to him so little worth repairing, his senses were there first opened to the real meaning of the words of the crucified Christ in San Damiano. Christ was setting him a task far, far greater than putting stone upon stone in disused churches. The repair needed was in the hearts of men, of popes, prelates and priests, of princes and magistrates and sol-diers and traders, of ordinary men and women, all bound together in the Mystical Body of Christ, which is the living Church, yet still for the most part living separate, lonely, misfitting, self-regarding lives in slavery to pride and money, in fear of insecurity, nursing hollow ambitions and the vicious circle of passions and distractions.

[23] Saint Benedict (c. 480-550), father of Western monasticism.

In such terms he must have meditated as he settled down once again to the repair of the chapel, already seven hundred years old and destined to endure unchanged for another seven hundred years, and — who knows? — perhaps seven hundred years more, the object of pilgrimage of countless millions, the treasure of all who have sought to live their lives, however distantly, under the inspiration and protection of Saint Francis of Assisi. Yet, by one of those strange paradoxes of human history, Francis himself would have been horrified by the size and richness of the immense baroque canopy which has preserved the humble Portiuncula by sheltering it from the ravages of the nature which Francis so much loved. But it did so preserve, in God's Providence, a shrine uniquely valued by the millions whose pilgrimage is to the *poverello*.

As a man grows older, nearer to his end, so does he tend to recall with a new vividness the memories of his youth. Francis, in his testament, we have seen, began by recalling the lepers and how he had dealt mercifully with them. The repair, actual and symbolic of the "little portion" was surely in his mind as he went on dictating to Brother Leo in the Portiuncula itself: "And the Lord gave me such faith in churches that I would simply pray and say, 'We adore Thee, O Lord Jesus Christ, here and in all the world.' . . . After that, the Lord gave me and He gives me so much faith in priests . . . that if they persecuted me, I would have recourse to them. . . . I am unwilling to see sin in them, because in them I see the Son of God, and they are my lords. I do this because, in this world, I see nothing corporally of the most high Son of God Himself except His most holy Body and Blood, which they receive and which they alone administer to others."

There was the solid foundation on which this passionate reformer and poet would seek in his own unique, extravagant but ever-living way to obey Christ's bidding: "Repair my Church."

By the year 1209, the work of repairing the Portiuncula had been completed. Francis was in his middle twenties.

Reading biographies which hurry through this early, but vital period, one may get the impression that the chapels were restored in the twinkling of an eye. It was not so. This period of conversion and manual work covered two or three years — a substantial portion of Francis's twenty-three years or so as a man of religion. During these years, Francis must have continued his solitary way of life, alternating his building and repairing with begging in Assisi for his food and for the tools and material he needed for his work. Assisi was a place where lay preachers, members of new sects, and oddities of one kind or another were to be met with. By comparison with some of them, this kindly *pazzo* of a well-known family must have come to seem a sane and modest person, however original his ways. Kindly people, having become used to him, would bring him food and gifts when they happened to be riding their mules and donkeys near where he was working. After all, if he was a beggar, he was a good beggar, not only restoring the worship of God where it had been neglected, but also playing a part, however small, in what we should call civic improvement.

Francis's solitariness during these years is harder to understand. The man who would soon be charming thousands and who in time was to have the largest progeny of any religious founder failed to attract a single disciple. It must have been his own wish to be spiritually alone at first. No one, as he used to say in his testament, "showed me what to do." Presumably, there were no more crumbling chapels to repair, and he was waiting for another sign from God. These months were certainly lived in the closest intimacy with God, an intimacy from which he acquired that mystical sense haunting him throughout a life that God wished him to live in an active apostolate. Meanwhile, it was up to Christ to give him his next orders.

He recognized these orders from his Master on the feast of Saint Matthias, February 24, 1209,[24] when he was serving Mass in his beloved, newly restored Portiuncula. This date is certain, for only on this day were the relevant Scriptural passages read in the missals of the time.

The priest was reading the Gospel. That Gospel told of Christ's commission to the Apostles: "Preach as you go, telling them the kingdom of Heaven is at hand. Heal the sick, raise the dead, cleanse the lepers, cast out devils: give as you have received a gift without payment. Do not provide gold or silver or copper to fill your purses, nor a wallet for the journey, no second coat, no spare shoes or staves; the laborer has a right to his maintenance."[25]

Francis must often have heard those words before, but as so often happens to us all, the place, the context, the association with some inner interest or wish caused him really to *hear* them for the first time.

The familiar sound and rhythm, the figurative sense, evidently not to be taken too literally, was suddenly transmuted, and the words were to him words of fire. God Himself was

---

[24] The feast of Saint Matthias is now celebrated on May 14. — ED.
[25] Matt. 10:7-10.

speaking through them, speaking them with all the significance which they suddenly seemed to have for *him*. "Cleanse the lepers!" This, at least, was a familiar password calling him forward. No gold, no silver, no copper — it was the counterpart, the authentic version of the former gestures of showering gold, silver, and copper on shrines and beggars and needy knights. The voice of the priest at the humble little altar of the wayside chapel was once again the voice of Christ.

After Mass, Francis, prompt as usual to assure himself of the authority of the ordained representative of Christ, asked the priest to expound the meaning of that Gospel, and the priest told him of the life of Christ on earth — a life in which those words had been literally followed. "But this is what I have always been searching for!" Francis exclaimed. "This is what I have been waiting to do — wanting it from the very depths of my heart."

The inference we automatically make when we read the detailed account in Celano is illuminating. We are reminded that even at this stage, after three years of semi-religious life, Francis remained ignorant of matters which today are the background of every reasonably educated layman. So unread was he and so unfamiliar with elementary Scripture that he accepted the single text as Christ's sole direction for a fully spiritual life, completely ignoring other texts which make it clear that Christ did not condemn all use of money, but gave advice varying with different vocations and circumstances.

This misunderstanding, which governs so much of Francis's life and example to his disciples, was later to prove a serious source of the troubles which were to mark the early development of the Franciscan order. All he could now see, however, was that his Lady Poverty was proving herself to be what he had always in his heart believed her to be — the lady who walked with the naked Christ, his Master.

There was no time to lose. "No sooner heard than done," Celano has the very phrase. There and then, he took off his shoes and threw his staff as far as he could. He undid his leather belt and took off his outer tunic. Around the patched, undyed, colorless undertunic he tied a piece of rope. Francis had become the first Franciscan.

Chapter Eight

Francis's Joyful Heart
Draws Followers

Henri Daniel-Rops, discussing the Church at this time, has well expressed in a single sentence where the Church's repairs were needed: "An ill-trained clergy, degraded in its lower ranks by lack of principles and contaminated at higher levels by lay influences, was poorly armed to meet the two temptations of man: the temptations of the flesh and the temptations of money."

Hence the constant effort of better men to repair the Church that showed so many cracks, so much neglect, and such dangerous signs of decay in Her dark corners. Great saints and holy men — Saint Bernard[26] had been dead only thirty years when Francis was born — and a great variety of "free-lance" local reformers of uncertain orthodoxy, as we have seen, were striving to effect the necessary repairs. The times were indeed ripe for a man who would combine sanctity, orthodoxy, and popular revolutionary temper: a man who had heard a voice from on high bidding him "repair my Church."

Not that there was anything of the modern revolutionary temper in Francis — in the sense in which we understand

[26] Saint Bernard (1090-1153), Abbot of Clairvaux.

such a phrase today, at any rate. The revolutionary has an itch to denounce; Francis, the sinner, wanted to repair and rebuild where reparation and rebuilding matter most and are most effective — in the hearts of ordinary men. It is remarkable that in his writings and in his legend, there would be little denunciation of the ways of the world around him. His strongest words — and they could be very strong — would be reserved for those of his followers who, having shared his ideals, wanted to water down his own uncompromising poverty and humility, the only effective solution to the state of the world entangled by the lust of the flesh, the pride of life,[27] and the acquisitive urge.

Men, he seemed to say, erred not so much through malice and weakness, but through failure to grasp the meaning of life as taught by Christ. God would doubtless have pity on human blindness, but God had called *him* at least to show in his own life the fundamental answer in the restoration of Christian hearts and wills through preaching nothing but the naked, humble, submissive, and loving Christ. He would never bother his head about new rules, regulations, and reform. Cleanse the heart, and the rest would follow.

Not that we can ever dissociate the revolutionary in him from the political and social struggles of the time. He had grown up in a turbulent city whose people had ceaselessly suffered from the conflict between the feudal *Majores* and the civic *Minores*, a city which suffered bitter wars itself with all war's consequences of misery, maiming, hunger, and hatred. The tradition has been to suggest that Francis sided with the

[27] Cf. 1 John 2:16.

Minores, perhaps because he was to call his companions *Minores* (the lesser folk) — but in a far more literal sense. But it is clear that the biographical tradition has misunderstood the true nature of the political *Minores*. These comprised the merchant and professional class, whose one idea was to amass wealth and become *Majores* themselves. Pride of life, yearning for position and glory, humbling a rival: these were the aims of the *nouveaux riches*.

Francis came to realize how much he had been influenced by the class to which he belonged, even though his search for glory had been very different and very superior to that of his family and his social equals. His spiritual message, his total turning away from the ambitions and values of his co-citizens, are in direct opposition to all that his family and class stood for. His search for the naked Christ was a rebellion against wealth and worldly honor and success. It sprang from his own experience of it. But his was not the mind to "universalize" his personal conviction. He would be interested in those who freely chose to live with him in evangelical poverty, and imitate Christ with him, but never would he attempt to establish a new Christian social class. His conversion was deeply personal, and it was always to express a personal conviction, a special vocation.

There is no reference in the sources to any such thing, but it seems possible that at this time, Francis again consulted Bishop Guido, seeing in him the bishop, not the man, just as Guido must have seen in Francis the simple goodwill, not the possible heresy. Francis must have looked for advice, as well as for some authority for his plan to carry out the precepts of the Gospel in their most literal sense: to preach as he went, telling them "the kingdom of Heaven is at hand" — a kingdom of Heaven which is hidden, however deeply, in the heart of each man created in God's image. In this first phase of his lonely apostolic mission, we hear no word of Francis's preaching in churches, and it is reasonable to suppose that Guido advised him to preach unofficially in public places and within such houses as would open their doors to him. At that time, there was nothing very novel about such freelance preaching.

Celano reports his manner of preaching: "His words seemed like burning fire. They entered right into men's hearts, and all the people were filled with admiration. He seemed entirely different from what he had been in the past, like a man who had once seen Heaven, failing to take an interest in the earth. . . . Whenever he preached, he introduced his sermon with a prayer for peace: 'May the Lord give you peace.' "

We also know that, like Christ, he preached with few words — and to the point. There was magic in his voice and words — a magic almost wholly absent from his written words as they have come down to us.

A student in Bologna who reported one of Francis's later sermons said that learned people in his audience were amazed at such eloquence coming from so simple a man, and his reported sayings and speeches from the various sources are always full of life and vigor. It was surely his words, as well as his personality, which induced so many thousands to follow him in his short lifetime, in what must have seemed to them a desperate way of life.

Because of his own extreme asceticism, which in his more profound and official moments seems to counterbalance his gaiety and common humanity with his own brethren, there may be a temptation to think of him as a grave and serious preacher. Celano, telling us that he preached penance and that he was entirely different from the man he had formerly been, leaves one with this impression. Yet we are also told that he was full of joy and that, in time, he won over his own people of Assisi, many of whom had been mocking and jeering.

Surely it is more likely that it was much the same Francis in manner: the Francis who delighted to break into song, with plenty of stories to tell, seeking his illustrations from the people, the town, the countryside, the birds of the air, and the animals; a lively, cheerful, mobile Francis easily turning from the grave to the light, from the warning to the encouragement — all this, and yet a man now possessing a new confidence and authority which brought a new respect and a new response.

His mind, ever since his turning to God, had been preoccupied with the paradox that in detachment, poverty, and penance, perfect joy was to be found, and we can imagine him neatly describing the helpless entanglements into which even the best of people got themselves by putting their trust in worldly cares and pleasures. Was he not himself, in his thin, drab clothes, without a penny with which to bless himself, a truly happy fellow, bursting into song and dance, as he would proceed to show?

Untrained, unlettered, and with a minimum of knowledge of what a preacher normally should know, he must have depended entirely on his native genius and his inner spiritual inspiration. He preached what came to his heart — that heart so filled with joy, so filled also with compassion for the blindness of people for the sake of whom his Master had suffered so much.

Later, no doubt, when his reputation was made, Francis's sermons would have borne more of the "missionary" character, with the church bells ringing and the people hurrying to meet the holy man. From the top of convenient steps, or on a convenient stone pulpit (some of which have been preserved), he addressed the masses who flocked to hear him.

Yet it was with reluctance on both sides that the repairing of God's Church through the establishment of a new society of disciples of Francis was begun. Francis, who was still content to fulfill the words of the Gospel as he had heard them on Saint Matthias's feast in the Portiuncula, had no desire to acquire disciples or followers. And it is hardly surprising that after all that was known of Francis in Assisi, puzzled admiration for his newfound powers, rather than any idea of committing oneself to him, expressed the feelings of the people.

We do hear of one unknown disciple in Assisi: "a certain man of Assisi, pious and simple in spirit and a devout man of God, the first to follow him." But we hear no more of him, and it may be that Francis himself, who in his testament said that even after he had acquired followers, "no one showed me what to do," parted from him.

As usual with Francis, it required something striking and unexpected to induce him to change his mind, although on this occasion, there was nothing miraculous about it. Still, the people of Assisi must have thought that this fresh development was as good as a miracle, for no less a personage than Bernardo da Quintavalle da Birardello wanted to throw in his lot with the crazy, if sympathetic, Francesco di Bernardone.

Bernard da Quintavalle's name has endured in the fine house and long, tortuous street winding around Assisi's steep hill. The Quintavalles, unlike the Bernardones, were of noble blood, although the two families were similarly wealthy. Bernard was a good man, but he moved slowly, only coming to decisions after lengthy examination and consideration and when perfectly certain of the best line to take. The *Fioretti*[28] tells us that he was "wise," by which they mean careful and calculating. Evidently, the story of the Bernardones and their good-for-nothing son who had impulsively repudiated a heritage for some wildcat religious ideal greatly impressed this man. The difference in age between them was not great, Bernard being a little older. What on earth had made Francesco, with his ambitions and promising worldly career, behave in this extraordinary fashion? Dreamer, poet, yes, but the rest was crazy. Yet there must be a reason, for Francesco was no idiot. Could there be anything in it? Bernard began to work it out for himself.

Obviously, a really wise man would want to be a success not only in this world, but in the far-longer-enduring next world. Could it have been this very sensible reflection which accounted for Francesco's behavior? Had he, after all, been wiser than his father, who had treated him so badly? Had he been wiser than Bernardo da Quintavalle himself?

So he kept his eyes on Francis, and he must have listened carefully to what he had to say in his street-corner preaching.

It was Bernard who took the first step. He wanted to investigate what it was that, in the modern phrase, made this son of

---

[28] That is, *Fioretti di S. Francesco d'Assisi,* or *The Little Flowers of St. Francis of Assisi,* a classic collection of stories and traditions about Saint Francis and his companions.

Bernardone "tick." So Bernard invited the self-made spiritual tramp to his own fine house.

There they talked together for many hours, Francis telling him the whole story of his life. Bernard gradually became convinced that Francis was genuine, with an outlook a great deal sounder than his own. But he was not going to be caught out without guarantees of solid spiritual solvency. He asked Francis to stay the night.

When the lights were out, Bernard pretended to be asleep, while keeping a wary eye on his companion. Ascetic by day, Francis might well be the kind of holy man who made up for it by snoring all night. But Francis, after falling into a light sleep, soon awoke. Getting out of bed, he knelt on the floor and remained in that position for a long time, praying — presumably for his host. That was good enough for Bernard da Quintavalle, who was to become his first disciple. They must have decided together on the next step, for two make a company. One stage in Francis's life was now turning into another.

As to the third Franciscan, there are doubts. He was, we know, a man called Peter, who is traditionally held to be Peter Catanei, a lawyer, although certainly not a canon of the cathedral, as he is always described. Peter Catanei was destined to act as Francis's vicar when Francis was away or too ill to carry the full burden of authority. Celano, however, says of the second companion, "Peter," that he was another man of Assisi, worthy of high praise for his manner of life, which "was closed shortly after, yet more holily than it had begun." It is hard to believe that Celano would thus have referred to the early death of the second companion, had he really been Peter Catanei, who, in any case, we know to have died in 1221, fifteen years later, predeceasing Francis himself by only five years.

Because of this and because, as we shall see, he could not read Latin or know very much about the Scriptures, the Bollandists,[29] followed by some later authorities, hold that the tradition is wrong and that we know nothing about the first brother Peter, except the little that Celano tells us.

The two recruits went with Francis to the church of Saint Nicholas one early dawn to consult the Gospels as to God's will for them, now that they had become a body or society, against, apparently, all of Francis's own expectations and even desires.

Francis would have known the parish priest well, since it was his own parish church. He asked for his help so that the three of them could hear the voice of Christ Himself through the words that Christ had left to the world in the Gospels.

It was another typical combination of common sense and search for divine inspiration. They prayed together, and Francis opened at random the book of the Gospels three times. The priest translated the first passage he saw: "If thou hast an eye to be perfect, go, then, and sell all that belongs to thee; give it to the poor, and so the treasure that thou hast shall be in Heaven; then come back and follow me."[30] He shut the book and opened it again. This time the message read, "Take nothing with you to use on your journey, staff or wallet or bread or

---

[29] The Jesuit editors of the series of lives of the saints known as the *Acta Sanctorum* were called Bollandists after John van Bolland (1596-1665), the first editor of the work.

[30] Matt. 19:21.

money; you are not to have more than one coat apiece."[31] And a third time, the book was closed and opened to read, "If any man has a mind to come my way, let him renounce self, and take up his cross, and follow me."[32]

Then Francis said, "My brothers, such is our life and our rule. Such is the life and rule of all who may wish to join our company. Go, therefore, and carry out what you have heard."

Had Francis had his way, these words of the Gospel, taken in their most literal sense and without reference to other qualifying texts, of which he appeared so ignorant, would have remained forever the sole essential rule of the order.

Bernard and Peter, having settled their worldly affairs — a complex legal business in Bernard's case, even though he gave the proceeds to the poor — put on the rough tunic and an old rope, and went with Francis to the Portiuncula to start their unique experiment in a human way of life.

Here was news indeed for the people of Assisi. Francis, half-mad and, thank Heaven, unique in his particular kind of madness, had actually succeeded in making disciples, one at least from the most solid and sensible people of the town: the looked-up-to Bernardo, a man who had known so well how to combine the spiritual and the temporal in a rational way. How could such men take so revolutionary a step? This question must have struck deeply into a young man called Giles.

Like Francis, Giles had had knightly ambitions. It being the vigil of the feast of Saint George, he had probably been preparing for the jousts and tourneys which were customarily

[31] Luke 9:3.
[32] Matt. 16:24; Mark 8:34; Luke 9:23.

held on the saint's feast day. How far he was from realizing that never again would he express his knightly ambitions in such a way!

"On the feast of Saint George in the year of the Lord 1209, very early in the morning," as the chronicler with unusual historical exactitude tells us, Giles went to Saint George's Church to pray for light. The church was crowded for the solemn Mass of the knights. How could *he* be a true knight, the young man wondered, and he found the answer where he least expected it. Francesco had wanted to be a knight. Could he not follow in his footsteps? He made up his mind to look for Francis. He said a special prayer that God would lead him to that holy young man.

He set out toward the country and ran into Francis. It was enough. He humbly asked Francis to let him be a member of his company.

In this shrewd, simple person with the smiling eyes who stood before him, Francis saw his true Knight of the Round Table and said to him, "If the Emperor Augustus were to come to Assisi and to choose some citizen to be his knight and lord of the bedchamber, such a knight would be delighted, would he not? Equally delighted should you be at having been thus chosen by God to be His knight and favorite squire to follow Him in His rule of the Gospels. Be strong and constant, then, in the calling for which God has chosen you."

No one was to take Francis more literally than Giles. Francis relished that literalness which made Giles a "character" even among so singular a company.

Giles, the perfect Knight of the Round Table, as Francis always regarded him, would have no use for polite and cautious subterfuges. Perhaps as characteristic as any in his "legend" was his retort, many years later, when the present grandiose basilica and convent of Saint Francis was being built by Elias. Looking at it, Giles said to one of the brothers, "I suppose all you require now is wives!" And when the brother tried to express his indignation, Giles explained, "You have evidently abandoned Holy Poverty, so you may as well abandon Holy Chastity."

He did not hesitate to twit cardinals who asked for his prayers yet continued to live in an unfitting manner and preachers who spoke much but practiced little. Giles, like the later disciple Juniper, represents for posterity the authentic strand of freedom and idiosyncrasy which was so characteristic of Francis's spirit.

Bernard, Peter, and Giles, the first three Franciscans: a rich man, a forgotten follower, and a simple young man putting his trust in God and Saint George. The worldly cares of a great business, the mass of forgotten people, the self-reliance of native shrewdness and simplicity: Francis, still making disciples against his intentions, had drawn a trio strikingly representative of the preoccupations which men must put aside in favor of the uncommitted freedom of the sons of God.

Others were soon to follow, and by autumn the numbers had been made up to twelve, a number in conformity with the Apostles, although Francis himself could have no interest in the efforts of Franciscan posterity to show a conformity between himself and Christ, which was a delight of his legend makers. In truth, we know very little about these first disciples. Even the conformity-seekers got muddled, since in some accounts Francis is one of the first twelve and in others he is not. There even had to be a Judas among the twelve or thirteen.

Except that all came from Assisi, we know nothing but the names of Sabatino, Morico, called the Small, John of San Costanzo, Barbaro and Bernardo dei Vigilanti. Of Philip the Long (a surname, not a nickname) Celano speaks, saying that although he had not studied the Scriptures, God had given him a wonderful power to expound their hidden meaning. John of Capello, of noble birth, was the Judas, although all we hear of his infidelity is that he objected to covering his head with a cowl and insisted on wearing a hat. The last of these first disciples was the rich and noble young knight, Angelo di Tancredi, an Assisian like the others and related to Clare, and not to be confused, as in most lives, with one of Francis's "Three Companions," Brother Angelo of Rieti.

This leaves Sylvester, who is named among the twelve when Francis's name is omitted. Sylvester was a priest, one in thirteen, a proportion in harmony with Francis's notion of a band essentially lay and uncommitted, yet living independently and therefore needing regular priestly ministry. He had not been, it seems, a very edifying priest, for when Bernard, after his decision to throw in his lot with Francis, was recklessly distributing his money to the poor of Assisi, Sylvester came to him angrily complaining. He told Bernard that he had given Francis stones for the repair of the three little churches and had not received a brass farthing in return. Francis, who was watching, smiled, and taking two handfuls of the money, he gave them to the priest.

An essentially good man, Sylvester was caught out by the most generous of hearts in an expression of petty meanness. He was left with much to think about. As a Franciscan, he was to live a life of solitude, reflection, and prayer.

Chapter Nine

❧

The Franciscans Console Hearts

Thus, haphazardly, had the first little company been formed, hardly knowing why or what it was all about. Francis did not plan it, but those first companions very soon came to realize that they had taken the most logical step in the world, escaping from the artificial worries and anxieties of conventional life to pursue together, without preparation or plan, the "one thing necessary."[33]

"Preach as you go, telling them that the kingdom of Heaven is at hand."[34]

The words of Christ and the imitation of His example were rule enough and purpose enough. Time had rolled back twelve hundred years, and in the "Galilee of Italy," the "good news" was being preached again in village square, on the hills and in the valleys where the people were growing their crops or tending their beasts. It was the dry and sunny season, when any man can live off the country and the generosity of its folk, being content with the shade of a tree or the protection of an outbuilding for his rest.

[33] Luke 10:42.
[34] Matt. 10:7.

These were the golden days when the brothers set out two by two on a holy mission which was also a delight.[35] The mood of the solitary Francis singing his way to Gubbio had become the mood of these first companions.

Francis himself had chosen as his personal companion his perfect knight, the dry-witted Brother Giles. Together they set forth in an easterly direction toward the busy port of Ancona. Was this a first expression of his longing to contemplate the sea which would one day carry him, not to the warlike Crusades, but to the land trod by his Master, the land that was to call him to spiritual knightly service in true service of the infidels?

There is a whiff of the sea in an early report by *The Three Companions* of the conversation that took place between the two holy men.

"Our work will be like the work of a fisherman who catches large numbers of fish, but leaves the small fish in the water and only puts the big ones in his basket." And the same authority tells us in so many words how thoroughly the new apostles enjoyed these days. "Walking toward the March of Ancona, they were in the highest spirits in the Lord. Francis, the holy man, walked along singing songs in French at the top of his clear voice, songs which blessed and exalted the goodness of the Most High." The same song of praise would one day be on his lips when, blind and broken, he was ready to go to his Lord.

No wonder the simple people, momentarily disturbed in their labors, thought that a couple of "fools or drunkards" were singing their way through those lonely parts. As for the pretty

---

[35] Cf. Mark 6:7; Luke 10:1.

Italian girls, they fled in terror when they saw these ragged, noisy tramps, "lest they should be led away by a foolishness or madness."

The Three Companions gives us a delightful picture of their evangelism. They did not formally preach to the people, but when they passed through the tight little huddles of houses and huts, they called upon the people to love and fear God and to be sorry for their sins. Or rather, that was what Francis did. As for Giles, he was content to go among the crowd with a knowing look, muttering, "You had better believe him. I promise you that no one gives better advice."

Alas, *The Three Companions* tells us that whether it was Francis or Giles or any other of these wandering spiritual tramps, "no one as yet followed them."

No wonder! This was not the way of the occasional itinerant reformist preacher who might pass by, wearing a severe and admonitory look and hinting of a dark future for Church and state. Nor was it the way of the professional cleric, too like a cleric at some times and too much unlike one at others. These new men, and especially Francis, in love with God and also in love with God's handiwork, frail as its human element too often might be, were in Heaven as they tramped under God's blue skies, treading God's warm, soft earth, at one with His radiant messengers: the birds singing above, the beasts browsing in the fields, the infinite variety of beauty in animal and vegetable creation. They saw the kindly, softened eyes of the older peasants, the willing patience of their hard-working womenfolk, the joy and the love of the courting couples, and the roguish innocence of the children, adored then as now by every Italian. The vision in these new men's hearts turned

God's world into a vision newly seen. They had to pinch themselves to remember that they had chosen Christ's naked-ness and penance because they knew that sin, greed, and self-centeredness lurked under every fair appearance. No, it was not the usual sermon they were preaching, and if the people could not believe their eyes, at least they were not to forget that something new and, on reflection, very wonderful had come into their land.

On these expeditions, Francis always insisted that the apostolic travelers should pay a special reverence to every way-side chapel and any wayside crucifix. Whether the Blessed Sacrament was reserved or not in any church they passed, they knew that every chapel and shrine was "a place of the Lord." We may safely add to this that so was every fine prospect, every tree, and every animal.

"Wherever they went, were it city, castle, farm, or house, they brought the message of peace. They consoled all whom they met, telling them to fear and love the Creator of Heaven and earth and keep His commandments. When asked who they were, they answered, 'We are penitents from the city of Assisi.' " The contrast between this evangelical peace and the wars, conflicts, and cupidities of Assisi — that "New Baby-lon" — could not have been more marked.

Bad as their reception often was at the hands of the many who began by mocking them and ended by loving them, it was when they were back in the shadows of the Portiuncula that these happy men of penance found themselves most consis-tently under criticism.

Living so close to Assisi, these unorganized and, literally, unruly tramps had a way of appearing in the most unlikely places, asking for food. Where once there had been a single madman, Francesco di Bernardone, who at any rate worked for his living by restoring chapels, now there were many — and the numbers were mysteriously increasing. Besides, Francesco at least could make them laugh, as when he would pick up two sticks and excitedly accompany his singing of the praises of the Lord with an imaginary fiddle. Compared with him, Bernardo, who, anyway, had let down proud Assisi, Pietro and Sylvestro and the others were boring beggars, although Giles could be relied on for the unexpected.

This kind of nonsense could not go on. A civic deputation to His Lordship the Bishop must be arranged. Religion itself, quite apart from Assisi's good name, was being mocked by these crazy eccentrics. Scandal is never more easily taken than by the respectable who are never aware of their own pompous self-centeredness.

So Guido sent for Francis and reported to him the complaints that had been brought to his notice. He must have kindly suggested that the penitents' way of living without any money or possessions was altogether too unpractical.

It was now that Francis made the famous reply, the spirit of which the world has ever since too little heeded, although it has had proof enough of Francis's common sense: "If we had possessions, my lord, we should need arms to protect them. Possessions cause disputes and lawsuits, troubles well calculated to destroy the love of God and our neighbor. That is why we are agreed about having no worldly goods in this world."

Guido must have been a very exceptional bishop even in those less-organized and rigid days. He did not say, "My son, your ideals are fine, but, after all, we have to be practical men.

Don't worry, leave it to me. I'll arrange it all and work out a rule of life for you and your friends which, I promise, will fulfill God's will for you as God means it to be fulfilled. God's Church comes first, and I'll give you a useful place within it." Instead, recalling, doubtless, the Francis who had stood stark naked before the crowd, he allowed him and his friends to follow the way of complete denudation and privation.

One has to guess the community way of life during these first months of this handful of men who felt themselves to be dedicated as none before had been. Their "two by two" missionary work in central Italy was based on the little chapel and shelter of the Portiuncula, where, under cover of the trees, they built rough huts of wattle. It was there that Francis had heard the Gospel of the apostolate and had its meaning expounded to him by the priest. That priest would have been a Benedictine of Monte Subasio, and he may have acted as intermediary when Francis was looking for a permanent base for the brethren as their numbers began to grow. The priests of the church of Saint Benedict near the Bernardone home would also have given him their view of Francis. Their references would have been more than enough, so Francis climbed the slopes above Assisi to find the abbot, who proved to be most willing to let him keep the chapel permanently. Francis, however, insisted on a loan, not a gift — a loan, the interest for which he would pay yearly by a jar full of *lasche,* the little fish to be found in great abundance in Lake Trasimeno. Not to be outdone, the abbot sent back every year a jar of oil.

This picturesque business transaction saved proprieties, but, thank Heaven, Francis's detachment was nothing calculated and inhuman. Although he would have given up the

Portiuncula immediately, had he ever been asked to, he made no secret of his love for his home and that of his brethren. The distinction between a legal possession and an attachment due to love in one's heart may seem academic, but, in this instance, it helps to remind us that it was never through lack of a deep human attachment to the men and places he loved that he set himself to go through life possessing nothing of the things in which he so much delighted.

An alternative home for the brethren was a rough horse-and-cattle shelter at Rivotorto on the banks of a twisting stream of that name, a mile or so from the Portiuncula. The winter rains and snow seeping into the woods around the Portiuncula may have caused this alternative use of a more solid shelter. Halfway between the two places lay the lazaretto, and it is unthinkable that the brethren were not often there.

It was at Rivotorto that the shelter was divided into cells by pieces of chalk. On one occasion, they were reduced to feeding on mangels through lack of any other food. But this asceticism, voluntary or imposed by necessity, was softened, as always with Francis, with a touching humanity and a sense of humor.

The famous story in the *Mirror of Perfection*[36] undoubtedly typifies the priority of love over penance in the mind of this pursuer of utter detachment. One night at Rivotorto, a brother woke up shouting, "I am dying! I am dying!" The brethren were awakened, and Francis asked for a light. Gently he inquired of the brother what was the matter with him. "I am

---

[36] That is, *Speculum Perfectionis*, a collection of stories about Saint Francis.

dying of hunger," he moaned. So Francis, rather than just feed him and make him feel an exception or a greedy fellow among ascetical company, ordered food to be collected and made them all have a meal together in the middle of the night.

This story is capped by the one in the *Fioretti* telling of how, at a later date, Brother Juniper cooked some gruel to ease Francis's throat, which, in Brother Juniper's view, must have become sore through rebuking him. Francis rebuked him still more for being so foolish. Then Juniper said, "Well, father, if you will not eat it yourself, please hold up the candle for me so that I can enjoy it." Then Francis, who loved Juniper's naiveté, saw that, in this case, they might as well enjoy it together. "And they were far more comforted by devotion than by their food," comments the writer.

From the beginning, Francis's attachment to certain places is clear. These special spots, preserved in Franciscan history as shrines, seemed for one reason or another to focus his wider love for nature in all its aspects. The man who had given up all for God found consolation in God's generosity to him with His free gift of places and spots that came to be especially dear to him. Earliest of them after Assisi and its immediate environment was Poggio Bustone above the valley of Rieti, where Francis met Angelo of Rieti and made him not only one of his company, but one of the three intimate companions, together with Brother Leo and Brother Rufino.

This long journey seems to have been planned as a major expedition, for many of the brethren went with him. Perhaps Francis had half a mind to carry on to Rome to see the Pope, but desisted on this occasion. What is certain is that he must have seen, as so many since have seen, a little settlement of small, brown, heaped-up dwellings nearly three thousand feet on top of the arid, stony mountainside to the east, where the snow-capped Monte Terminello stands guard. His love of solitude and barren heights, which, in his nature, balanced a love of cozy sheltered peace, prompted him to climb upward.

After the climb, he was happy to greet the people of this desolate mountain village with the words that can be read today on a tablet in one of the terraced lanes: "*Buon giorno, buona gente!*" ("Good day, good people!") The good people, mysteriously earning their bread in these barren parts, were doubtless amazed to see a beggar arriving at the end of the world for no obvious reason. It must be some saint coming down from Heaven, they thought. In some such way, at least, one has to reconstruct the scene, since we know that it was here that Francis, preaching against hypocrisy, confessed that so far was he from being a saint that he had eaten lard in Lent. Never, as we shall see, did he have a head for formal rules.

The cheerful "Good day, good people" and the surely jocular confession of how greedy this supposed saint was tells us almost all we need to know of the early Saint Francis, still in relatively good health, as he moved from one spot to another.

But we need also to remember that above the little village lay the wilderness which had first attracted him to a spot far from men and near to God. It was in solitary, silent prayer that he gained strength to endure the far-less-cheerful reception that too often faced him when the crowd laughed at him instead of smiling with him.

"You will find some that are true, gentle, and gracious. They will gladly accept what you say. But you will find far more who are faithless, proud, and blasphemous. These will mock and oppose you, and you will have to do your best." Such was his own warning to his followers.

The times were rough, and Italians have a habit of speaking their mind — and Francis, there is no escaping it, must have seemed very odd. It may be that, so human was Francis in his reactions, that the spots where he was happiest, whether in the north, not far from Assisi, or in Italy's heart, near the valley of Rieti, with its charming little lake of Piedi Lucco, were the places like Poggio Bustone, where the people quickly took him to their hearts.

Chapter Ten

❧

Francis Wins the Pope's Blessing

Francis, the spiritual tramp, the freelance religious, the knight with his brother Knights of the Round Table, always surprises us when we least expect it.

It seems extraordinary at first sight that this humble little man of Assisi, with his handful of companions, in the good books of the local bishop, a good enough man in himself, should now decide that he must personally see the Pope — and so tremendous a figure of a pope as Innocent III. After all, who was Francis, and what had he to tell the Pope?

Religious groups like his positively pullulated across Christian Europe. Francis had no idea of a rule, save that of the Gospel, and no idea of a way of life and work, save that of the disciples of Christ. His biographers retrospectively cause him to have foreseen the immense following of the future, but this seems most unlikely and most uncharacteristic. And yet he insisted on seeing the Pope. Why?

Surely, first, because he was Francis; second, because of his simple understanding of the Church, and third, because of his connatural orthodoxy of mind. Francis had the fearlessness of true simplicity and vision. He never recoiled from ideas and gestures that overawe petty, self-regarding minds; he never seemed to reckon with the possibility of defeat or snubs injurious to a man's complacency and pride. And he had been commissioned by someone far greater than any pope — by Christ's word: "Repair my Church." To have the idea and to carry it out were one and the same thing with Francis. The Pope was the head of the Church, his father in God, and Francis, as it happened, lived quite near Perugia, a papal city, which was often the pontifical residence. If he was to continue with his companions to live the religious life which he instinctively felt to be God's way for him, his friends, and any further friends who might wish to join him — well, the Pope was the obvious person from whom to seek advice and approval.

Rome, the capital of Christendom, and the object of universal pilgrimage, had already been visited by him. He made up his mind to go there at once and seek audience and permission to continue along the religious way to which Christ had called him.

Had he consulted the Bishop of Assisi? We do not know. We may doubt, however, whether Guido would have thought the plan a wise step at that particular moment. Celano says that Guido was unhappy at the thought of Francis's leaving Assisi, where he could do so much good. Guido, as we shall see, was to be in Rome when Francis reached it. Had that wise man and protector traveled there posthaste to prevent disastrous consequences that must have seemed to him only too likely? The sources say that he knew nothing of the journey. Yet once he knew of Francis's decision, he must have been terrified by the possible consequences.

Francis, of course, knew the way. Probably some of the others had been on pilgrimage to the tombs of the apostles, for

Assisi is only a little over a hundred miles from Rome. Possibly Bernard knew the Eternal City well, for he was chosen as leader of the expedition — another example of Francis's humility. It was in the early summer of 1210 that the little company trudged their way southward.

Innocent III was perhaps the mightiest of all the popes. Certainly the claims which he made for the power of the papacy over secular nations were the highest ever made, before or since. Innocent III, in the words of Don Sturzo, "always claimed a wide and decisive power over Christendom, as unifying the social structure in a religious center which, inasmuch as religious, was also political."[37] Yet it was Innocent's claim which furthered the liberation of the common people of Europe from the shackles of feudalism and indeed would make possible the social changes carried through in such large measure by the friars, of whom the most important in this respect were the Franciscans. But if Innocent conceived his papal powers and duties in grandiose terms, he was personally a man of deep and mystical spirituality, one of whose sayings is always worth remembering: "The sin least worthy of being pardoned is the sin of despairing of God's goodness."

Despite his grandeur, he must have been a very approachable pope. According to one version, Francis is said to have met him unannounced at the Lateran Palace,[38] and Matthew Paris,[39] the English Benedictine who did not approve of friars,

[37] Luigi Sturzo, *Church and State* (Notre Dame, Indiana: University of Notre Dame Press, 1962), 98.

[38] The basilica of Saint John Lateran is the cathedral church of Rome.

[39] Matthew Paris (c. 1199-1259), medieval chronicler.

tells us that Innocent was so outraged by the sight of Francis that he told him to say what he had to say to the pigs. Much to the Pope's surprise, Francis went and did this. The Pope therefore granted him all he asked.

This late account is almost certainly untrue, but Matthew Paris's description of what Francis looked like when the Pope first saw him cannot have been very far off the mark: "a brother wearing an ill-fitting habit, looking like nothing on earth, with a straggling beard, unkempt hair, and black, hanging eyebrows."

The Three Companions, on the other hand, tells us that the travelers, having arrived in Rome, found the Bishop of Assisi, who "received them with delight." At once he introduced them to the Cardinal of San Sabina, John of Saint Paul, "a man full of the grace of God, loving above all other things those who served God." This holy prelate heard from Guido the story of Francis and his friends, and asked to see them. He invited them to accept his hospitality, not only out of kindness, but also to have the opportunity of becoming more fully acquainted with these outwardly unprepossessing and possibly dangerous men. No one, given the chance of getting to know Francis and seeing how he lived and prayed, could ever resist him, not even, in time to come, the nephew of the great Saladin. No wonder the cardinal, so far from judging his visitors, asked them to pray for him and begged to be included (in an honorary capacity) among their company.

The cardinal then went to tell the Pope of the strange but sublime penitents whom he had been studying, informing the great statesman-pontiff, perhaps, that whereas other reformers, who seemed as strange as Francis, insisted on more rigid laws, more severe interpretations of the Commandments, and often preached a condemnation of the body and nature as evil, Francis wanted only to speak of salvation through love and liberation, the beauty of even the least-regarded insect, flower, or stone in the world that God had made and had sent His Son to redeem from man-made sins through the pursuit of man-made ambitions.

"I believe I have found a man of truly perfect life who only desires to live according to the life and ideals of the Gospel. He, I think, is someone whom the Lord can use to reform Holy Church across the face of the world," the cardinal ended, as *The Three Companions* reports.

Innocent, who had a high regard for the Cardinal of San Sabina and who wanted to see a Church spiritually and morally worthy of its mission, needed to hear no more. Let the man and his friends be brought in to see him. Francis, the humblest man in Christendom, was to speak to the most powerful of all the popes. It was the case of Guido of Assisi all over again. What the brothers looked like as they made their way across the mosaic pavements and through the marble-lined apartments has not been recorded.

Kneeling at the feet of the Pontiff, Francis explained their way of life and their purpose. The great Innocent, only too well aware of the heady nature of the wine of absolute spiritual poverty, so often indulged in by emotional men on their way toward heresy, was not impressed.

He said, "My dearest children, I think the life which you are leading is too rigid and hard. Do not misunderstand me; I am persuaded that, filled as you are with true fervor, you are determined to fulfill with all loyalty the promises you have made. But our responsibilities do not end with you. We have to think of those who will follow in your footsteps, and many may not share your enthusiasm."

Unperturbed, Francis answered the firmness of the ruler with the even greater firmness of the God-enlightened man. "My lord Pope, I find myself entirely in the hands of my Savior, Jesus Christ. It is He who has promised us eternal life and everlasting happiness. It is not likely that He would refuse so small a thing as the crumbs which are all that we have need of while on this earth."

Still Innocent was not convinced. "We do not doubt, my son, that what you say is most true. But you must not forget that nature is frail. It rarely remains consistent for long. We want you, my son, to ask the Lord to make clearer to you exactly to what degree your present ideals are in accordance with His will."

Francis would have been lost but for the Cardinal of San Sabina, who, after the audience, reminded Innocent that to refuse the request of these poor penitents just because their ideals seemed to be too harsh and unpractical was very like condemning the evangelical life itself. If evangelical perfection is irrational and beyond the bounds of possibility, then its author, Christ, must be responsible for such absurdities. This would be blasphemy. The cardinal could only have taken such a view because of some intuition about the holiness of Francis and his companions — an exception that for once proved the rule.

Innocent found it hard to get around the argument and agreed to see Francis once again. Meanwhile, Francis, surely in despair at the Holy Father's apparent inability to follow his simple argument — the learned and the good could at times be strangely obtuse — decided to help the ruler of the world by putting it all in a language that even a small child would understand. So he invented a fairy tale.

When he was called for the next audience, he dropped onto his knees, and almost before the Pope could speak, he started telling his story. "Once upon a time, there lived a wondrously beautiful lady who was extremely poor. She lived in a desert. The king of that land saw her one day and thought that she was so beautiful that he married her. Their children grew up as beautiful as she was. She said to them, 'I know you are very poor, but do not be ashamed of it, for you are the children of a great king. Now is the time for you to present yourselves at his court, and he will give you all you need.' The children did as they were told, and when they were brought into the presence of the king, he was full of admiration for their beauty. Noticing that they looked very like him, he said, 'Whose children are you?' And when they answered that they were the children of a poor lady who lived in the desert, the king embraced them with great joy, and said, 'Don't be afraid. I am your father. If I invite so many strangers to my house, how much more ready I am to invite my own sons!' The king gave orders to the lady of the desert to send all her children to the court."

Francis then explained in detail to the Pope that the lady of the desert was himself, whom the Lord had called to bring him many children — the King of Kings had assured him that he would look after them all. If the King of Kings was ready to provide for everybody, how much more ready must he be to provide for those bound to follow the Gospel.

Whether Francis's fairy tale would have persuaded Innocent, we cannot be certain, but luckily it reminded him of a dream he had recently had. He had dreamed that he had seen the Lateran Palace shaken to its foundations, its tower leaning over, and its walls on the point of crumbling. He had tried vainly to cry out, but his hands refused to move when he sought to join them together in prayer. Then a little ugly man with a cord around his waist came along, running toward the church. As he put his back to the leaning wall, he grew larger and larger until he became strong enough to push the wall back and, in this way, saved the church.

"This is a truly religious and holy man," the Pope declared. "By word and example, he will restore and sustain the Church of God."

Innocent then approved the primitive rule of the company, the wording of which has not come down to us, but which is only a collection of Gospel texts. He went on to say, "My brothers, go with God, and preach penance as the Lord leads you. When the Most High has multiplied your small numbers, come and see me again without hesitation, and I will grant you more favors and entrust you with more important missions."

Celano tells us that on another occasion some years later, when Francis went to see the Pope (then Honorius III[40]) he spoke to him while tap-dancing, "not in wantonness, but as glowing with the fire of Divine Love; not provoking laughter, but extorting tears of grief." This reaction cannot have been other than an instinctive reverting under stress of emotion to the dancing in which he had delighted as a young man in the

[40] Honorius III (died 1227), Pope from 1216.

celebrations of the Company of San Vittorino. It is another extremely important link between his early years and the spirit which he wished to inculcate into the Franciscan Order — a spirit which he was bringing into being by a quality of piping which puts into profound shade the piping of the yellow and red Pied Piper of Hamelin. Although there is no mention of this dancing at the present interview, the feeling that was to prompt it, even in the presence of a pope, must have been in Francis's heart.

Francis, then, vowed obedience to the Supreme Pontiff, and the others vowed obedience to Francis. They were authorized to preach repentance wherever they went. The Cardinal of San Sabina conferred the tonsure on the brothers, and it has been suggested that perhaps it was now that Francis received the other orders up to the rank of deacon. He was too humble ever to seek to be ordained priest, or to seek ordination for his followers.

Wonderful as the story is, what took place was, in a sense, entirely unofficial as though in keeping with Francis's own unofficial mind. The papal approbation of the *Regula Primitiva* ("primitive rule"), as it is called, was not confirmed by a bull, and the new congregation had no name. These were the last things to worry the founder. The miracle was not that Francis had accommodated himself to the pontifical and canonical ways of the Holy See, but that the great and majestic Pope had allowed himself to bend down to the level of a handful of spiritual tramps whom he recognized as potential saints and the kind of single-minded followers of Christ of which the medieval Church was so badly in need.

Chapter Eleven

Clare Runs Away to Join the Franciscans

Francis, in his simplicity, had never doubted that Innocent would approve his evangelical way of life. In his present sublime assurance of Christ's guiding hand, in such marked contrast with the changing moods of his preconversion life and the fits and starts of the period of his conversion, he could not even have understood any seeming rejection of Christ and the Gospel. It may well be that Francis himself had prompted the Cardinal of San Sabina to use this unanswerable argument. He could leave Rome, therefore, looking confidently to the future of his little community, although we are told that, on the journey back, he was assailed by a temptation — one that would increase with the years: the temptation to substitute a hermit's life of contemplative prayer for an apostolic mission.

His personal devotion to our Lord and to the rigors of a way of living cut off from all creaturely attachments, would increasingly bind him in heart and spirit to God until the day when, high up on the mountain, his love would have to overflow from spirit into flesh and stamp his body with the wounds of his Beloved. This choice between contemplation and action would haunt him all his life, and it would prove to be another source of misunderstanding among his followers.

The temptation on this occasion having been overcome, the travelers returned to Assisi, at first, it seems, to Rivotorto.

Even after Francis himself had been accepted as a novelty in Assisi, the people murmured at the begging of his brethren. Although it does not seem that he would ever have thought that begging for food, as distinguished from money, in case of necessity, was wrong or improper, the man who had restored the churches with the hands of an experienced mason in exchange for food and stones would always prefer working for his keep and that of his companions to begging.

He expressed his feelings in the story of Brother Fly, the brother who was so fond of eating. "Go your way, Brother Fly, feeding as you do on the sweat of your brothers and remaining idle in God's works. You are a brother drone who will not share the toil of the bees, but expects to be the first to eat the honey."

Organization by this time was sufficient to allow of manual labor in the fields around Assisi as the means by which the community were enabled to obtain the little they required. But payment for such manual labor had to be in the form of real wealth — food and other necessities — and never in the token of wealth — money. Celano, saying that, for Francis, "money and dung were of equal value," relates the story of his order to a brother who threw a coin found in the Portiuncula onto the windowsill. The brother was told to take it away in his mouth and deposit it on some ass's dung beyond the confines of the property. With anyone else, this sort of behavior would seem mere crankiness, but Francis was not a reasoning nor, in our ordinary sense of the word, a reasonable person. "The earth is the Lord's," he would say, "just as every man belongs to the Lord — not to himself." If he was in spirit a Christian communist, the qualifying word was *communist*, not *Christian*, for communal property was just as abhorrent to him as private property. He only recognized the Lord's property to be used by man to find freedom in the Lord's service. Money forever continued to be for him the symbol of men's enslavement to the false values of the world and to their own self-regarding passions. He could not understand how it could be taken to be a claim for more than one's fair share of the world's goods. It was the cause of envy, hatred, and war. It was the opposite of love and peace.

The wisdom that lay behind his rebellion against the way of the world, against the *Majores* and *Minores* of all times, must appeal to any thoughtful person, but only Francis and those close followers of his, living under the direct spell of his inspiration, could turn theory into the practice of a way of life that made no concessions whatever, and yet made no claims that this was the *only* Christian orthodoxy.

By this time, it must have become known in Assisi that their religious maniac, Francesco di Bernardone, had been to Rome with Bernard, Giles, and the others, and that they had been received by the Pope himself and his cardinals. His status suddenly changed, and he was asked to preach in the churches, even in the cathedral itself, in its exterior then what it remains today: an exquisite jewel in stone. His sermons would be in no way different from the earlier harangues, as from equal to equal in the open air, but now he was a celebrity, and the canons would nod as sagely as the common people when he gesticulated and cooed and cried over their stupidity and how they brought all their troubles onto themselves by living as though God did not matter.

Toward the end of the year 1210, the interminable ("cold" and "hot") wars from which the Assisians suffered through the quarrels between the emperor and the Pope (the Ghibellines and the Guelphs), and focused in particular on the long struggle with Perugia, came to an end. For the little city itself, this meant that the great tension between the *Majores* and the *Minores* would tend to die out, since it had been fed by appeals on both sides for external military aid. On November 9, 1210, the citizens met together (the father of Brother Angelo di Tancredi was one of the representatives of the *Majores*) to sign a solemn pact "for the furthering of peace and concord" by pledging themselves not to appeal to outside factions, nor to make outside alliances, whether with Pope or emperor or city or castle or lord, but to work together for the honor, well-being, and growth of the Commune of Assisi.

Because it so happened that at about this time, Francis decided to call his brothers "lesser brethren [*fratres minores*], so that they be poor and humble folk" and "subject to all, seeking ever to be lowly, doing menial things despised by others," historians have believed that the Assisian pact was the occasion for Francis's decision to give his followers that name. His example, it was suggested, had influenced the great men of the town. But this is extremely unlikely, for there was nothing whatever in common between the growing ambitions of the political *Minores* and Francis's ideal of "a new people, small, special, unlike their former selves in life and words, content only to have God."

The Rivotorto shelter, as an alternative to the Portiuncula, was not destined to endure, although the reason it did not last beyond the early part of 1211 is, as so often in the story of Saint Francis, an accident. *The Three Companions* relates the story.

"Once, where the brothers were together there, a countryman with his donkey came to the shelter and noisily pushed his donkey into it, shouting, "Get in! Go on, right in! This is the place for us!' " He had seen the brothers and thought it wisest to push the donkey in first. Francis, who more than once in his life, as we shall see, could show his feelings in no uncertain manner, was furious at this disturbance of the brothers in their time of prayer and silence. So he turned to the brothers and said, "I am sure that God has not called us to live together apart from the world in order to provide a stable for a donkey and a parlor for men. Our way is to preach salvation, to give men sound advice, and especially to pray and to give thanks to God."

It seems a little strange that a nervous countryman's shelter for himself and his donkey should have been enough to cause the community to give up a home for prayer and work, but Francis always tended to be unpredictable, and he may well have feared, as his words implied, that they would all once again fall for the temptation of substituting contemplative life — the vocation of Mary — for the active apostolic life — the vocation of Martha.[41] It was just like him to make a grave

---

[41] Mary and Martha, friends of Christ, represent, respectively, the contemplative and active sides of the Christian life; see Luke 10:38-42.

decision because of a donkey. It was the sign he needed — the outward sign of inward certainty.

It was after the community was thus finally established at the Portiuncula, probably in sounder conditions, suitable for the stream of new followers and an organized community life, however simple and rudimentary, that a fresh development of great significance took place.

We have already had occasion twice to mention the girl Clare, who would have known of Francis di Bernardone by repute and who, we may guess, had taken a special interest in the unique career of this puzzling citizen of Assisi. There is no evidence that Francis himself had known anything of her, although he may well have done so. Assisi was a small place, and Clare a daughter of a great patrician house. Clare, we cannot doubt, had followed with absorbed interest the gossip about the way in which Francis had taken to religion in so novel and picturesque a fashion, had gone to see the Pope, and had returned to be a preacher in Assisi. With her younger sister Catherine, she would have stood in San Giorgio and later in the Duomo, craning her neck to see the little bearded man whose words blazed forth like a crackling fire — whose words, above all, seemed to be so true, so full of common sense, so strangely in harmony with certain secret aspirations of her own, when one thought over them quietly on the way home or in the dusk of an evening.

Who was this Clare? She was, as Fortini has shown, the granddaughter of a certain Faverone, the son of Offreduccio, members of a great family of Assisi, living in a fortress-like house at an angle of the Piazza, in front of the new cathedral of San Rufino. This family of lords and knights dominated that quarter of the town. Their comings and goings, often in clanging armor, must often have disturbed the peace.

Faverone's brother was called Scipione, a name which has led the biographical tradition to suppose that Clare belonged to the great house of Scefi. The mistake, however, was not important, for Clare's people were equally of the class of feudal nobles who had sided with Perugia in the war. Faverone had married a woman of the same feudal class named Ortolana, of whom we know that she made a pilgrimage to the Holy Land after the peace with Saladin. Probably because of this, she called one of her daughters Catherine, after Saint Catherine of Alexandria, protectress of crusaders.

Clare, the eldest daughter, was thus brought up on the stories of the Holy Land and the courage of the crusaders. Her father, Faverone, was probably dead by the time she was growing up and under the guardianship of his eldest brother, Monaldo, a tough warrior who, if not the wicked uncle, was one of notorious severity and bad temper. His brother Scipione had a son, Rufino (Clare's cousin), who, as we shall see, became one of the closest of Saint Francis's companions in religion. Faverone and Ortolana had three daughters: Clare, born in 1193 (therefore eleven years younger than Francis), Catherine, to be called in religion Agnes, and Beatrice.

It is difficult to conceive of Clare as other than a beautiful young woman with regular features and clear, brightish skin, intelligent, and strong-willed. Her mother, Ortolana, on the other hand, suggests a rather more homely person with an interest in gardening (which Clare was to inherit).

Whether Clare as a child was as holy as she was serious-minded, we do not really know, despite the legends. We do know, however, that when she was about seventeen, her uncle wanted her to make a good marriage — a kind that a handsome knight's daughter could aspire to. Clare, however, either disliked her uncle's choice or found someone else, and realizing the hopelessness of her position and the futility of a violent quarrel with her uncle, she sought the counsel of her mother's great friend, a certain Bona, whose sister Pacifica had accompanied Ortolana on her pilgrimage to the Holy Land and other more recent pilgrimages.

Interested as she may have been in the story of Francis, it is unlikely that the daughter of a proud family, living amidst the clang of arms and despising these *nouveaux riches*, would have begun by having a great opinion of him. Yet she may have seen him in his glory and been told of his ambitions to become a knight and go to the Holy Land. To the pilgrimage-loving Ortolana and Pacifica, this ambition would have meant a great deal, and Clare would have shared their feelings.

However this may be, Francis's fantastic conversion made the deepest impression on them all, and Clare confessed to Bona her growing attraction to the holy man and all that he stood for. Her cousin Rufino must have shared these feelings. Bona took her to see Francis, and for a year, Clare and Francis met secretly at the Portiuncula without the knowledge of her family. Again, we can only guess at what happened during these clandestine meetings. Clearly, Clare appreciated the fact that Francis's religion was something far deeper and more genuine than the religious conventions of the time, just as hers would have to be, if it was to be true to her deepest self.

In Celano's second life, written for edification and in the hagiographical convention, we are told that Francis viewed "familiarity with women" as "honeyed poison." He once said that there were only two women whose faces he would recognize if he looked at them. The conventions of medieval hagiography did not permit of an extensive description of the relations between a religious, least of all the founder of the great order, and the women he may have met in life. Clare, of course, would be an exception, but apart from Clare, we know that he must have met numberless women to whom he would have spoken in the course of his apostolic missions. Can we imagine that courtesy and love were absent when he spoke to them of God, of the way of holiness and detachment, of their families and their bambinos? We are in Italy after all! When the Third Order came into being, he must once again have had a good deal to do with women.

Apart from Clare herself, we know that Francis came to be especially attached to the patrician Roman widow Giacoma dei Settisoli (whom he may already have met at this period). Another woman in whom he was interested was Praxedis, a Roman anchorite. Some say that he knew well a Lady Columba, who donated to him the property around Fonte Colombo, near Rieti, which would become the Sinai of the order.[42]

Yet we know that Francis came more and more to avoid unnecessary contact with women. This may have been connected with his knightly troubadour hero-worship of woman, symbol of poverty, and of our Lady, rather than flesh-and-blood women. It may also have been a remembrance of his

---

[42] It was on Fonte Colombo that Saint Francis would write the rule for his followers, just as on Mount Sinai, the Law was given to Moses for the Israelites to follow (Exod. 19:16-20:17).

early weaknesses and a godly fear that the weakness must always be guarded against. The longer he lived, the keener was his realization of the sins of his youth and the greater was his determination to atone for them by maltreating Brother Ass.[43] One tradition states that right from the beginning of his conversion, he planned to found a community of women and that, when repairing San Damiano, he had a vision of the chapel becoming one day a home for nuns. Allowing, however, for all this — and indeed implicit in it — can we believe that a man so understanding and appreciative of all God's creation shared any of the medieval puritanism about the relations between good men and good women? One of the most touching features at Francis's saintly deathbed was to be the presence there of Giacoma dei Settisoli — "Brother Giacoma," as she was called in the order. With all this evidence, we may surely safely discount the conventional ascetical tones of the early sources and believe that his own extreme personal asceticism in reparation for the sins of his youth was never inconsistent with all that courtesy and love demanded, whether it was the case of a man or a woman.

Francis, at any rate, was certainly at this time free from the extreme rigorism which grew as his life came to be lived closer and closer with God. The free, spontaneous spirit of the early days could not be better illustrated than by these meetings between Clare and Francis at the Portiuncula. Was it not an extraordinary thing that in the year 1211 or 1212, a religious leader of growing reputation and outstanding spiritual power should incite a girl of nineteen to set out, unknown to her

[43] "Brother Ass" was Francis's name for his body.

mother and guardian, to spend hours with a religious community and its founder? Perhaps this is an example that enables us to understand what one of his followers, Brother Jordan, wrote about him afterward, namely, that it had never occurred to him that Francis was a saint. He meant, of course, a saint according to the conventional notions of saints. We ourselves may well meet deeply holy men and women in our lives, and yet never think of them as saints. Convention has tended to create a mold of sanctity, never to be seen in a living man or woman.

During those secret meetings over about a year when Clare came, accompanied by Bona, Francis must have got to know her intimately. He could discern that she was of a mettle capable, not just of becoming a nun, but of sharing his own ideals of the spiritual adventure of total dedication and denudation to find true joy in this world.

Little by little, she learned the secret of Francis, a secret for which she was more than ready, if we trust the early writers, who sanctified her youth and insisted in particular on her likeness to Francis in respect to generosity to the poor. Both Clare and Francis must have had conferences with Bishop Guido, for he was clearly primed for the dramatic happenings of Palm Sunday, March 27, 1212.

The mystery is how all this was kept secret from her uncle Monaldo and perhaps even from Ortolana, her mother.

That morning, we are told, Clare, instructed by Francis, dressed with special care and went to the crowded cathedral with her family for the joyful blessing and distribution of palms, at which Bishop Guido himself was officiating. So overcome was she that she could not trust herself to go up to the altar to receive her palm — or was this a prearranged signal for the bishop that she was well decided to run away that evening? Anyway, the bishop came down from the sanctuary to bring the palm to Clare as she knelt in the body of the church. For the rest of that Palm Sunday, she managed to behave as though nothing was in the wind, for no one at home, except Bona, suspected what was to happen.

Late that night, when the household had retired, Clare and Bona, avoiding the main door at which a man would be posted, made for the "door of death" — the door to be found in many houses which was only opened when the dead were carried out. Francis and Clare had evidently planned this practical but deeply symbolic detail. Clare was to accomplish her elopement to a living death, as the world saw it, to be Christ's bride, as she saw it. Outside, Pacifica took over the escort's duty from Bona.

Together, they made their way by the light of a lantern on the cold evening of an early spring day down the path through the woods that led to the Portiuncula. Not long after they had entered the forest, they began to hear the distant chant of Matins. As they drew near, the voice of Francis could be heard exultantly singing above the rest.

Soon, accompanied by the brothers, the two women were approaching the little chapel. As they entered, Francis came down from the altar to greet Clare. He led her, dressed as a bride, to the steps to the altar, and there, after having removed her jewels and covered her with a rough, undyed cloak like his own, he ratified her dedication by cutting off her hair, no doubt with the permission of the understanding bishop.

When dawn came, Francis and the brothers, again by previous arrangement, escorted the first woman Franciscan down into the marshland where stood the Benedictine convent of San Paolo of the Abbesses, on the way to Perugia, two miles distant.

The disappearance of Clare naturally infuriated Monaldo and the other stupefied relations. A day or two later, this wicked uncle, accompanied by a cavalcade of his kinsfolk and friends, rode to the famous monastery. Celano tells us that they were determined to carry her back by main force — a dastardly intention in view of the monastery's privileges. In the canonization account, we find the more likely story that their intention was to tell her of the shock which she had given them and of the grief of her mother and all her relations. The whole adventure was quite unthinkable where a girl of Clare's birth and prospects was concerned. She must return home at once.

Clare's answer was decisive. She raised her veil and showed her shorn hair — an unanswerable argument if, as we must believe, Francis had acted with episcopal authority. But if Celano's version is truer, it seems that Clare's ability to stand up to the party of rough, bullying kinsmen was an example of a willpower which, for the rest of her life, enabled her to override with gentle firmness all from the highest to the lowest who would seek to betray the ideal of Francis. She was only beaten by the conventions of the times which forced a nun to live enclosed. Otherwise, in her, we would have seen a wonderful example of the apostolic spirit which in our day enables women, especially in modern orders and secular institutes, to devote themselves to the service of Christ in the person of the poor, the destitute, and the sick.

The Benedictine convent could only be a temporary shelter, yet Clare, given the fury of her powerful relations who were ready to fight tooth and nail to get her back, had only one idea in mind — namely, to share with Francis, insofar as a woman might, the ideal of literal evangelical perfection in complete denudation. She at least would not yield, nor would Francis. Soon she moved, we are told, to another Benedictine convent, that of Sant Angelo in Panzo, to the east of Assisi on the slopes of Subasio.

This convent was a worldly one, its inmates being engaged in active work and in business negotiations about their properties, and it far from suited Clare's needs. It became, however, the stage on which the second act of the drama of Clare and her family was to be played.

Clare's sister Catherine had always been close to her and was deeply affected by her. When Clare fled from home, Catherine wanted to follow her. Clare prayed that she might share the same vocation. So it happened. The young girl, only fifteen years old, managed to elude her family and make her way to Sant Angelo. It was now mid-April.

This second abduction, as it seemed, was altogether too much for Monaldo and the relations. Indeed, we must, even at this distance of time, feel some sympathy with them. Two eligible daughters in a fortnight! They could hardly understand that after those long evening discussions between Francis and Clare, it was their very eligibility — in other words, their marriage to the social conventions and position — which had been shown up to be utterly false and a school for misery. The young man from the Gospel had gone sadly away.[44] They at least were not going to make the same mistake. In the minds of

[44] Matt. 19:22; Mark 10:22.

Francis and Clare, there was nothing metaphorical about the call to leave father and mother and follow Christ.[45]

Inevitably the relations were going to make a bid to save Catherine by any means, even if they had now to give up where Clare was concerned. Possibly, in Catherine's case, Guido had shrugged his shoulders. He could canonically protect Clare, but hardly Catherine. Anyway, in this case, there was no question of arguing. Once again the relations came riding to the convent. They were in a state of fury and hardly paused to persuade Catherine to come quietly. The state of her mind being obvious, they seized her and dragged her physically down the hillside through the thorns and briars. Clare ran after them to find Catherine torn and bruised, lying on the ground. The story was that she had miraculously become too heavy to bear. But perhaps even those rough men were suddenly appalled by their cruelty to a young girl and hesitated to complete their mission. Perhaps Clare's imperious voice had made them pause. Her presence, in any case, was too much for them, and they ran away.

So Catherine was to become Agnes in religion. The convent itself which housed the two sisters at this period was to become a house of Poor Clares, and a descendant of Francis's brother, Angelo, would a century later become its abbess.

The arrival of Agnes made it all the more necessary to find accommodation where the two sisters could live and receive, as Francis had been receiving, recruits eager to find joy and fulfillment in the human realities of fellowship, in the service of Divine Truth, and in escape from the self-deception of

[45] Cf. Matt. 19:29; Mark 10:29.

worldly ambitions and passions. The solution turned out to be the spot sacred in Francis's mind, the church of San Damiano, where the Crucifix had bade him "Repair my Church," and which he had repaired with his own hands. The church and the house where the chaplain lived belonged to the bishop, and Guido, so loyal in his support of Francis, was glad to give over the property to these "poor ladies of the Lord." Clare and Agnes, soon to be joined by many others, settled into the little property, the simplicity and beauty of which were the inevitable and proper outward expression of the spirit within. Clare herself was never to leave San Damiano except to visit the Portiuncula, although Agnes would leave one day to rule a sister convent.

The golden days never shone more richly and softly than in these months when the two communities planned, lived, and prayed the perfect life of supernatural and natural happiness together. Francis and the other brothers would often visit the quickly growing community of sisters, for these had to depend on the produce of their little garden and the alms which the brothers obtained for their work, gladly sharing the proceeds with them. We have too little record of their conversation, perhaps because the chroniclers, looking back, did not feel that this early close relationship between the Portiuncula and San Damiano would be properly understood. But the *Fioretti* tells us that "Saint Francis often visited Saint Clare and gave her saintly advice." The writer, for example, relates how Clare had on one occasion "great longings" to have a meal with Francis. She was supported by the brethren, and Francis said, "What seems good to you seems good to me also. But to please her more, let us have this meal in Santa Maria degli Angeli [the Portiuncula], for she has been shut up in San Damiano for a long time."

Clare therefore came down to the Portiuncula one day with her fellow sisters. They all took their places around the sparse food. But when the first dish was brought, Francis began to talk so marvelously about God that very soon the whole company was "rapt in God." At the time, the people of the district thought they saw a great fire burning, and they rushed over to put it out. But all they saw was the company at table, rapt in God. After a long while, Saint Francis and Saint Clare and the others "returned to themselves, and being greatly comforted with the spiritual food, they gave but little thought to bodily food."[46]

It is Celano who tells us that later "the father little by little withdrew his bodily presence (from San Damiano), but continuing to love them in the holy spirit, he never ceased to take the greatest interest in the sisters . . . and, having promised them and those who joined them, professing the same rule of poverty, his aid and counsel as well as those of his brothers, he kept his promise with great diligence until his death."

"Do not believe," said Francis on one occasion, "that I do not love her with a perfect love."

---

[46] If this charming story in the *Fioretti* seems incredible to us, given that Clare was a cloistered nun, should it not have been incredible to the original storyteller? Even though it can hardly be taken literally, it illustrates the tradition of the closeness between Francis and Clare, as well as the geniality and spontaneity of their saintly relationship.

Chapter Twelve

❧

Francis Leads His Followers in Joyful Simplicity

The gradual giving up of the joy of seeing and talking to Clare was, of course, the measure of the delight which he had taken in her company. Francis's life was to be a steady process of giving up to God, little by little, every joy he had found in the very process of yielding all that the world holds to be desirable. Thus he would find in the end the one joy of enjoying only God. Nevertheless, this retirement, even right up to the end, was never to be inconsistent with a visible joy in the company of his brethren and what one can only call a lightness of touch that made him a boon and sweet companion to his brethren.

But these were still very early days, and it will be well if we take a brief look at some of the more famous of those who joined his company, so that we may form a picture of the happy, holy brothers, who, through Francis, had been liberated from the "New Babylon," which Assisi, as we have seen, was deemed to be.

We have given the names of the "first twelve" — every one of them from Assisi. In contrast with all of these was the highly controversial figure of Brother Elias, who would have been far better fitted to the role of Judas than poor John of Capella, but Elias, of course, was not among the first twelve.

We shall get to know Elias better later in the story. It is sufficient to say at present that he was an Assisian, despite the name Elias of Cortona. He was called Elias Bonusbaro (Bombarone). Fortini points out that in 1198, a Bonus Baro was in fact the ex-consul, then aged about twenty-five, Francis himself being sixteen. Miss Rosalind Brooke thinks it more likely that Brother Elias was the son of the consul. Either way, this theory would account for the high regard which Francis was always to have for Elias, and it would be consistent with the quite unproved view that Elias was Francis's first unnamed friend after his conversion.

Elias was to prove to be a man of exceptional intelligence and executive ability — a "top person," as one might say to-day. Celano, in his first biography, says that Francis had chosen him to take the place of a mother to himself and a father to the other brethren. The very close friendship between Francis and Elias, who one day would incur excommunication and be widely viewed as the evil genius of the order, in particular betraying the founder's own ideal, is a major puzzle, but Elias incontrovertibly began as a good Franciscan. He certainly attached himself to Francis in all honesty and with a full heart. We know how much he loved the Celle di Cortona, whose beauty and solitude inspired him to live his life unknown to men, and in communion with the God of nature — but the ideal in his case may well have had a little too much of the outlook of Omar Khayyám,[47] a jug of wine, a loaf of bread. . . .

[47] Omar Khayyám (died 1123), Persian poet and mathematician.

Francis, too, may not have been a first-class judge of men. One feels that he may too easily have believed that others, because they loved him, shared the height of his spiritual ideals. Nor is it difficult to understand Francis's veneration for an old friend, substantially senior to himself, intelligent, able, and experienced. Indeed, that the consul or the son of the consul should have joined the humble brethren so early may have made Elias all the more beloved by Francis.

Of a very different nature was Francis's love for Brother Leo, the alternative name suggested for that early friend. Leo, to be the secretary and confessor of Francis, is a far more difficult person to see clearly after seven hundred years. Francis called him the *pecorello di Dio* ("little lamb of God"), an appellation which strikes us in translation as unbearably sentimental and rather ludicrous. For us today, perhaps the comparison made between our Lord's "beloved disciple"[48] and Francis's "beloved Leo" is nearer the mark. Leo, like Elias, lived to a good old age. His strong, beautifully formed medieval script in no way suggests sentimentality or softness, any more than does Francis's own rough hand. Leo's personal loyalty to Francis was absolute, and of him Francis said that "whoever possesses the purity and single-mindedness of Brother Leo will make a good friar minor." Leo's fidelity to the ideals of Francis and his closeness to him were to make him the symbol of the true followers, the "Spirituals," or *Zelanti*, in the great disputes that followed Francis's death. In this respect, he stands opposite to Elias.

By now, the delightful Juniper would have joined the community: a simple soul with his disarming and always amusing

[48] John 19:26.

habit of taking everything in its most literal sense. Perhaps it was as early as this that Clare called him "God's toy."

Then there was the silent, humble Masseo, at whose expense Francis liked to play tricks, as when he spun him around and around on a road to determine which of the four ways they should take. Masseo of Marignano was a tall, handsome, portly, and cheerful man. He often blurted out his feelings even to Francis and then was deeply sorry that his tongue had got the better of him. He once grumbled at all this praying at the shrines of dead saints when one could get sound advice by consulting living ones — a sentiment which Francis, who rarely referred to saints, might not have disowned. We are told that when he was praying, he was heard cooing like a dove. All this led him to direct his spiritual efforts to acquiring self-control and a proper humility. He was by way of being one of the best preachers in the company, so Francis thought it wise to exercise him in the virtue of humility.

One day, Francis assigned him all the humbler offices of the community, so as to leave the others free to devote themselves to prayer for longer times. After some days, the rest of the community felt rather ashamed of themselves when they thought of burly Masseo washing up, mending, and sweeping all day. They asked Francis to let them take turns with him. Francis passed the message to Masseo who said, "Whatever you tell me to do, that I take to have been said by God." Francis devoted his evening conference that day to the subject of holy humility, and Masseo was restored to normal community life.

Very different in both appearance and temperament was Brother Rufino, Clare's noble cousin. He was nicknamed

Francis Leads in Joyful Simplicity

"Saint Rufino," and we are told that this was because Francis once had a revelation that he was one of the saintliest people on earth. But one cannot help suspecting that this introspective person was one of those lanky and rather gloomy and terribly serious souls to be found here and there in religious communities. Certainly he was subject to dreadful scruples.

One of the chapters of the *Fioretti* gives a lively account of how he was prey to the temptations of pride and despair. Only with great difficulty could he drive away the temptation to think that Francis was no more than an ignorant simpleton likely to land him in the end in Hell. Better for him to go away and become a hermit, devoting his life to prayer and solitude. All Francis's reassurances seemed to be in vain, and poor Rufino began to fear that he was, anyway, predestined to damnation. In the end, the temptation was repelled by a brute act of force, contrary to Rufino's refined nature. Rufino answered the Devil in the coarsest possible language. So furious was the Devil, that he engineered an earthquake on Monte Subasio, the rocks crashing together so that "they shot forth horrible beams of fire through all the valley." And the chronicler who tells this tale, in preternatural terms which make us smile today, yet ring so true to the character of an overscrupulous religious, ends by saying that the cure was so complete that Rufino would have "continued day and night in prayer and contemplation of divine things if only the others had let him alone."

Another story about Rufino reminds us how strongly Francis insisted throughout his life on the keynote of his conversion: an absolute revolt against all that he and his family had stood for in the world. One day, Francis tested Rufino's obedience by commanding him to preach naked to the waist. But the thought that he, Francis, had dared to impose such a penance on the noble Rufino caused him to call himself a "horrid little man." He pulled off his own shirt and shared "Saint Rufino's" preaching experiment.

These brief character sketches of some of the best known of the early companions illustrate the diversity of outlook and character of those who first followed Francis. However holy, they remained, like Francis himself, intensely human, for Francis was the last person to try to fit men into one mold. It was the spirit, not the external behavior, which mattered to him. His complaint about the world was the conformism that dominated it. All those people, who thought themselves free and original, were each bound to the pursuit of the conventional, the fashionable, the inevitably fallacious and disappointing. His companions, on the other hand, whatever their character and quirks, were one together in finding joy in God and therefore joy in their own hearts. The chroniclers aimed at edification, but they could not hide the truths which showed that the friars shared Francis's own freshness and humanity.

Their common life was most certainly one of constant prayer, discomforts, and self-imposed austerity, but in the Portiuncula and other foundations, or tramping the roads in pairs, as they preached and consoled the people, they were happy and often ebullient Italians whose peace with themselves expressed itself in a jolly companionship as they worked and toiled in the fields (for they still lived largely by their own work) or sat around a crackling fire of a winter's evening, conversing with a full heart.

It is said that Francis himself never laughed. It is true that one thinks of him rather as someone with a merry twinkle in his eyes and a winning smile of inner understanding. Yet laughing must have been a strong Franciscan tradition, if we are to believe Thomas of Eccleston, who wrote of the early Franciscans in England: "The brothers were always so merry and glad together that they could scarcely look upon each other and abstain from laughter." That tradition surely reflected the spirit of the early days even if Francis himself only smiled his approval of the laughter which burst out when this strange assortment of spiritual tramps in those strange garbs suddenly saw themselves as they were.

To balance this and indeed to help explain the paradox of uninhibited joy in sorrow, we may anticipate here and quote from the famous chapter of the *Fioretti* in which Saint Francis was one day to describe in immortal words the quality of perfect joy. This well-known passage, no doubt rewritten and polished by the chronicler, may well be taken as a key and unifying factor in all that we know of Saint Francis.

One day, when Francis was walking with Brother Leo, he said, "Brother Leo, in every land, the Friars Minor set a fine example of holiness and edification. Even so, I want you to write down and consider that not in this is perfect joy."

They walked together a little farther, and Francis called again to Brother Leo: "Brother Leo, let us suppose that the friar minor should give sight to the blind, straighten crooked limbs, cast out devils, enable the deaf to hear, the lame to walk, the dumb to speak — let us suppose that he can even raise a man four days dead;[49] write down that not in this is perfect joy."

[49] Cf. John 11:39-44.

When they had moved farther on, Francis, speaking more loudly said, "Brother Leo, if a friar minor could speak all languages and could know all there is to know in science and the Scriptures so that he could prophesy the future and see into the secrets of consciences and souls,[50] write down that not in this is perfect joy."

And again, after moving on, Francis yet more emphatically said, "Brother Leo, my *pecorello*, suppose that a friar minor could speak with the tongue of angels and knew the courses of the stars and the secrets of all herbs; suppose all the treasures of the earth were revealed to him, and he had the secret of birds and fishes, of all animals and of men, the trees, stones, roots, and waters; write down that not in this is perfect joy."

For two miles, Francis and Brother Leo continued their dialogue. At last, Brother Leo, very much surprised, asked, "Tell me, then, in the name of God, wherein lies perfect joy?"

This was Francis's answer: "When we reach Santa Maria degli Angeli, soaked as we are by the rain, frozen by the cold, covered with mud and desperately hungry, suppose that when we knock at the door, the porter comes out angrily and asks us who we are, and that we answer, 'Two of the brothers.' Suppose, then, that he answers, 'You are lying. You're no better than vagrants who go about telling lies and robbing the alms of the poor. Get out!' Let's suppose that he closes the door in our faces, forcing us to stay outside in the snow and rain, cold and hungry until the night. Then if we bear with patience the wrong done with such cruelty and insults — bear it with equanimity and without murmuring, humbly and charitably

[50] Cf. 1 Cor. 13:1-2.

believing that the porter truly thinks we are what he says we are, God having inspired him to speak against us — O Brother Leo, write down that in this is perfect joy."

The *Fioretti*, which gathered together, over a hundred years after Francis's death, the unwritten memories through three generations, cannot be relied upon for accuracy. Least of all can they be relied upon for verbal accuracy, but only Francis himself could have acted and spoken with that rhythmic crescendo and driven home so beautifully the paradox of perfect joy.

Once Brother Leo had written it down, it became a treasure to be safeguarded, whether in the actual writing or through his closest followers and those who followed nearest in spirit to them. Although it is dangerous to take any so literal a man as Francis otherwise than literally, we may suppose that his object was to drive home, here as always, the mystical and ascetical teaching that to him was only common sense — common sense because he meant literally to follow the naked crucified Christ and because he knew that this made for fulfillment. Do we not know that the only relief to frustration, anger, and passion is to cool down quietly and make the best of a bad job? What else was Francis saying under the inspiration of the love of Christ who, after all, made our human natures? To be free from slavery to the outer forces that drive and distract us is to have the chance of finding and knowing ourselves and the God within us — to find perfect joy.

The other factor which helps to explain the unique spirit of Francis is perhaps the best known of all to the world. When we say that it was the love of all dumb creation and of all the beauty of the earth that God created, we shall misunderstand him unless we realize the reason for that love. Francis was not to be an animal lover in the modern sense. He did not, strictly speaking, love animals for their own sake or for his own. He loved them because they were God's handiwork, God's gift to man. He loved them because, for him, they talked of God, just as the beauty of the countryside reflected the beauty and goodness of God. This, of course, was by no means inconsistent with a natural love for all the beauties of God's creation: man, animals, and nature. Francis never found any difficulty in fusing his own natural love and joy with his far more important supernatural love and joy. In this case, we can hardly doubt that this sanctity strengthened and developed to an unprecedented extent an inborn power over animals.

The stories are, of course, endless, but doubtless the most famous took place at Cannara in the great green plain to the south of Assisi. There it was that Francis preached his sermon on peace — and preached it not to men, but to the birds. As he was walking along the flat roads of the sun-drenched valley, he noticed that the trees by the roadside were filled with chirruping birds. He told his companions to wait for him while he went nearer in order to preach "to my sisters the birds." As the story is told in the *Fioretti*, the birds awaited him, their beaks open, their necks stretched, and their wings hovering.

"My sisters the birds," Francis said, "you owe so much to God your Creator that you must always and everywhere sing His praises. You are free to fly just where you want to. You have been clothed with two and even three thicknesses of vesture. You also owe Him thanks for the air which is your element and which He has appointed for you. You do not have to sow or reap, for God feeds you and gives you rivers and fountains where you can drink; mountains and valleys where you can rest in safety; high trees in which you can build your nests. Because you do not know how to spin and sow, God has clothed you and your little ones. All this shows how much your Creator loves you, so prodigal has He been in the good things He has given you. Remember, then, not to fall into the sin of ingratitude and always remember to praise God." Francis then blessed them, and they all rose up into the air singing lustily.

In preaching to the birds, Francis was also preaching to posterity. His sermon was not on kindness to animals, and he would probably have been stupefied to hear that one day people called vegetarians would exist.[51] His sermon was on the lesson to human beings which was to be read in the life of the birds. God had given them all they needed, and they lived in peace and freedom. God has given to man infinitely greater gifts of intelligence and spiritual destiny, and they live in servitude and war. The birds own nothing and sing their happiness. Men thrive to amass as much as they can, and happiness eludes them.

Stories of the silencing of the swallows so that the people could hear him speak, of the taming of the cicada, of the removing of a worm from the path lest a passerby tread on it, and of taming a lamb which he saved from being killed and cooked, illustrate his very real love of animals and an inner closeness to animal life. But there is also the story of Brother Juniper, who went into a wood and cut off the trotter of a pig in order to cheer and comfort a sick friar. Juniper thought he

[51] His insistence on eating meat was the occasion later, as we shall see, of a crisis in the order.

had acted in the kindest way, given his motive and his very Franciscan belief that the pig belonged to God rather than its nominal owner. But Francis rebuked him for the trouble he had caused, not apparently for his cruelty to an animal. It is very possible that this story is apocryphal or muddled up in the telling, but it does at least indicate that Francis's closest disciples did not learn from him kindness to animals in the modern sense.

Nevertheless, the stories wonderfully illustrate how much the uninhibited Francis differed from the typical saint or founder of a religious order. He looked outward as much as inward (or perhaps more than inward) to find God. His simplicity was not the painfully achieved detachment from the complications of life in the great mystical tradition of the Pseudo-Dionysius school,[52] but a natural, spontaneous seeing of God in all His works. The spiritual life was for him a breath of God's free fresh air, not the external repression of the dark cloister driving thought inward.

---

[52] The Pseudo-Dionysian writings, attributed to Dionysius the Pseudo-Areopagite and written around the year 500, emphasize the union of God and the soul. To attain this union, the soul must leave behind the perceptions of the senses and the reasoning of the intellect.

Chapter Thirteen

Francis Wins Souls for God

Clare, settling down in San Damiano, a short walking distance from the Portiuncula, completed the first establishment of the order which came to be known as the Franciscans. The men would come to be known as the "First Order"; the women as the "Second Order." The "Third Order," in which laymen and laywomen would share the ideals and way of life of Francis and Clare insofar as is compatible with celibate or married life in the world, was to be established later, but the time and manner are uncertain.

Some historians claim that the Third Order was started at this early period, but it is generally held that it was created some ten years later. Jacques de Vitry, an especially valuable eyewitness writer, since, not being a Franciscan, he was not tempted to exaggerate or edify, and because he was a contemporary, wrote in 1216 that the new order consisted of men without property who lived praying and working, preaching by day and praying in their hermitages by night, and of women living together in convents near towns, earning their food by the work of their hands. He mentions no Third Order for layfolk.

However, it is not impossible — rather, it seems likely — that Francis at this period would not have withheld from people in the world his ideal of evangelical life insofar as it could be lived consistently with the responsibility of their state. He was no visionary or anarchist, but a man with a genius which could see through the self-contradictory fallacies of simply living for the artificial and showy rewards of the world, for money-making, security, satisfaction of passion, the pleasure of mere dissipation, in terms of the "thing that is done," of success, or of the then-prevalent false codes of honor. Thus the germ of the Franciscan tertiary, whose social influence, especially in ending feudalism and the oaths which bound so many of the common people to military service for their lords, was to be immense, may well have existed by now.

However this may be, we can say that by this period, Francis had in his own mind virtually completed the work he had set out to do. The Pope himself had blessed the new way of religious life and the simple evangelical rule. His trusting and obedient nature, strangely compounded as it was with a vivid imagination and the determination of genius, had no qualms about the lack of any written confirmation. Innocent's words sufficed. The company of men and women were proving every day that their way of life — the only sensible way for people who understood where happiness really lay — *could* be lived, whatever Bishop Guido may have thought, and that in it was to be found a wonderful spiritual fulfillment. Only factors outside Francis's control could change the idyllic picture of spiritually newborn men and women who had dared to take the words of Christ quite literally.

One such factor was that Francis was proving too much, and becoming the victim of his own success — and this in two ways. The first way was in the wholly astonishing rapidity of the growth of the movement which he had so amateurishly started. The second was Francis himself, so long hesitant before the choice between the life of Mary and the life of Martha, before, that is, the life of mystical prayer and the life of apostolic preaching. In seeking in himself and in his first followers to combine both, he would fall a victim in the end, in the literal sense, to the mystical way, as we shall see.

It is impossible to trace the detailed circumstances in which the order grew in those early days. Jacques de Vitry gives us a general description of the First and Second Orders: "There are people of both sexes, rich and of the world, who have given up everything for the love of Christ, left the world and called themselves lesser (minor) brethren. The Pope and the cardinals have a high opinion of them. These brothers are completely uninterested in the affairs of the world. Instead they labor all the time with great fervor and all their strength to rescue from worldliness souls that will perish unless they follow their example. By God's mercy, they have been most successful and gained many, the example of one leading to the conversion of another. They live in the spirit of the primitive Church, of which it was written, "There was but one heart and one mind among the believers.'[53] By day they go into the cities and houses to labor hard to win a few souls; by night they return to their hermitages and lonely homes to engage in contemplative prayer."

When we are told that within just a few years, a chapter general[54] of the order would bring five thousand souls to the

---

[53] Acts 4:32.

[54] A chapter is a meeting of the members of a religious order for handling important affairs of the community.

Portiuncula, when we know that within forty years of Francis's early death, over sixteen hundred Franciscan houses had been established, we begin to understand why the early biographies of Saint Francis seem almost from the start of the story to be studded with Franciscan foundations or *luoghi* (places, denoting in some cases only a few mud huts, where two or three of the brethren might temporarily settle as a base for preaching in the surrounding country) cropping up without rhyme or reason almost everywhere. The growth was fantastic and unique, especially when one thinks of the unorganized way in which Francis founded his company. It was not only a tribute to Francis's spiritual and human attraction, but also a sign of the thirst for supernatural peace and happiness in those troubled, dangerous times. Providentially, the orthodox Francis had done even better than the heretic rebels who sought to change the religious face of the earth.

He seems to have tramped indefatigably through Umbria and Tuscany, including Florence, the marshes and the country around Rieti, where he founded a community and received into his company John Parenti, who would succeed him one day as the minister general, or superior, of the order. Bernard da Quintavalle went even further afield to Bologna, there also to found a house.

The story of the rich man and his entry into the order, with Francis's famous words about courtesy, shows better than any chronicle of detailed activities the true reason for his success. This rich man received Francis and his companions with a fine sense of hospitality. The dusty, barefooted travelers in their tattered rags were greeted as princes. Their feet were washed and kissed. A great fire was lighted, and the table was spread with the best of food. The host, avowing himself a very rich man, assured the visitors that anything he had was at their disposal now or whenever they should need it. "For the love of God, who has granted me so much, I willingly do all I can for His poor."

It was when they left that Francis said to his companions, "Know, beloved friar, that courtesy is one of the attributes of God Himself, who in courtesy makes a present to us of His sun and His rain, which fall both on the just and the unjust.[55] Courtesy is sister to charity — charity which causes hatred to vanish and keeps love alive. Now that I have experienced so much of godliness in this good man, I would like to see him in my company. I would like therefore to return to him to see if God may have touched his heart and inspired him to serve God with us. Meanwhile, we shall pray that God may put this desire into his heart and give him the grace to act on it."

So, of course, it happened. But Francis's words, the fruit of the marriage between the knightly ideals of his preconversion period and his subsequent spiritual enlightenment, may have achieved even more in reminding posterity that true sanctity is a matter of supernaturalizing all the natural virtues; that courtesy, which we think of as a natural virtue, is as much a mark of holiness as is charity. It was this breadth and freshness of Francis's religion which made him so attractive in those rough, ill-mannered days — and keep him so in ours, when sanctity is too often thought of either as a remote eccentricity or a mere ascetical discipline bound by a multitude of laws and precedents, rather than the full flower of the good life.

[55] Matt. 5:45.

But perhaps the most breathtaking aspect of these early years of Francis's apostolic ministry is to be found in an ambition and resolution which no one could have foreseen.

It is true that Francis, from his earliest years, had been brought up to think far beyond the walls of his native city — and this was not so exceptional in those days when Christendom, rather than countries and provinces, was the natural territorial unit. France, whether he actually went there or not, was the country of his heart and imagination, rather than Italy. Chivalry and the sons of the troubadours had no frontiers within Christendom. Even so, we could hardly be prepared for his reaction to the news of the bloody victory of Las Navas de Tolosa on July 16, 1212, at the eastern foot of the Sierra Morena in southern Spain, when the heavily armored Christian knights went through the Moorish ranks like a tank division of our own days. That victory broke the Moorish power in Spain and opened the way for a new crusade. But for Francis, humbly tramping the lanes of central Italy, and for him alone in Christendom, it opened the way for the conversion, rather than the killing or the capture, of the infidel.

Unpractical as Francis had always been by any worldly standard, this idea of his was surely the craziest of them all. In the centuries of endlessly complex three-cornered relations between the Latin Christians, the Byzantine Christians, and the Turks, no one had ever thought of sending a priest or a missionary across the seas to convert anyone in the name of God. As between the Western Church and the Eastern, now in schism, the ideal, when it was not fighting, was what we call the restoration of Christian unity, of which Innocent himself was the most intelligent champion. As between either and the infidels, it was a case of bribery or the sword in the name of Christ.

Francis, who, before his conversion, dreamed so much of knighthood, gained on an infidel battlefield, did not doubt that the crusades were holy wars. In 1099, the great knight Godfrey de Bouillon had conquered the Holy City. Ninety years later, in 1187, Saladin reconquered it. This was when Francis himself was five years old, and he must have shared with the rest of Assisi something at least of the universal grief which overwhelmed Christendom. The shock had led to the immense idealism and self-sacrifice of the crusades, however unworthy of that ideal had been so many of the actual crusaders. In this very year, the pathetic crusade of the children had revived the purity of the original ideal, although it was doomed to disaster. The *chansons de geste*, the quest of the Holy Grail: these had molded the young Francis's mind to see the glory of the deliverance of the Holy City and of the holy places of Palestine as something sublime.

It was in the teeth of all this spiritual romanticism that he, now a man wedded to Lady Poverty, saw clearly what no one else saw, even the great and holy Innocent: that there was a better way which in the end must be the only way. It was to go east as Christ would have done, armed only with the sword of the spirit. In his mind, he was not even thinking of anything so clear-cut as a missionary enterprise. With the breadth of mind, which was native to him, where God and man were concerned, it was the thought of peace, of reconciliation, of the reign of Christ again in Bethlehem, Nazareth, and Jerusalem, above all, of walking in the very footsteps of his crucified Lord, that impelled him to cross the seas and carry on his work beyond them as though merely exchanging the Galilee of Umbria for the Galilee of Christ. Yet his instinctive desire made him the first foreign missionary in the modern sense, just as his foundation of the Friars Minor had made him the first of the home apostolic missionaries who to this day have preached, as friars and other religious, the heart of Christianity to the man as such, whether rich or poor, just because Christ's call was to the man, not to his rank, status, or country. So great was the mysterious, untamed spirit of the *poverello* of Assisi, the playboy son of Pietro di Bernardone.

Yet so ridiculous from the point of worldly common sense was this first plan to convert the heathens that it turned out to be an utter fiasco. He went with a companion, whose name has not been recorded, to Ancona and there got himself onto a boat bound for the Syrian coast, at this time still rather insecurely occupied by the Christians.

Alas — although perhaps fortunately for posterity — the ship was driven by a storm east instead of south and to the Dalmatian coast. Francis could find no ship to take him to Syria, and no one, it seemed, was willing to afford the travelers a free passage home. So, as Celano puts it, "trusting entirely in God's goodness, he and his companion smuggled themselves aboard." Providentially, an unknown person carrying a quantity of food came along and, hailing a member of the crew, bade him take the food and feed the stowaways with it. Bad weather once again delayed the journey, so that a time came when only Francis's secret food remained. Then, Celano tells us, God miraculously multiplied this remnant, and all on board were able to enjoy excellent meals until they reached Ancona.

Fresh from this sorry adventure, which must have depressed Francis not a little, for he was certainly far from free from normal human emotions, Francis's spirits were wonderfully raised by an adventure which must seem to our age much more obviously providential than the sail home from the Dalmatian coast.

The *Fioretti* tells us how Francis and Leo found themselves one day in the wild country of the Apennines under a huge rock, above which stood a great castellated fortress. The *Fioretti* gives the date as 1223, three years before Francis's death. It has now been established by a legal document that the date was ten years earlier, 1213, when Francis was still living well within the memories of his preconversion period.

From above, the travelers could hear the echoes of music and singing, of the clash of arms in the jousts, of the guests' applause — all of which denoted that a great festival was being held in the home of the Lord of Chiusi della Verna, Count Orlando dei Catanei. Orlando was a local potentate who combined personal piety with all the pride and tradition of a great and powerful family.

On that day, one of his cousins was being initiated into the order of knighthood. Twenty-four hours earlier, the local lords and their families had been making their way as guests to the splendid festivities. That morning, Mass had been sung and the new knight clothed and invested with sword and spurs.

When the travelers were passing by, they heard the sounds of the knightly pageant and the celebrations that followed the religious rites. Was it the opportunity of a sermon or the echoes in his heart of all he had so much loved in the past which prompted Francis to take Leo with him up the steep path to watch the merry scene? Surely both motives.

Anyway, the two travelers made their way toward the castle. With light steps, they padded along with bare feet and watched all that was to be seen and heard. With their patched tunics and old rope, they would hardly have been noticed in the glare of the bright banners, the shining metal, and the bright dresses. How long they watched the festivities unseen we do not know.

Did Francis have any temptation of regret for all that had once been his life, a life from which he had only broken so slowly?

Francis, we should never forget, was not the kind of saint who could cut himself off absolutely from the past. It was from the past that he shaped his future. The qualities of his past, with their necessary complementary weaknesses, remained essential ingredients in the whole man, a fact which explains so much of his charm and ever-attractive personality. He must have meditated hard on this occasion, as he watched the pageant and heard the music, and out of his meditation came his sermon.

Perhaps someone recognized him, and word went around that the famous preacher of Assisi was present. It was a new and unexpected attraction in days when preachers had to fill the place of the great variety of means of communication — papers, books, radio, and television — which fill our contemporary life.

Francis asked for nothing better, and, climbing onto a wall, he entered into the spirit of the day and took as his text a couplet of a minstrel song. Typically, it was the kind of song he used to sing, a song of worldly love: "So great the good that I foresee, that pain itself is joy to me."

Alas, we can only imagine for ourselves what else he said, but he would have had no difficulty in showing — and from his own experience — that the self-sacrifice and idealism for earthly love which the dream and code of chivalry and glory imposed on its votaries were efforts wasted as compared with the inner peace and fulfillment that resulted from dedication to the crucified Savior — a dedication that alone could make a man free and truly happy.

His words, whatever they were, deeply moved the lord of the castle. Count Orlando dei Catanei himself went up to Francis and told him that he would like to discuss with him his own spiritual future. Insisting on the courtesy that he had once so highly praised, Francis replied, "Of course! But now you must not be rude to your guests. Enjoy the show, and dine with them. Then we can talk together as long as you like."

In gratitude for what Francis had to say to him that night, Orlando made Francis an extraordinary — and providential — offer. His property included a wild, rocky, and heavily wooded mountain — a mountain from which the snow only disappeared late in the spring; a mountain dark, strikingly shaped, remote from the normal paths of men — a place eminently suitable for solitary life and meditation. Its peculiar shape made it stand out even in that land of mountains and hills. It stood about halfway between Monte Feltro and Florence. It was called Alvernia, or La Verna. Orlando said that he would like to donate it to Francis and his company. Francis was delighted, telling him that he would send some of the friars to this spot to see if it was suitable for the purposes which his friend had in mind. Subject to that, he would accept the generous offer.

La Verna was to be one day the scene of the greatest outward mystical event in Francis's life, the receiving of the Stigmata. When we look back, it seems almost inevitable that the solitary heights of La Verna should have come to Francis straight from a pageant of worldly chivalry. His life was summed up in the transference.

Doubtless, he had even then some intuition of its mystical importance, for even in those days of endless evangelization, covering hundreds of miles of the country, he still remained subject to the great stress of not being able to convince himself that he was called to the active life. He was certainly happiest, most fulfilled in his inmost being, when he could find an excuse for long periods of retirement to solitude and prayer, as when about this time he had had himself secretly rowed to a deserted little island in Lake Trasimeno, there to pray and fast from Ash Wednesday until Maundy Thursday. For shelter, he had built himself a kind of hole in a dense thicket; for food, he took only two loaves of bread. The *Fioretti* tells us that, when the brother came to fetch him, one and a half loaves were still uneaten.

North of Lake Trasimeno and below the hill on which stands Cortona, there is an exquisite valley down which runs a river breaking the rocky banks into a series of caves. Those caves, above which today stands a friary, now called the Celle di Cortona, rivaled the Carceri on Monte Subasio as a favorite place for retirement and meditation. Heights and depths, *alphas* and *omegas*, as it were, of the earth's configurations, both seemed to appeal in a special way to Francis. The stream of worldly life was on the flat, where everything seems easy; to find God and happiness, one must walk away from the trodden paths of men.

For Francis, the attraction of the mountains and the valleys would be stronger than that of the towns and villages, even though, to the end of his life, he would never cease from the work of evangelization wherever people called for his help. Yet in his heart, there was always conflict, as there would indeed be within the order he founded.

It may have been the gift of La Verna which especially set his mind on the subject at this period. However this may be, we have a full description of the crisis at this time both in the *Fioretti* and, with greater authority, in the *Legenda major* of Saint Bonaventure.

> Francis, that most faithful servant and minister of Christ, in his desire to fulfill all things as faithfully and perfectly as possible, wished to live by those virtues which he believed to be most pleasing unto God, guided as he would be by the Holy Spirit. It was because of this that he found himself greatly worried by a doubt in his heart. In order to settle the matter, after he had spent many days in prayer, he put the problem before his brothers.
>
> "What is your advice, my brothers?" he said. "What do you suggest? Shall I spend my life in prayer, or shall I go about preaching? In truth, I feel, I who am so little and simple and unversed in speaking, that I have been called to prayer rather than to preaching. In prayer, it seems to me, is to be found spiritual profit and acquirement of grace; in preaching, we pass over to others the gifts we have received from Heaven. Besides, in prayer, our inner feelings are purified, and we attain to union with the one true and highest good, just as we

strengthen our virtue; in preaching, our spirit may grow dusty and ourselves distracted, so that discipline is weakened. In prayer, too, we speak with God and we hear Him, and while we live with angels, we also speak with them. On the other hand, when preaching, we must accommodate ourselves to men, and living among them, we must think, see, say, and hear all the things that go with men. Besides all this, there is one matter which in God's sight seems to carry more weight than everything else — namely, that the only-begotten Son of God who is the highest Wisdom, left His Father and came down to save souls. Thus He taught the world by His example and preached salvation unto all whom He had redeemed at the cost of His precious Blood. He purified and fed them, keeping nothing back of Himself, giving instead everything for our salvation. Since we should do everything in imitation of His example, it seems that it would be more acceptable to God, if, giving up the leisure of prayer, I should undertake work."

For a long time, Francis discussed these matters with the brothers and yet could not reach a clear conclusion as to which alternative was more truly pleasing to Christ.[56]

The crisis was sharp enough to make him turn for advice to the soul he most trusted and most loved: Clare. To her he sent a message through Brother Masseo. All we know of it is that Clare was to pray and tell him what was God's will in this matter. But we may be sure that the message must have recounted his own anguish of mind. To Sylvester, too, the priest among the first twelve, reputed for his powers of contemplative prayer, a similar message was sent.

[56] Saint Bonaventure (c. 1217-1274; Franciscan theologian), *The Life of St. Francis of Assisi*, ch. 12.

Such importance was attached by Francis to the answer that Masseo, on his return, was treated like an ambassador, with the ritual dignity and flourish which meant so much to Francis when matters of the highest importance were at stake. Masseo's feet were washed, and a meal was eaten. Then Francis went with him into the countryside council chamber — a clearing in the thick wood. Francis knelt on the ground and raised his arms in the form of a cross to hear the ambassador's dispatches from God. Both Clare and Sylvester had told Masseo to inform him that God's vocation for him was to preach the Gospel and to work for the good of souls. Not for his own spiritual benefit had God called him, but for the spiritual benefit of others.

But God, we may say without irreverence, was playing a game with Francis. Through the mouths of Clare and Sylvester, he was officially bidding Francis, as the first Franciscan, to be the leader of an apostolate that would carry and wonderfully spread through the ages the love and example of Christ to the meanest of men, as well as to the highest. But God, for all that, did not withdraw the intimacy of His own presence deep within the heart of Francis, an intimacy far, far stronger than the capacity of the will of Francis to give his whole mind and energy to the external labors of preaching and the arduous business of organizing and ruling the flood of men who were drawn to his ideals and insistent on sharing them with him. One might almost say in hopelessly inadequate human language that God, while ordering the external way to success, could not withdraw himself sufficiently from His loving son to enable him fully to obey his orders.

The Franciscan tradition, in seeking to work out an external pattern of conformity with Christ in the events of Francis's life, missed the point which must so strongly strike us in this day, as we try to analyze what made Francis so saintly and so attractive a man. It was, if we may so put it, the least imitated part of the life of Christ which Francis most closely imitated. Francis began by kissing the leper, just as Christ cured the leper.[57] His sermon to the birds instinctively echoes the "see how the birds of the air never sow or reap or gather grain into the barns and yet your heavenly Father feeds them" of the Gospel.[58] Francis, like Christ, rebuked sin but loved the sinner. Like Christ, Francis saw men as living, spontaneous beings, essentially free to live their divine destiny, not as creatures bound by the conventions of fashion, success, and power. Christ loved poverty, and He loved living from day to day, just as Francis did. Christ, in His parables and in His tender sayings, was a poet; and Francis began by being a poet, and never ceased to be one. But while many can appreciate (yet without imitating) the freedom of the unconventionality, the beauty, and the deep sympathy which were so outstanding in the life of Christ, they recoil from the dedication to the heavenly Father and the sacrifice, so willingly accepted, of which all these were the flower.

So it was with Francis, although we often tend to forget it, and the spiritual dilemma which faced him was one of appearance rather than reality.

Communion with Christ, sacrifice and austerity — it was because of these that his evangelization was so irresistible and so astonishingly fruitful. Francis, like Christ, was no copybook

[57] Matt. 8:2-3.
[58] Matt. 6:26; Luke 12:24.

leader of a movement. Nor was Francis's withdrawal from the world of men a copybook withdrawal. Because he was so close to God, he captivated men. Francis was never to change very much (save through the infirmities of "Brother Ass") from the light-hearted jongleur of religion, the jongleur who expressed in delightful spontaneity and simplicity the inner joy that grew within him; he was the friend among his friends, the spiritual tramp, the man who could not but be a magnet to all who knew or even met him. It was Brother Masseo, perhaps, who accidentally gave to posterity the best "profile" of his leader.

One day, Masseo, doubtless after a long tiring day of preaching with Francis, a day with hardly a moment when men, women, and children were not mobbing this delightful man of God, muttered half to himself, half to Francis, "Why after you? Why always *after* you? Why, why, why?"

The reporter says he spoke as if in raillery to test Francis's humility, but we may be allowed to believe that so human a question was prompted by more natural motives.

"Why does all the world go after you?" he went on. "Why does everybody, absolutely everybody, want to see *you*, to hear *you*, to do what *you* want? You are not good-looking or very intelligent or a nobleman. Why, why, why, then, should the whole world rally around *you?*"

Francis's answer was, of course, the correct one — that, seeing how naturally unsuited to holiness and success he was, his success must be all the more due to God and not to any merit in himself. That was true, but for once it is the words of Masseo which remain in the memory, not those of Francis.

One of the most charming and significant examples of the Christ-like attitudes of Francis, which won him so much love from men, is the story of how he dealt with a band of thieves who lived in the woods near the Franciscan hermitage of Borgo San Sepolcro. These apparently rather unsuccessful thieves were in the habit of going to the hermitage to ask for food. The brothers naturally quarreled as to whether it was right to give food to thieves, or whether, even in this case, the duty of almsgiving was paramount. When one day Francis himself came to the hermitage, the brothers asked him for his advice.

Francis said, "Do as I tell you, and I think that, with God's help, we shall win their souls. Get some bread and wine, and take it to the thieves in the wood. Shout to them and say, 'Brother thieves, come to us, for we are your brothers and we have some good bread and wine for you.' " They would not delay in coming, he assured them. He went on to tell them to spread a cloth on the ground and put the bread and wine on it, and serve it humbly and gladly to them so that they could have their fill. After their meal, when they were feeling good, it would be the time to speak to them of Christ and to ask them, for the love of God, to give up their bad habits. In that mood, they would be bound to promise. Then, later, the thing to do would be to invite them again and this time to add some eggs and cheese to go with the bread, just to show that their first promise had been rewarded. Now, at last, they should ask them why they were so foolish as to live in the way they did, always hungry and always suffering so much hardship. Why, too, did they behave so badly, thus risking the loss of their souls? Would it not be far better for them if they served God, for God would give them what they needed in this world and save their souls in the next. The kindness and consideration of the brothers would move them to repentance.

The friars did what Francis had advised them to do. The result? The thieves not only did as Francis had foretold, but for just measure, they took it upon themselves to come and serve the brothers and make them as comfortable as possible, carrying logs on their shoulders to give them the warmth they needed. It is a simple story, yet typically Francis, the natural as well as supernatural philosopher, and one that charmingly expresses the real meaning of "turning the other cheek," and of repaying evil with good.

One cannot forbear somewhere in a life of Saint Francis to retell the story of Brother Juniper, of whom Francis said, "Would to God that I had a great forest of such Junipers," and "He would be a good friar minor who had conquered himself and the world as Friar Juniper has done." It is not that the story in itself reflects Francis's own instinctive imitation of the life of Christ, but rather that perhaps one can think of Juniper as not being unlike one or another of Christ's Apostles, had we known more of them.

On one occasion, all the community went out preaching, leaving Brother Juniper to cook the supper. It occurred to Juniper that if he cooked for a fortnight, a great deal of time would be saved for the more serious business of prayer. So he went out to borrow great saucepans and to obtain meat, fowls, eggs, and herbs. "Into the fire he put everything, the fowls with their feathers on, the eggs in their shells, and everything else similarly." Soon the place was like an inferno, and Juniper, with a large plank tied around his waist, kept jumping from one pot to another to do the skimming. The friars returned home, and the feast was served. Juniper "all ruddy with his exertions" proudly told them, "Let no one think of doing any cooking for a while, for I have made so great a banquet today that it will last for more than a fortnight."

Alas, Juniper's cooking was such that one of the friars exclaimed, "No pig in Rome, however starved, would eat that mess." Poor Juniper was heavily reprimanded and teased, but he took it all so well that the superior said, "I should be quite happy if Juniper wasted as much as this every day, so long as we had it, on condition that he edified us as much as he has done, for after all, he only did it out of simplicity and charity."

Chapter Fourteen

❧

The Pope Approves
the Portiuncula Indulgence

Looking back on his life, Francis was to say, "The Lord revealed to me what I must say when meeting anyone with a good wish: 'The Lord give you peace.' " It was that message of peace, never forgotten and insistently maintained, which drove the order along in those unsettled times. There was no need of formalities in order to join the order. Francis's message seemed to sweep through the country.

From the start, as many of the brothers as could arrange it returned twice a year, at Pentecost and Michaelmas,[59] to the mother house to refresh their spirits and make decisions called for by this rapid increase. Francis, who wanted no rules save such as sprang directly from the Gospels, nevertheless had a keen sense of community, just as he had so deep a feeling for friendship. These were his Knights of the Round Table, and, dispersed as they were in their evangelical work, they needed, as much for comfort and refreshment as for their captain's

---

[59] Michaelmas, the feast of Saint Michael the Archangel, is now celebrated on September 29 as the feast of the archangels Michael, Gabriel, and Raphael.

spiritual direction and exhortation, to gather around him as often as they could.

We have to remember that even after the numbers grew, the brothers possessed no property and no secure means of living, and when we are thinking of the first foundations, we are not thinking of stone or wooden convents, of furniture, however meager and plain, of any collection, however humble, of necessary books; we must think of a rough shelter or a few hastily built huts with the earth for flooring and ample spaces for fresh air. From the beginning to the end of his life, the champion of peace (spiritual and temporal) between men had a particular aversion to books and book-learning. The *Mirror of Perfection* has many stories illustrating something near to an obsession in Francis about the possession of books.

Perhaps the most significant is to be found in Francis's dealings with a novice "who knew how to read a psalter" (a passing reminder that, although many well-educated people entered the order, far more were semi-illiterate). Francis said to him, "Pay no heed to books and knowledge, but only to godly works; knowledge puffs up, whereas charity edifies." And a few days later, "Once you get your psalter, you will desire and covet a breviary, too. And once you get your breviary, you will sit in a chair like a great prelate and say to your brother, 'Fetch me my breviary.' "

Francis had found all he needed in a few texts of the Gospel, in the book of the hearts of men as he saw them around him, and in Shakespearean "sermons in stones."[60] Learning, for him, was only another sort of possession, driving man into

---

[60] William Shakespeare, "As You Like It," Act 2, scene 1.

himself and separating man from man. Books only told of what great, good, and brave men achieved, and substituted for the good life the false satisfaction of supposing that to know about sanctity, religion, and heroism was much the same as living these.

To us today, it must seem a strange and cranky point of view. But it harmonized with his rejection of money and property, on the ground that these divide men and create the need for self-protection, which ultimately leads to faction and war. Books, too, he thought, separated and divided men, who, as individuals or in groups, should follow naked the naked Christ, who possessed no property or books.

We need to remember that Francis's outlook was not one which he viewed as being universally valid. It was for the few. When we remember this, we can appreciate that his conviction was well founded and contained an invaluable warning: not to sidestep real living for the illusion of life at second-hand, with its consequent temptations to be other than one is.

It was to the Pope that he looked for guidance. He was content to abide by the authority of Innocent. We are told that as early as 1212, he journeyed again to Rome to report progress where his order was concerned. It was probably on this occasion that he first met Giacoma dei Settisoli, the recently bereaved widow who heard him preach in the streets. He had preached his sermon of peace, and Giacoma was never to forget it.

Three years later, he was to make another and much better-known journey to Rome. In November 1215, Innocent III inaugurated the Council of the Lateran with a sermon. Francis, it is believed, was among those who heard it, and one sentence of the Pope's made an enormous impression on him. "Go through the midst of the city, through the midst of Jerusalem," Pope said, "and mark *Thau* upon the foreheads of the men that sigh, and mourn for all the abominations that are committed in the midst thereof."[61]

With his vivid imagination, Francis could visualize the scene, the great T-symbol of the Cross of Christ before Pilate's inscription was added,[62] marking the foreheads of those who "understood" the true secret of life.

In the chronicles, we are told more than once of how Brother Pacifico, the troubadour, crowned before his conversion "king of song," frequently saw the sign *T* shining on Francis's own head, and Saint Bonaventure reported that "with this signature, Saint Francis used to sign his letters as often as holy charity led him to dictate any written message."[63] One such autograph, we shall see, remains.

Unfortunately we have no record of Francis's life in Rome during the period of the council — indeed, with that indifference to history which marks the writings of the early chroniclers, no reference to the council is made by them. But we know that Francis, doubtless through the help of the Cardinal of Santa Sabina or possibly because it was the Pope's own idea, secured an astonishing triumph, as though under the sign of *Thau* nothing became impossible to him.

Innocent, sensing the dangers inherent in the unofficial reformist religious movements, accepted the advice of the

[61] Cf. Ezek. 9:4.

[62] John 19:19.

[63] Saint Bonaventure, *The Life of St. Francis of Assisi*, ch. 4.

Lateran Council that no new religious orders should be approved. Fresh efforts and initiatives to meet the difficult problems of Christianity in a changing age must be made within the scope and traditions of the existing religious rules. Innocent would make only one exception. It was the exception in favor of this company of Lesser Brothers, the last, one would have expected, to be so privileged, seeing that it had virtually no rule at all, except the counsels of the Gospel. Could anything have been more surprising?

Once again, one is conscious of the strange and, but for the example of Christ himself, unique paradox of Francis's life — namely, that despite his embracing the unconventional, the exceptional, the unique, he drew to himself a whole world of the conventionally great, the rank and file, and the humblest.

Tradition tells us that it was on this historic occasion that Francis, the humble, who would have no book learning, no organization, met another man with whom his work would be bracketed through the centuries to come.

This man was eleven years older than Francis, and an altogether different type of person, who, at the age of thirty-four, had accompanied his bishop on a journey to Rome to ask the Pope for permission to preach to the infidels in central Europe. The young man was already a canon and a subprior of the bishop's chapter. Innocent had not been greatly interested in the proposed mission to the barbarous Hungarians, but he was deeply disturbed by the Albigensian heresy which was making alarming progress in southwest France. Such generous and learned religious volunteers should labor nearer home and see if they could make any impression on a heresy which was sweeping through a corner of Christendom because its apostles were leading lives far more Christian in appearance than the too-often decadent true believers.

This man had also discovered that progress could only be made if would-be apostles forgot all about the trammels of clerical dignity and worked on foot and alone in a spirit of evangelical poverty, comparable with that of the Albigensian heretics. The work, he discovered, needed a combination of the spirit of the Gospel with a learning necessary to demonstrate the fallacies in the persuasive Albigensian teaching. Continuing to work through the horrors of the 1208 Albigensian crusade, but never compromising himself by any share in fighting or in the acts of injustice on the part of the defenders of orthodoxy, he gradually recruited a small band of fellow apostles.

His name, of course, was Dominic Guzman, and the little band were the "preaching brothers," the future Dominicans.

But Dominic, whose order had not yet been founded, did not obtain from Innocent the same privilege as Francis. He was not allowed to develop the order's work under a novel rule. Instead, he had to choose from the older rules, and he chose the one he thought most adapted to his own purposes, the rule of Saint Augustine as lived by the Premonstratensian Canons.[64]

How was it that little Francis succeeded where the great Dominic failed? This is one of the odd pieces of evidence

---

[64] The Premonstratensian Canons, known as the Norbertines, were founded by Saint Norbert (c. 1080-1134), Archbishop of Magdeburg, and followed the rule of Saint Augustine (354-430), Bishop of Hippo.

which make us wonder how far we really know and understand Francis.

While the council's work was proceeding, this Dominic, aged forty-six, and Francis, aged thirty-three, ran into each other in Rome. They may have met by accident. They may have met because Dominic, as we are told, had a dream in which he saw the Blessed Virgin presenting Dominic himself, together with another unknown small, bearded friar, to our Lord. As a result of the dream, Dominic sought out Francis. They may have met — and this one would like to think — because the Pope and the cardinals already realized that the man in gray and the man in black and white were destined, between them, to effect one of the greatest reforms in history through the creation of the friars, just in time to meet the two-fold lack in the Church: a spirit of poverty and social justice for the common people; and a spirit of learning and humanist understanding which would organize man's growing intellectual and emotional restlessness within the Christian revelation. An inner, rather than an outward, Christian piety, a piety that consciously took into account the changing values of social evolution; Christian scholarship and discovery; Christian art and culture — all these were to be the fruit of the lives of Francis and Dominic.

Alas, we always tend to read history backward, and it is most unlikely that even so brilliant a pope as Innocent, now already a sick man and near his early death, had any such visionary conception of what these least-regarded men in the Rome of 1215-1216 would mean to the story of Christendom. The needs of the Church, however, he saw, and some at least of his hopes providentially rested on these two men.

The most we can do is picture to ourselves the outward con-trast and inner concord as the two men embraced one another, a meeting visually immortalized by Andrea della Robbia's[65] terra-cotta on the loggia of San Paolo in Florence. Dominic was good-looking, ascetic, with fine intelligent eyes: the pic-ture of a learned, saintly Spanish priest. Francis, with his large dark eyes, unkempt hair, and straggly beard, must have made something of a ludicrous contrast with the religious hidalgo. But under the contrasting clothes of torn, undyed homespun and impeccable black and white, both bore the same marks of men of the spirit, with their spare frames and their long, thin, delicate hands.

We cannot doubt that Francis's days in Rome in connection with the work of the Lateran Council proved to be another stage in the deepening of his vocation and of his awareness of the crying needs of contemporary Christendom. For him, these would be symbolized by the figure of the *Thau*, of the Cross, to be mystically inscribed on the forehead of the faith-ful whose lives had been renewed and enlightened so that they could appreciate, in their enormity, the fatuous worldliness and sinful infidelity of so many who led spiritually heedless lives. His penances would have to increase yet further, as would the number of the night hours of passionate prayer.

He had never forgotten that he, too, had been a sinner, and whatever sins he may have committed in his youth, these he now increasingly saw with the saint's insight, as a hideous deformity for which he must make amends day and night throughout his life. But while so severe toward himself, the

[65] Andrea della Robbia (1435-1525), Italian sculptor.

breath of charity and understanding and courtesy guided him when dealing with others. This is well brought out in perhaps the most famous of all the stories about Francis: the story of the wolf of Gubbio.

As one day he went to preach in that enchanting town which he knew so well, he found its inhabitants living in a state of abject terror because of the wolves that were hungrily prowling around it, devouring cattle and other animals and even attacking the citizens themselves. One wolf in particular seemed already to have earned almost legendary fame for its boldness and its ferocity. When Francis arrived and was told the dread tale, he undertook to walk out and seek the dangerous beast. The wolf, we are told, rushed at the saint, and everyone watched in terror. But Francis made the Sign of the Cross and, as the beast stopped, said, "Come to me, Brother Wolf. In Christ's Name, I forbid you to continue in your evil ways."

Preaching to the wolf, Francis went on to accuse him of the crimes which he had committed and tell him that he deserved no more than to perish in torment like a murderer. "But," he went on, "I want you to make peace with the people so that they should no longer fear you, nor fear for their dogs and for themselves." He then promised the wolf that if he agreed to behave in the future, he would be fed to the end of his life, since it had been hunger which had driven him to commit these crimes. "Will you promise never to harm anyone again, neither man nor beast?"

The bad wolf, we are told, nodded to show his agreement and put his right paw in Francis's hand. He then followed Francis into the center of the town, where the people, dumbfounded, watched the extraordinary sight.

Then, preaching to the people, Francis explained that sins, like those of the wolf, brought a more fearful punishment than the attacks of any wolves. Calling on the people to do penance, he said, "Brother Wolf has sworn never to worry you again, if you, on your side, promise to feed him for the rest of his life."

The *Fioretti* tells us that the wolf came to die naturally of old age, mourned by everyone in the town.

It is hard not to believe that this story was founded on fact, since it squares so well with Francis's undoubted power of taming animals. No doubt, what happened was vastly exaggerated in the telling. However this may be, its moral is clear. The secret of happiness and success lies in reconciliation between man and man and, above all, between man and God — reconciliation which is attained, not in a niggardly way, but in a generous and chivalrous way. Love, not fear, generosity, not niggardliness, guides man Godward, both in spiritual and material things.

The mind of Francis was thus torn between his deepening appreciation of the intrinsic effect and consequences of sin and his pity for stupid sinners whose minds were so often obscured rather than vitiated and corrupted. In this mood, his thoughts would turn to the power of God, who alone could forgive sin and remit its consequences, whether here on earth or in the hereafter.

He knew of the great indulgences accorded by the Church to those who made an offering for the Crusades and volunteered to participate in them out of devotion. The fifth crusade had just been proclaimed by Innocent at the Lateran Council.

Francis, of course, would not for a moment have questioned this indulgence, initiated by Urban II,[66] which enabled sinful warriors to fight in infidel lands with the moral certainty of salvation. This first plenary, or total, indulgence[67] demanded, like any other, true repentance, although, in later years, the ambiguous phrase of remission of "pain and guilt" led many to believe that an indulgence actually pardoned like the sacrament of Confession. But Francis's heart was less and less in fighting crusades and more and more in the idea of pacification and conversion overseas and in the spiritual enlightenment of Christians in Italy and in the rest of Europe.

If the Pope, he thought, could proclaim a great indulgence for crusaders, why not one for his beloved, weak sinners at home? If these could be relieved of the burden of their past by a great indulgence, following on a genuine will to reform expressed by receiving the sacraments of Penance and the Eucharist, would they not make a completely fresh start with a determination to live the same joyful life, the secret of which was Francis's "good news" to his countrymen? Naturally, too, Francis could never have felt happy about the need to make a monetary offering as one of the conditions for obtaining the indulgence. Such, we must surely believe, were the thoughts that lay behind the mysterious event which occurred in 1216, only a short time after the Lateran Council.

The sick Innocent was residing in nearby Perugia, and one night, while he was praying in the chapel of the Portiuncula,

---

[66] Urban II (c. 1042-1099), Pope from 1088.

[67] A plenary indulgence is held to remit the entire temporal punishment due to an individual's sins.

Francis heard Christ telling him that he must go to the Pope and ask him to grant a plenary indulgence, similar to the indulgence granted to the Crusades, to anyone who visited the Portiuncula chapel.

It should, of course, be understood that the plenary indulgence which he had in mind was not a slot-machine pardon for sin, but a remission of all punishment in the next world for sins committed, but absolved in a sincere confession to a priest. The purging power of Purgatory was taken very literally by Catholics; apart from this, the obtaining of a plenary indulgence could not have but a considerable psychological effect in helping the Christian to feel that the burden of the past was well and truly over, so that a real fresh start might be made.

Early next morning, Francis, accompanied by Masseo, covered the few miles to Perugia and saw the Pope. Innocent died on July 16 of that year, so it may be supposed that it was the dying Innocent whom Francis then met. If so, we do not know what happened. Perhaps Innocent was too ill to deal with the request, and Francis came to him only to see him die, for he was present at his deathbed. The next Pope, Honorius III, was elected in Perugia two days after Innocent's death, and it was to him that Francis was to make his formal request for this unprecedented indulgence.

Honorius III, a compromise candidate, chosen not only for his personal piety, but because he was not expected to live long, was destined to reign for nearly eleven years more, by which time he must have been nearly a hundred years old.

In his Perugian palace of San Lorenzo, Honorius must have been taken aback when Francis reminded the Pope that he had built and restored the Portiuncula and now was asking His

Holiness to grant it an indulgence obtainable on the anniversary of its dedication each year and without the customary offering. But Francis's fame was well known to the new Pope, and he did not dismiss him for bothering him by asking for the impossible. Instead, he patiently explained, backed up by the less tolerant cardinals present, the difficulties in the way of granting anything of this kind.

But Francis, as usual, was not to be put off by impossibilities, and in his typical way of putting things differently from anyone else, he asked the Pope to "grant him not years of indulgence, but souls." In other words, he wanted the kind of plenary indulgence which would free from all punishment and guilt for all past sins those who, having sincerely confessed their sins, visited the Portiuncula. And he added, "It is not I who ask, but the Lord Jesus Christ who has sent me to ask you."

The cardinals were not slow to murmur that if an indulgence like this were granted, one might as well give up the crusade indulgence altogether. Who would bother to get it at the cost of such sacrifices if a similar indulgence could be gained by simply journeying to Assisi? But the Pope cut them short: "We grant you what you seek."

However, the indulgence was only to be granted for one day each year, the anniversary day of the chapel's consecration, fixed for August 2. Further pleas that the indulgence might be gained during the eight days after the consecration and its anniversaries were refused.

Francis was content with having obtained what he believed he had been supernaturally bidden to seek. He turned to leave the room, but the Pope called to him and said, "You are altogether too simple-minded. Where are you going? You have nothing in writing to prove that this indulgence has been granted to you." Francis, in the same spirit as he had accepted Innocent's verbal confirmation of the rule, answered, "I have your word, Holy Father. If God wants this, He will see it through. I need no document. The Blessed Virgin shall be the charter and Christ the notary; and the angels will be the witnesses."

A fortnight later, the chapel of the Portiuncula was consecrated by the bishops of Assisi, Perugia, Todi, Spoleto, Nocera, Gubbio, and Foligno, and Francis himself proclaimed the indulgence in the following words: "I would like to send you all to Paradise. Our lord Pope, Honorius, has granted me by word of mouth the following indulgence. Those of you who are present here today and those who will be present in this church on this day in the years to come, so long as their hearts are well disposed and truly penitent, will be forgiven all their sins."

The most astonishing aspect of this story is that it is nowhere referred to in the early sources of Saint Francis's life. It was not until some sixty years after his death that there is any record of it, although the records do suggest that it was then well established. Moreover, many would say that the seeking of an indulgence of the kind was unlike Francis, while a new Pope's granting it against the advice of his cardinals was almost unthinkable. We have already given reasons why Francis might well have expressed in this original way his feelings about the Crusades and the crusade indulgence, and not least about the money which had to be offered to obtain it. It was so like him to feel that the sinners whom he was converting would have their good resolutions better confirmed by "indulgences" than by the customary severity. Moreover, we know how highly he always regarded the outward symbols of the Church's divine commission.

As for the Pope, captivated by Francis's charm and faith, he may well have met his cardinals' practical objection to the new indulgence by telling Francis that the privilege was special to him and to the Portiuncula and not to be spoken or written of in the future.

If such arguments are not very strong, they at least serve to support the strongest evidence for the authenticity of the indulgence — namely, that it grew steadily in fame and popularity during the years to come and that it was never prohibited or condemned by the Holy See. It is difficult to believe that this would have been the case, had there not been an extremely strong tradition about the original establishment passed down through two or three generations of friars.

Chapter Fifteen

禁

The Franciscans Bring Christ to Foreign Lands

At this time — about the middle of the second decade of the thirteenth century — the future of the rapidly growing numbers of those who had thrown in their lot with Francis all over Italy was beginning to be a problem. The Lateran Council had had universal and ecumenical significance, and it had marked the friars for a new destiny within the universal Church. The Portiuncula Indulgence, given by the Pope and, as we are told, "ratified by Heaven itself in a vision," symbolized the privilege and scope of Francis's company, equaling as it did the great indulgences only granted in connection with the Crusades — the great "international" question of the day. Yet within the Church's rigid hierarchy, these loosely bound, ruleless friars made a strange picture, and it is a measure of Francis's extraordinary personality that they could so long have remained what they were and what the visionary Francis wanted them to be.

Dotted about Italy in very small communities or in twos and threes, they had no visible status and no normal clerical rule. They worshiped and said their regular prayers in any neighboring church or monastery. The vast majority were not priests, and, toward the beginning, we only know of Sylvester

and Leo as members with any pretension to full priestly education or even any knowledge of Latin. Francis was later to say in
his testament, "Those who accepted my way of life gave all
that they possessed to the poor and were content with a single
habit, patched all over, with a cord and breeches. Those of us
who were in Holy Orders recited the Office like other clerics,
while the lay brethren said the Our Father."

The *Fioretti* gives us a curious story of the way in which
Francis, a tonsured cleric and then a deacon, and Leo, a priest,
were to say their Office. Francis was to be the first choir and
Leo the second. When they began what they called their Office, Francis made up the first versicle: "Brother Francis, you
have committed so many sins in your life that, no doubt, you
deserve to go to Hell." To which Leo answered in the second
versicle: "But now that you have done so much good, you will
most surely go to Heaven." "No, Brother Leo, that is not what
you have to say. You should repeat the versicle I recited." Leo
answered, "Well, Brother Francis, in the name of God, let us
try again."

Then Francis started the second versicle: "Brother Francis,
the sins of which you are guilty before the Lord of Heaven and
earth are so great that you deserve to be damned forever."
Then Leo answered, "Thanks be to God, you will advance so
rapidly in virtue that you will be blessed among the blessed."
Francis now became irritated at Leo's insistence on not repeat-
ing the self-deprecating verse, but capping it with the truth. But
Leo had his way.

Francis, whose apostolic vision had no bounds, began to
see the spread of his followers not only all over Italy but over
Europe and right into the lands of the infidels. He personally

had no qualms at seeing his followers at work across the face of the known world without any other rule and organization than the literal following of the Gospel and the regular coming together of as many of his followers as could make the sometimes long journeys on foot to the Portiuncula. He himself had not hesitated to take a ship to preach to the infidels, gaily leaving his followers fatherless and, in common human prudence, risking the future of his whole work. "Tomorrow" never worried him. Tomorrow was God's business, not his.

The generosity in his nature which made him throw money about before his conversion and curse it after, as inconsistent with true freedom and true sharing between man and man, was the guide to the apostolic labors of his company as a whole. They must be free; they must share their "good news" with all the world and be prepared, therefore, to set out two by two to France, Spain, Germany, and Hungary. No preparations seemed necessary to him, no learning of foreign languages, no study of alien customs. God would guide and guard — and if they fell by the wayside, He would care for them on earth or in Heaven.

No one before Francis, and no one since, has planned the future of an organization with such sublime abandon. The Knights of the Round Table had sworn loyalty to their leader, and between him and them, as among the knights between themselves, the religious law of obedience had been miraculously transmuted into a spirit of brotherhood and trust, so that practical decisions, while they were outwardly the responsibility of the "mothers" or "guardians," seemed to emerge from love and mutual understanding in the spirit of Francis himself.

Yet, in a strange way, this utopian dream was rooted in a very practical reality that grew out of Francis's simple and spontaneous love of obedience to the Church. Bishop Guido, the Cardinal of San Sabina, Innocent himself, his successor, Honorius — with all these great rulers of the Church Francis had maintained an intimate contact. Now, at this critical formative moment in the expansion of his work, Francis was to make a new friend and find a new counselor in the highest ranks for the Church. It was Cardinal Ugolino.

This cardinal was a man of the deepest personal piety with a serious desire for the reform of the Church and its adaptation to the conditions of the times. Nonetheless, he was a great prelate of conservative temper and realistic outlook. Francis may have first met him in Rome when Innocent approved the *Regula Primitiva*, at the Lateran Council and, a year later, when Innocent III and his successor were in Perugia, the latter conceding the Portiuncula Indulgence. On all these occasions, Cardinal Ugolino was present, but sometime in the year 1217 or 1218, Francis came more directly under Ugolino's sway.

At a chapter meeting, usually assigned to the year 1217, at either Pentecost or Michaelmas, it was decided to expand the work of the order by sending brothers to various countries of Europe.

Little account was taken of the practical difficulties of this missionary work. Sixty brothers were sent to the barbaric Germans, as Italians thought of these northern folk. The Germans may have taken a different view, for the friars in Germany, knowing no word of the language except, apparently, the words "*Ya! Ya!*" used this affirmative as an answer to every question put to them. As one of the questions was "Are you heretics?" the answer "*Ya!*" caused them to be beaten and persecuted. Others who went to Hungary fared no better, despite their readiness to appease the local population by the gift of practically all they were wearing.

Francis, always ready to share with his brothers the "hard labor, being mocked, hunger and thirst, and other troubles of all kinds," was determined to take part in the great adventure. After prayer, he declared to the assembled brothers, "In the name of our Lord and the Blessed Virgin Mary and the saints, I choose the province of France. They are a Catholic people, and, more than other Catholics, they show a special reverence for the Blessed Sacrament. That touches me, and that is why I would like to talk with them." He planned to take Sylvester, the priest, with him.

There are few things more touching in Francis's life than this moment. He had said his prayers and left the choice of country to God. God had chosen Francis's beloved France, where he would go in appreciation of edifying French Catholics. Dear, human Francis: did his own mind and feeling have no part in the revelation? But, alas, Francis's dream of singing once again in the sun of Provence the old songs of the troubadours along some tree-lined French road was destined to be shattered. God, he must have realized, was determined to have His way after all.

Francis and Sylvester made their way north through Arezzo (a city at the time in such a turmoil that it seemed to Francis that it was under the spell of devils — devils whom he solemnly commanded to leave the town, thus restoring peace and order to it). From Arezzo they tramped to Florence.

There, they met Ugolino, who was in residence as papal legate to Tuscany.

It was during this meeting that Ugolino evidently made it clear that he was prepared to take the order under his personal protection and guidance. He would lead them along ways which, while preserving their particular spirit and spontaneity, would safeguard them from the dangers and criticisms they might meet at the hands of churchmen shocked by a freedom and lack of ecclesiastical discipline that would seem to be out of keeping with the Church's regulations and traditions. This plan, for example, Ugolino pointed out, was an excellent illustration of the sort of adventure which the new order should *not* undertake. To send out missionaries to foreign parts without due preparation was asking for trouble. Did Francis himself realize that his proposed journey to France would deprive his companions in Italy of his protection and play into the hands of prelates known to be hostile to the whole experiment?

Francis replied that, having sent his brothers away to those dangerous countries, he could not remain safely protected in Italy. The cardinal took the opportunity of pointing out that the original plan of sending these brothers on such adventures was far from wise. To which Francis answered, as he had so often done before, that the Lord called for the salvation of all people in all places — and he underlined, "not of Christians only, but of the very infidels themselves." This fantastic and unprecedented vision, no doubt, edified the cardinal. He maintained his prohibition, however, and Francis was, for once, dissuaded from his intention to leave Italy.

Disappointed in his hopes of visiting France and, for the love of God, evangelizing in the Provençal tongue, Francis chose Brother Pacifico as his substitute. In one of his chapters, Celano tells us of the fame of Pacifico as a "king of song" in his unregenerate days, when his renown earned him the crown of laurels at the hands of the great emperor Henry. Then he came under Francis's influence, having chanced to meet him in a convent. Francis, when Pacifico first saw him, seemed to be adorned with two bright swords, one from his head to his feet and the other across his breast. Francis spoke to him of a greater emperor, and the "king of song" was soon under his sway. He, too, as we have seen, was one of those privileged to see Francis with the great *Thau* on his forehead. If Francis could not go himself, he chose the obvious substitute.

So earnest was Pacifico in his practice of poverty in France that he came under suspicion as a possible Albigensian. He was examined by the Sorbonne,[68] but he had no great difficulty in satisfying his examiners about his orthodoxy.

Cardinal Ugolino's refusal to allow Francis to go to France was extremely wise. Both the first and the second lives by Celano underline the way in which the new order was finding itself beset by critics and enemies. "Oh, how many, especially at the beginning of the undertaking, were plotting to overthrow the new order," Celano wrote in the first life; and in the second: "At that time, he saw very many raging like wolves against the little flock and then, grown old in evil, taking the occasion to do it harm. He foresaw that even among his sons, things contrary to holy peace and charity might occur, and he

---

[68] The Sorbonne, a theological college in Paris noted for the severity of its examinations, came to be consulted on theological and political questions.

doubted that, as often happens among the elect, some, puffed up by carnal feeling and in spirit quarrelsome and prone to discord, might rebel."

Faced with these grave problems, Francis realized how valuable would be the personal assistance which could best come from a cardinal who so clearly shared the ideals of the brothers.

What he did not and could not understand was that the mind of an experienced cardinal was necessarily something totally different from his own. Francis was a Christian revolutionary with a heart as large as the world. Therein lay his immense strength and attraction.

Ugolino understood the vision, and he liked nothing better than literally to share, when he could, the simple lives of these saintly first friars who, in bringing so many back to Christ, themselves lived with Christ. He is said even to have contemplated resigning his high position to join the brothers as a humble friar.

A story is told of his imitating the brothers so literally as to wash the feet of the poor. On one occasion, he did this so badly that the poor man asked him to stop since the friars themselves did it so much better.

Like Francis, Ugolino ministered to lepers and, even after becoming Pope, he would on occasion put on the Franciscan habit and accompany them in their door-to-door visiting.

But his love and imitation of the brothers came from the heart rather than from the head. In reality, he was an experienced man of the Church who understood very well the practical limitations of Francis's ideals. What he really wanted was somehow to get hold of this outpouring of pure spirituality and fresh apostolic zeal and with them, fire the Church's complex, heavy, and, too often, cold organization. That is why it seemed to him to be a fruitful idea to try to persuade the friars to accept episcopal sees. He could not understand that the idea horrified a man like Francis as utterly incompatible with the very meaning and soul of their movement.

To the cardinal's pleading that, in the primitive Church, bishops had been poor men, glowing with charity and not with greed — why not therefore Franciscan and Dominican bishops today of the same caliber? — Francis answered, "We have been called *Minores* that we may never presume to become *Majores*. If you wish us to bear fruit in the Church of God, keep us in the state to which we have been called, and force us back to lowliness even against our wills."

Although Francis himself could not help continuing to be the effective father and ruler of his followers until the end of his days, he hated from the start the position of eminence which he held. Even on the first journey to Rome, he chose Bernard to be the leader of the pilgrimage. So now, only about seven or eight years later and he still in his thirties, and not yet markedly afflicted by physical weakness, he formally resigned his official headship, and appointed Peter Catanei to that office of minister general — nominally his own superior.[69]

Cardinal Ugolino showed himself even less understanding of the ideals of Clare and her foundation of Poor Ladies. Clare, like Francis, was determined to maintain the practice of absolute and corporate poverty — not just individual poverty within corporate ownership. Ugolino failed to understand that

[69] I follow here the chronology suggested by Rosalind Brooke.

for both Francis and Clare, there was liberty and emancipation, as well as great spiritual enrichment in the practice of total poverty. Freedom from all ties, from all business, allowed for complete liberty of spiritual action and removed all temptation to enter into the complexity of business and property-owning which corporate ownership involved. We know only too well, in regard to Francis's own times, as well as in earlier and later times until the Reformation, how corporate ownership could lead to the greatest abuses among religious communities both of men and of women. Francis had seen it all around him in Assisi, and he would fight until his death against reforms and rules which involved imposing it.

Another example of Cardinal Ugolino's failure fully to understand Francis was his conviction that the spirit of Francis would be more effectively spread if he consented to adapt his order to one or another of the great monastic rules, as Dominic had been prepared to do. Pope Innocent, we have seen, allowed Francis to be a unique exception in this matter, but now that the order was so rapidly growing, it seemed to Ugolino that there would be much greater safety for Francis and his followers if they conformed to the Church's ruling.

Once again, Francis was adamant. "The Almighty," he said, "has made it clear to me that I must live according to the manner of the Gospel." Later, he explained even more clearly: "My brothers, the Lord has called me by the way of humility, and He has shown me the way of simplicity. I do not want you to mention to me any other rule, neither that of Saint Augustine, nor that of Saint Benedict, nor that of Saint Bernard. The Lord told me that He wanted me to be a new fool in the world and that He did not want to lead us by any other way than by that Wisdom, for, by your learning and your wisdom, God will confound you."

This apparent stubbornness, unthinkable in our days where Church matters are concerned, was, of course, the counterpart of the complete originality which manifested itself in every action and decision of Francis where he and his followers were concerned. Christ had spoken to him — that was enough.

It is probable that no great churchman could have acted otherwise than Cardinal Ugolino. Yet no one else could have been so patient and understanding of the problems. One is compelled to believe that but for the providential intervention of Cardinal Ugolino, the future of the order would have been even more troubled than it was actually to be. It could have come to disaster.

For the time being, the cardinal acceded to nearly everything on which Francis insisted, and was content as a "father," "lord," and "benefactor" — the words used by the early writers — to do what he could to safeguard the brothers and to protect Francis, so far as he was able, by issuing instructions which made clear to all their orthodoxy and the regularity of their ecclesiastical status.

Chapter Sixteen

Francis Tries to Convert the Sultan

Meanwhile Francis, so far from paying heed to the spirit of Cardinal Ugolino's prohibition of the journey to France, was planning a far more extravagant adventure, as the world of the time would think it. It seemed to him to be no more than the next logical step along the lines he had always envisaged — namely, the preaching of the Gospels without thought of any limits other than those imposed by insurmountable circumstances. His spiritual élan knew of no bounds, whether in Christian or pagan lands. He must move farther and farther along the one way which, he believed, God wanted. He must oppose all that delaying action which human prudence dictated — the docketing, the ticketing, the classifying, and the organizing.

He had already, as we have seen, been inspired to undermine the old spirit of the crusades (much as he loved the knightly ideal which underlay it) by thinking out the better way, the only way, Christ's way. He must convert, not conquer; preach the love of Christ, not kill Christ with the sword which Christ ordered Peter to sheathe.[70] The fact that, in trying to

---

[70] John 18:10-11.

put the plan into operation, he had once made a fool of himself as human judgment would see it, makes no difference. That was God's business, not his.

Biographers tell us that he was seeking martyrdom at the hand of the infidels. But here, too, he would surely have been indifferent. If martyrdom were the will of God, he would welcome it joyfully, for martyrdom meant the privilege of sharing physically in Christ's own sacrifice — the lover united with the Beloved as closely as any earthly experience could reach. But Francis was also supremely alive, and his primary desire must have been the natural one of winning that living, radiant, yet fallen infidel world for his Beloved, just as he had gladly labored among the crowds at home, good people with the mark of Baptism on them, but weak and sinful — just as he had moved through the fair countryside filled with God's creatures; just as he had looked up to the heavens to see God's light-bearing sun, singing his praise of the Creator, who had made the brilliance of the reflected colors, the warmth of the evening's soft shadows.

Therefore it was that Francis, at the Pentecost chapter of 1219, decided that the sending of his brothers through Italy and then across the mountains must now be followed by sending them across the seas to the lands of the infidels, the lands where his Master had lived and died. They were to be the new crusaders, God's crusaders. His old friend Giles, the third Franciscan, was to head a mission to Tunis. Five others were to cross to Morocco, a mission destined to produce the first Franciscan martyrs who would die very much in the spirit of Francis himself, since they could easily have escaped. If their blood did not become the seed of the Church in that land, it was not wasted, for it brought into the company of Francis the best-known Franciscan saint after Francis: Anthony the Portuguese, to be known for all time as Saint Anthony of Padua.

The most sensational and fateful news to be given to the chapter was kept until the end. Francis himself would lead the third missionary enterprise. With twelve brethren, he would go to Egypt, where he could preach to the crusaders who were besieging Damietta, at the mouth of the Nile.

The plan had evidently long been in his mind. Two years earlier, at the chapter when Francis himself hoped to go to France and other brethren were sent to different parts of Europe, he had selected Brother Elias to head a mission to Syria. Francis's close friendship for Elias cannot be doubted, and he must have considered him the most able of his earlier companions. Syria comprised the Holy Land, and Francis must have intended to see the way prepared for his own dream of visiting and converting those who lived where Christ had lived.

He was also to choose as one of his companions no less a person than Peter Catanei, who had recently (if we are to believe modern chronological reconstruction) been made his vicar. Can it have been that he secretly planned to transfer the center of the order to the Holy Land and the lands of the infidels? If so, it would seem that he never breathed a word of it, since there is no suggestion of such a plan in any of the records.

Hardly less strange is the fact that no objection seems to have been made to so highly dangerous an enterprise. The father and founder might well have been drowned on the way; he might be held captive by the Saracens; he might — indeed, most likely he would — be martyred, given his ideas about personal missionary contacts with the most dangerous and bloodthirsty of enemies.

He must also have been troubled in mind as to what would happen to his followers while he was absent for a period likely to be critical in regard to the future of the order.

However, no objections seem to have been made to the daring plan even by Cardinal Ugolino. Taking with him, in addition to Peter Catanei, two of his first companions, Barbaro and Sabatino, as well as the ex-feudal lord Brother Leonardo di Ghislerio and Brother Illuminato, Francis sailed, according to tradition, from Ancona, although it is more likely that the party sailed from a port in Apulia, the more normal route to the East, calling at Crete and Cyprus, and eventually reaching Acre, where they probably made contact with Elias and his companions. Setting sail again with Illuminato, Francis reached Egypt.

The siege of Damietta was an episode during the fifth crusade, called for by Innocent III and supported by his successor, Honorius III. The ill success of more direct attacks on the Moslems had led to the plan of taking Damietta and then exchanging that fort for Jerusalem. It was a good plan, thought out by the best of the crusaders, John de Brienne, King of Jerusalem — John de Brienne, brother of Walter, whose name had inspired the young Francis to seek the glory of knighthood.

By February 1219, the sultan, Malek-el-Kamel, nephew of Saladin the Great, the hero of the East, was ready to make the exchange. Alas, the courageous but foolish Spanish papal legate, Pelagius, would not hear of so cowardly a plan. He insisted that Damietta must be captured and, after it, Jerusalem itself.

So when Francis reached the shores of Egypt, at the height of the summer of the same year, what he saw was the army of crusaders maintaining a dreary siege of double- and triple-walled Damietta, with its hundred and ten towers, forty forts, and provisions for two years. It must have seemed strange to Francis to find himself once again in a field of war, and one on so much larger a scale than the small, but bloody, battle of Collestrada. So determined a seeker of peace, he could not have been surprised to find the Christian army, enervated by climate and boredom, to be something wholly different from the pictures of knightly crusading romanticism which he had once so assiduously nursed in his imagination. The commanders were quarreling, and the men were given over to drunkenness and every kind of license. Yet, amazingly, this "simple unlettered man, so lovable and so dear to God and man," as Jacques de Vitry, who was sent out as bishop to rouse the crusaders, described Francis, was able to show himself once again the true crusader, the true leader capable of calling men to their duty.

Soon many were clamoring to join his company. "Master Regnier, the prior of San Michel, Colin the Englishman, Don Matthieu, Michel, Henri le Chantre" are named by de Vitry, and "many others whose names escape me."

Francis, the apostle of peace, like so many other apostles of peace, turned out to be a better general than the generals. When, near the end of August, the generals planned a great assault on the city, quarreling among themselves as to the best tactics, Francis's advice was asked for. He warned them that they would be driven back, but they would not heed this defeatist view of an amateur friar. We are told the story of how, while the battle was being waged, Francis prayed as Pacifico went a little ahead to see what was happening and to report to Francis. What Francis had foretold took place. In a terrible battle, with heroic deeds on both sides, the crusaders were driven back, and some six thousand of them were killed or taken prisoner.

Extraordinary as was this apostolic achievement of an unpresuming and odd friar lost in a great military concentration, it amounted to little in comparison with the plan he was nursing in his mind in that Egyptian summer, turning to the autumn of the year 1219. Here was the real purpose of Francis in leaving Assisi and his brethren — an idea so startling, so preposterous, that no one but Francis could have entertained it.

His crazy plan was to make his way with Brother Illuminato right through the Moslem forces and convert Malek-el-Kamel himself. The idea caused the best laugh of the campaign among clergy, officers, and men.

Saladin's nephew, like Saladin himself, was anything but a barbarian, but whatever his personal views, the cause of Islam was held by him and his followers with a far greater tenacity and pride than the vast majority of Christians were showing for their Faith. Moreover, this, at the moment, was the battle line, and no one could hope to make his way through the Moslem ranks without being captured or, more probably, killed. Francis and Illuminato, with their usual humility, went to the papal legate to ask for his consent to the plan. To a great churchman, the suggestion was not only ridiculous in that there could be no hope that the friars would ever return, but it was also immoral. What the average Christian thinks today of Communism pales in comparison with what a papal legate at that time would think of the Moslems. There could be no question of any sort of personal relations or coexistence with these cruel, evil people, who forced their captives to spit on the cross and whose vices were a byword. Yet Francis's personality somehow overcame once again the objections of men in high places. Pelagius, faced with Francis, found it impossible to maintain his prohibition. Doubtless, he eased his conscience with the thought that the brothers were already as good as dead, and death was common enough in that encampment.

"Very well," he said, "try it if you must, but remember that you go without my mandate."

So Francis and Illuminato, in their gray tunics and barefoot on the hot sand, made their way toward the Moslem lines. Francis, as usual on such occasions, when he felt himself to be a knight of Christ fighting desperate spiritual battles, walked along singing the praises of the Lord. The extraordinary sight of these two beggarly men at least prevented the Moslem soldiers from cutting them down there and then. They thought they must be a couple of lunatics, wanting to abjure Christianity and accept the Koran. So, guarding them, they took the queer Christians to the sultan's tent, for Kamel was curious about oddities.

Given the nature of the religious and the ideological differences between the Christians and the Moslems, the chances of these nondescript Christian friars reaching the sultan's headquarters with the idea of converting him to Christianity were exceedingly slim.

Yet, once they had arrived, we may well imagine that Malek-el-Kamel had no difficulty in realizing that this little man with his dark, intelligent, smiling eyes and his drawn, ascetic features was no ordinary person. The sultan enjoyed religious controversy, and he asked for no better distraction than some long talks with this unusual Christian, who seemed so utterly different from the masses of his enemies. Probably there were a number of meetings which amounted to a miniature ecumenical conference, the first to overstep the boundaries of Christianity since the early days of the Church.

Francis won the first round. Kamel was standing with him on the carpet with a pattern of crosses. "I see you have no objection to tramping on the cross," the sultan laughed. Francis, the unlettered, answered easily: "You should know that there were many crosses on Calvary, the Cross of Christ and the crosses of the malefactors. We venerate the Cross of Christ, but as for the others, you may keep them. If you want to cover the ground with them, why should we have scruples about walking on them?"

It was time for the sultan to send for his theologians. As is not unknown with some theologians, these saw little advantage in arguing about the truth. This man's attempt to expound the Christian Faith within the Saracen camp was a scandal not to be tolerated. They pleaded with their broaderminded master.

"Your Highness is the arm of the law, and it is your duty to keep and defend it. We bid you in the name of God and Mohammed, who gave us the law, immediately to cut off these men's heads, for we shall never listen to what they say. We enjoin you also not to listen, for the law forbids us to listen to preachers of other laws."

With this, the theologians retired, but Francis had a splendid suggestion for the sultan. "Light a great fire," he said. "Let your priests and mine enter it, and you will see by what happens which of our two religions is the more saintly and true."

The sultan expressed his doubts about the readiness of his theologians to enter any furnace, so Francis said he was ready to go in alone if they would promise to abjure their religion should he come out unhurt. "If I am burned up, impute it to my sins. If God protects me, acknowledge Him to be the true God and Savior of all."

So far from ordering the death of these infidels, Malek-el-Kamel was undoubtedly greatly moved by a faith and a trust that compared favorably with that of the best of his own people. He invited Francis and Illuminato to stay with him, promising many rich presents. Whether Francis stayed or not, we do not know, but he refused everything but a little horn, which he was to use to call people to his sermons.

When they finally parted, the sultan arranged for the brothers to be escorted to the Christian lines, bidding them farewell with the words: "Do not forget me in your prayers, and may God reveal to me the Faith which is most pleasing to Him." Francis was also, we are told, given a safe conduct to travel freely in Moslem lands.

This episode is said to have been commemorated on the Moslem side by an inscription on the tomb of a Moslem mystic, the Fakir al Farisi, a counselor of Malek-el-Kamel, which reads, "His adventure with Malek-el-Kamel, and all that happened in regard to a monk are very well known." No one else but Francis could, it seems, have been that monk.

Francis had failed, and perhaps he had never expected to succeed in the sense of actually converting the sultan, but, as in so many other ways, he opened a way. His magnificent gesture was in the end to bear greater fruit than any local conversion could have done. His spirit and courage had pointed forward toward the days when his own Franciscan followers would be missionary pioneers. Love, understanding and trust for Christ's sake, not self-regard and the letter of the law: these are the way to truth and unity.

A month later, we are told, the two friars returned to Damietta, escorted by a troop of Saracen horsemen. We know nothing further of Francis's stay with the crusaders before Damietta, nor what part he played when the city finally fell in early 1220. In the spring, Francis set sail again for Acre — to walk in the actual footsteps of his Master.

The plain truth is that nothing whatever is known about the months spent in the Holy Land. It is one of the many oddities about the records of Saint Francis that his early biographers, who dwell on so many details, authentic or not, are silent as to what Francis, with his passion for the symbolism that entered by the senses to carry infinite inner meaning, did during these supreme moments of his life, and what they must have meant to him.

Perhaps it is as well, for so much of Francis's life after his conversion is more or less of an enigma, the record falling so far short of the reality, that we have to infer the latter from the extraordinary impression which he made both on his contemporaries and on posterity. If what really went on in the mind and heart of Francis during his missionary life is so intangible, how much more would it be so if we knew of the outward detail of this little humble man's following in the footsteps of his Master and echoing the life and spirit of Christ as the Gospels tell it? His was no abstract, inquiring, philosophic mind, able to communicate in detail with posterity, but a mind in tune with reality, the concrete, the touch and hand of God. These months, like the mystical union which was to be expressed in his very flesh on Mount La Verna, would anyway be beyond our comprehension.

Francis, in this eastern journey and pilgrimage, did not share in his body the Passion and death of Christ, but it may well be that it was in the prolonged exposure to the glare of the eastern sun, cruelly reflected from the golden sand, the harsh ocher earth, the white glare of town and village, that he further weakened a body never strong after his Perugian captivity. His own extreme asceticism must have prepared the way for the bad effects of these months. Thus he contracted the disease of the eyes which was quickly to obscure forever the loveliness of the world which sang to him of its Creator. It may be that the last sights of this earth which he saw quite clearly were the spots trodden by our Lord, eleven hundred years earlier. With weakened body and darkened eyes, he would live on for a few more years, singing all the more exultantly the praises of the God who had given him strength and vision and now wanted to give him only Himself.

At Acre, moreover, when he returned there in the shortening months of 1220, Francis showed that there was still plenty of spirit left in him. Saint John Acre, then a great port and capital of the kingdom of Jerusalem, already had its Franciscan foundation well established under Brother Elias. One of the brothers under Elias was a new recruit of great promise, one Caesar of Speyer, so successful a preacher of crusades that his German countrymen drove him from his native country lest he denude it of warriors. Francis, as we have seen, had taken Peter Catanei, his vicar, to Palestine. Acre, therefore, at that moment could have boasted of the finest of Franciscan communities.

One day, another Franciscan brother, who must have been very close to Francis's own temperament, came hurrying through the dusty streets to find the founder. It was Brother Stephen, named "the Simple," although the word *candid* would be more appropriate. Brother Stephen had been desperately seeking Francis, for he had appalling news to give him.

The worst had happened. The provincials in Italy, Matthew of Narni and Gregory of Naples — the first reputedly a saintly man; the second, we know from his later life, a very hard man — had taken advantage of Francis's absence from home to put into operation the reforms against which Francis had so long been fighting. The brethren, deprived of their father, seemed to be slipping into factions. Those who were determined to remain closest to the ideal of Francis himself were being persecuted and dispersed. Some, under John of Capella, were trying to devote themselves together to the service of the lepers in an extremist community in loyalty to Francis, although, no doubt, without his spirit of freedom. Cardinal Ugolino was insisting on the adaptation of the rule of Clare to the precedents of other convents for women, while the vicars themselves were forcing on the main body of the order a more formal rule expressly contrary to all that Francis had been striving for: the primitive rule of perfect imitation of Christ as He had lived in Palestine.

Brother Stephen, who had brought with him a copy of the new regulations, was the spokesman for those brethren who had been opposing the changes and had even been threatened with expulsion for their pains. It was the old story now come true. Rome, in the person of Ugolino, wanted to see the followers of Francis assimilated to the traditions of the older orders, as were their spiritual cousins, the followers of Dominic. They should have new constitutions. The days of Francis's evangelical texts were long past. There was much work to be done for the Church by the later recruits, many of whom were scholars, lawyers, churchmen of promise, men of business, and administrators before they had followed Francis. Wattle huts, haphazard shelters, spiritual tramping as the spirit moved them, the lack of sanctions — such ideals had indeed molded their wonderful spirit and outstanding devotion, but now it was time to get down to the real business of raising the standards of Christendom under the planned leadership of the Holy See and its constituted officers, among whom Franciscans themselves would be outstanding.

Such would have been the gist of the message which Brother Stephen brought. Francis knew it all, and he realized in his heart that there was little he could do about it, save insist that this was not the commission which he had received in his heart from his Master. His inspiration had been to simplify, to show the world the way of freedom by rejecting the enslaving cares of the business of a great world, even a great ecclesiastical world, and to proclaim the joy and peace of utter denudation — to save the living, actual man, here and now present, not to plan a better future for mankind with better versions of the old entanglements. He did not judge others. He only knew his own way.

But his actual response was wonderfully typical of his genius in disregarding generalities and putting his finger on the present, the vivid, the actual. When Brother Stephen showed him the draft of the new constitutions, his mind fixed at once on the paragraph dealing with new fasting laws — fasting laws similar to those of the other orders. According to this draft, this very day of the week was one on which they should not eat meat. As it happened, a dish of meat was lying on the table at which they were about to sit down for their meal. "What shall we do?" Francis said to Peter Catanei. "It is for you to decide," answered Peter, "for you are the superior." "Well, then," said Francis, "let us eat what is set before us, according to the Gospels."[71]

With the simplest and the most practical of gestures, Francis had made his feelings clear. As always, he could do no other, where his inspiration and beliefs were in question. As soon as possible, Francis, Peter, Elias, Caesar, and Illuminato sailed for Venice to engage in the melancholy struggle to maintain the old ways. It is to be noted that Elias, so often associated with undesirable reforms and changes, was still on Francis's side.

As soon as they had reached the city on the water, Francis took Illuminato to a deserted little island off the coast to spend some days in prayer and preparation for the struggle that was to come. As the two companions were praying, we are told, the birds gathered above them, accompanying their recitation of the psalms and hymns of the Office with their chirruping.

[71] Luke 10:8. This conversation may seem difficult to reconcile with the view that Peter was already minister general. But Francis, to his death, would remain father and founder, and Peter, on a critical occasion like this, would surely look to Francis for a ruling.

After a time, Francis bade the birds stop and fly away, that they might be left to their silent contemplation.

The breakdown of Francis's health in Palestine and the fatigues of the journey made it impossible for him to tramp along the many miles of flat country between Venice and Bologna. He had to ride on a donkey, while a brother walked along beside him.

The brother, who had been a nobleman, was not too pleased to find himself walking while the bourgeois Francis rode. Francis could read his thoughts, and he offered to change places with him. The poor brother was filled with confusion at being caught out in his unedifying daydreams, and so they carried on, as planned, toward their destination.

During this journey, Francis's mind must have been full of apprehension. What had they done to his Knights of the Round Table, bound to that poverty, freedom, and companionship traced in the steps of his Master, as he himself had been physically tracing them in Jerusalem, Bethlehem, and Nazareth?

But all his doubts and worries left him utterly unprepared for what he was to see in Bologna.

Bologna, the great university city to which students in law made their way from all over Europe, had especially happy memories for Francis. Years earlier, his first companion, Bernard da Quintavalle, had traveled to Bologna to bring to its restless and ambitious students and citizens the ideal of Franciscan humility and poverty. But Bernard was made a laughingstock, and the more men, women, and children mocked him, the more he showed himself to the passersby, taking his stand in the center of the town with all the ruffians making sport with him. Among them was one man, a doctor of the law, who realized that this was no madman, but someone dedicated to a higher way of life. Bernard, instead of arguing with him, simply gave him Francis's book of rules. Having studied it, the doctor realized that his intuition had been correct. He became a firm friend of Bernard and helped him to found a Franciscan convent in Bologna.

With such memories, Francis could not have helped looking forward to seeing the brothers who symbolized in that city of learning another way of understanding where human happiness and fulfillment lay.

As at length he reached the city, he eagerly inquired where his brothers were to be found. "The Lesser Brothers? Everyone knows where they are. They are housed in a fine new building near the university." Francis remembered that Peter Stacia, Provincial of Lombardy, had been a Doctor of Law of Bologna. His vivid imagination saw it all with horror: a comfortable house with a library; the brothers walking to the schools; superiors hoping to do better than the sons of Dominic; and, worst of all, the murder of Lady Poverty in the taking of possessions for their use, comfort, and education. Francis, as we have seen so often, was no conventional saint.

When he saw the reality before his eyes, he reacted with all the emotional strength of his character. On this occasion, we can say that he simply lost his temper. He would not have been the first saint to do so. The *Mirror of Perfection* tells us that when he saw the spiritual house he had built crumbling at his feet, "he turned back on his steps and went out of the city." He thought he had seen before his eyes the collapse of all that he had striven and suffered for: the triumph of his Lady Poverty.

The accounts at this point are neither clear nor consistent, but it seems evident that the news of the father's arrival had reached the brothers — some, we are told, thought he was dead. They must have sent a delegation to explain the situation and to try to pacify him. If so, they were unsuccessful, for Francis's wrath was not a matter of a few moments only. He called for Peter Stacia, and Peter must have received one of the stiffest dressing-downs in ecclesiastical history. Others were to do penance, leave the convent, and never return to it. "But what about the sick?" he was asked. The record tells us that Francis would make no exception for them either. "Out they must go!" The place, to Francis, had become accursed.

One may feel rather scandalized by this infuriated reaction of a man of so gentle temperament — a man, above all, of peace. But at least it reminds us that his gentleness and charm were not merely inborn qualities. His extravagant youth should make that clear. Francis had chosen what he believed with his whole heart to be the way of the Lord and, in prayer and penance, had canalized his naturally passionate disposition along the line of love. The strength of the principles which had made this possible was also the strength of will, the strength of indignation, the strength of misery which caused this outburst at the evidence of the overwhelming betrayal of those values which, as he firmly believed, could alone restore the Church and bring peace and joy to men, as they had done to him.

He was no visionary, and he did not indict others, least of all the Church, but he knew himself to have been commissioned to live with his followers the only and the better way. His own brothers had spectacularly taken advantage of his absence to let him down. Months of doubts and miseries and anxieties were ahead of him. Broken in health and hurt in mind and soul, he must now, in prayer and suffering, try to follow his Master's way of the Cross, and through it learn what God's will for him and his brethren should prove to be. This was to be his true Passion.

Chapter Seventeen

※

Francis Preserves the
Purity of the Order

As Francis continued his journey south, it became more and more clear to him that neither the Bologna scandal nor the new fasting laws were mere eccentricities imposed by the vicars during his absence and that of Peter Catanei. They were instances of a deliberate policy to assimilate the work he had created to the established traditions of the older orders. They represented a point of view held in the main by later recruits, inspired certainly by the glamour and wonder of Francis himself, but intent, with their learning and more established conventional traditions, on making the order a more efficient force in the service of the Church at a time when heresy and weakened discipline were endangering the future.

Whereas Francis had insisted that the Franciscan *luoghi* should be small and makeshift, sheltering but a few brethren, the policy was now to build all over Italy large communities living in proper houses, in which the ideal of corporate poverty could no longer be maintained. Whereas he had insisted on a simple evangelical rule, observed by love, devotion, and a free spirit of idealism, rather than by discipline, with the brothers in large measure choosing for themselves the itineraries of their wandering preaching, although with all possible respect for priests, churches, and constituted authorities, the policy now was to accept as far as possible the traditional disciplines and rules. Whereas he had insisted with absolute determination that the order and its members should not be protected by ecclesiastical letters of authority, clearly double-edged credentials, the practice of accepting such commendatory letters had been growing and was officially being made compulsory for all.

In Francis's view, it was the spirit that kept a brother faithful, but now the Pope insisted that recruits should do a year's noviceship before profession, and they could not leave the order for another.

Inevitably, these changes would tend to split the brethren into parties; the veterans, nearly all of whom stood by Francis; the reformers who welcomed the changes, believing that only so could the order be maintained in being and do its full work; and even smaller groups which revolted against the reformers by forming themselves into bands which wanted to outdo Francis in extravagant ways of penitential living.

Francis, moreover, realized perfectly well that, however good the motives which had prompted these changes, they must lead to competition and ambitions for success and distinction in the Church and in the world — in other words, the very thing of which he had always had most horror. He saw it all as indicating that the whole of his work would collapse, and the order would suffer the fate of many others which had started with seemingly exaggerated and unpractical zeal in protest against ecclesiastical decadence, but had either drifted into heresy or conformed to established monastic traditions.

Francis Preserves the Purity of the Order

It must have been his feelings at this time and later which Celano expressed when he wrote, "When Francis saw how some of the brethren were seeking high office, brethren whom this alone made unworthy, quite apart from other matters, he used to say that they were no longer *Minores*, but that they had fallen from glory, since they had forgotten the vocation to which they had been called. And when some of these unfortunate men showed how much they resented being removed from office, for they had been seeking the honor of office, not its burdens, he would silence them by many a talk. . . . Office, he would say, leads to a fall, just as praise leads to headlong destruction; it is in the humility of subjection that the soul perfects itself." And Celano quoted the saint as saying, "The best brothers are confounded by what the bad ones do. Even if they have not done wrong themselves, the example of the bad ones brings them also under judgment. That is why they are piercing me with a cruel sword and plunging it into me all day long."

Faced by this terrible crisis, Francis did two things — two things so typical, that they go far to enable us to understand still further his originality of spirit and extraordinary effectiveness, despite his own lack of all the acquired gifts which the more learned brothers wished to see more effectively expressed in the order.

The first of these must have cost him a good deal, since he must have feared that its effect on the future of the order might well be out of harmony with the inspiration which, he was sure, God had given him. Yet he could not possibly have avoided it. It was formally to ask Cardinal Ugolino to become the cardinal protector of the order, even though at that time there was no need for this kind of official protection where a religious order was concerned.

We have already seen how sympathetic the cardinal was, but he had never pretended that as a Church official he could entirely approve of Francis's seemingly anarchic inspiration. Yet orthodoxy had been at the very root of all that Francis had done, and only from Rome could he obtain a guarantee that the order could survive and prosper. So, with the cardinal's official backing, he would once again journey to Rome.

His whole mind was illustrated by the story of the little black hen and her chicks which Celano tells: "While the man of God was often meditating on these and similar things, one night he saw a vision in his sleep. He beheld a little black hen, like a tame dove, whose legs and feet were feathered all over. She had countless chicks, which pressed eagerly around her, but could not be gathered under her wings. The man of God arose from sleep, recalled what he had seen and himself became the interpreter of his vision. 'I am this hen,' said he, 'small in size and black by nature, who ought, through innocence of life, to have that simplicity of a dove, which wings its rapid flight to Heaven, even as it is most rare in the world. The chicks are the brethren, multiplied in number and in grace, whom Francis's strength suffices not to defend from the disturbance of men and the gainsaying of tongues. I will therefore go and commend them to the Holy Church of Rome, that by the rod of Her power, the ill-disposed may be smitten and the children of God enjoy full freedom everywhere, to the increase of eternal salvation.' "

It is from Celano, too, that we have the charming and so typical account of how Francis, having made up his mind, went to Rome and preached to the Pope and cardinals. When Cardinal Ugolino heard that Francis had decided to put his position before the Pope personally, the cardinal "was filled with apprehension as well as with joy, admiring the fervor of the holy man and beholding his simple purity." But he was also "in an agony of suspense, praying to God with all his might that the simplicity of the blessed man might not be despised." The cardinal need not have feared. Francis was one of those persons who find it far easier to get his mind over to the "top people" than to the class of minor officials and subordinates. Everything was to go well. "Such was the fervor of his spirit as he spoke," Celano says, "that, unable to contain himself with joy, as he uttered the words in his mouth, he moved his feet as if in dancing, not in wantonness, but as glowing with the fire of Divine Love; not provoking laughter, but extorting tears of grief."

This, we recall, was the occasion when Francis instinctively reverted to his preconversion life, and found himself, in his faith and excitement, dancing as he had danced in the streets of Assisi during his unregenerate days.

The wheel had come full circle, and all that had made Francis the most attractive personality in Assisi was now, turned to the highest spiritual ends, radiating an unanswerable attraction in the papal court itself. Just as, having convinced Bishop Guido where others could not be convinced, and then having bypassed Guido to go to Innocent III with his companions and obtain the approval of his primitive rule, so now in his difficulties he instinctively acted along the same line and asked Pope Honorius to give him and his growing order permanent assistance, which could best come from a cardinal protector who seemed in so many ways to share the ideals of the brothers. What he did not and could not understand, any more now than when he first met the cardinal, was that, in the long run, the mind of an experienced cardinal was necessarily something totally different from his own.

But this difficulty did not daunt him. He set, as it were, his second plan in action, although such a phraseology would have meant nothing to him. His plan can best be described as simply carrying on as always. It had never been his way to take thought, to balance pros and cons, or to try to compromise. Never did he want to alter anything by rational argument. He just quietly went on doing what he believed he had to do, and what he believed God had inspired him to do. He proposed to solve this crisis in the same way, remaining himself, but allowing others to remain different, so long as they did not think he really approved of them. The simplest solution was also the most brilliant one. Indeed it was the only one.

So long as Francis was there and remained himself, his spirit would endure in spite of all, and the Lesser Brothers would remain authentic Franciscans at least in the sense that they would have been utterly different without his presence, actual or in spirit. Changes might be necessary, but Francis, by remaining himself, was a living witness to the fact that the changes were not really his, not what he would have approved. Illogical and inconsistent by canons of reason and sensible behavior it may have been, but such canons were never his. He believed in both God and man, and he believed that the two together could find ways forward where brains, prudence, and law must block them. Had he been anything else, history would never have heard of Francis of Assisi.

Francis Preserves the Purity of the Order

There is a passage in the *Mirror of Perfection* which manages to convey the full illogicality and yet the full effectiveness of Francis's way of coping with contradictions:

A brother once said to Francis, "You know how, once upon a time, the order, by God's grace, flourished in the purity of perfection. That was the time when the brothers, with great fervor and care, observed the fullness of holy poverty. They lived in small and poor buildings. They had few books, and those in a poor state. In all these outward things, they zealously conformed with our profession and vocation. Similarly, they held together in the love of God and their neighbor in a truly apostolic and evangelical way. But now, all this has greatly changed, although excuses are made on the ground that there are too many brothers to live together in that way. . . . We firmly believe that you disapprove of this despising and disregarding of the way of the holy simplicity and poverty which was so marked when we started together. Yet we cannot understand how it is that if all this displeases you, you tolerate it and refuse to correct it."

"As long," Francis answered, "as I held the office of superior and the brothers remained true to their vocation and profession, I tried as well as I could (despite my weak health ever since my conversion) to do all I could for them by my example and by my exhortation. But when I saw how God multiplied our numbers and how many grew lukewarm and weak, losing the right and safe path, forgetting their calling, not heeding good example, and deaf to exhortation, admonition, and my example, I resigned the superiorship and the government of the order to God and the ministers. When I did this, I did explain to the chapter general that it was because of my weak health that I could no longer bear the change. And I said that nevertheless if they really wanted to follow me for their comfort and utility, I would see to it that they would have no other superior until my dying day. So long as a good and faithful subject knows and observes the will of his superior, the superior need have no worry about him. So much so that, realizing how both subject and superior can profit together where the brethren are good, even if I were in bed sick, I should find no difficulty in satisfying them. For my office as superior is a spiritual office only, to control evil ways and spiritually to correct and amend them. And if I cannot correct and amend them by exhortation, admonition, and example, I am not minded to take over the role of executioner to punish and scourge them like the magistrates of the world. Until the day of my death, never will I cease, by good example and by good works, to lead the brethren to walk in the way the Lord pointed out to me, the way that I have taught and pointed out by word and example. They will then be without excuse before God, and I shall not be bound before God to render any further account concerning them."

In other words, Francis had been saving the order by resigning an office that had become intolerable to him because it could no longer be the office he had known and understood. But he fully intended to remain a living conscience to those determined to do things otherwise than he knew to be right. In a sense, we may say that he intended to have it both ways, with the simplicity of a dove and the wisdom of a serpent.[72]

The date traditionally given for this formal resignation of office is the chapter of 1220, the date when, in fact, he went to Rome and asked Cardinal Ugolino to be the order's cardinal protector.

[72] Cf. Matt. 10:16.

"That he might observe the virtue of holy poverty," wrote the author of the *Mirror of Perfection*, "in a certain chapter, before the brethren, he resigned the office of superior: 'From now onward, I am dead unto you, but here is Brother Peter Catanei, whom I and all of you will obey.'

"Prostrating himself on the ground, Francis then promised Peter obedience and reverence. All those present were in tears and bitterly lamenting the fact that they had thus been made orphans of such a father. But Francis raised his eyes to Heaven and, joining his hands together, said, 'Lord, into Thy hands I commend those whom Thou hast committed to my care. Most dear Lord, my infirmities are such that I can no longer look after them, so I commend them to the minister. In the day of judgment, they shall answer for them before You, O Lord, if any brother perish through their negligence, bad example, or overseverity.' "

As we have already pointed out, this date has been disputed on the grounds that it leaves no time to cover all that Peter Catanei did as minister general. In fact, Peter Catanei died in 1221. It is also argued that Francis could not have been personally present at the Michaelmas chapter of 1221, since he and his companions did not leave Syria until September. Moreover, as we have seen, when he did reach Italy, he made his way to Rome in order to ensure the official protection of Cardinal Ugolino. It looks, therefore, as though Francis's resignation took place before the journey to the East.

But whether before or after the journey to Syria, Francis's resignation could hardly be understood in the same sense as such a resignation would be understood today. He could not but remain the father of the order and, as we have seen, its conscience. Peter would have closely shared Francis's ideals and would have fully understood Francis when he said, "Charles the emperor, Roland and Oliver, and all the paladins and puissant men who were mighty in war, pursuing the pagans with sweat and mighty labor even until death, achieved over them an immortal victory and died in battle, and are holy martyrs of the Faith of Christ. And now there are many who expect praise and honor of men for merely telling the tale of the deeds they did. So it is among ourselves. Many expect to be praised and honored for merely acting and preaching what the saints actually did. Pay no heed to books and knowledge, but to godly works; knowledge puffs up, but charity edifies."

He confessed that he, too, had been tempted. "I also have been tempted to have books," just as he had been tempted to have money and a merry life. And in the decadence of the Church around him, he saw learning as a ladder to success and vainglory, arrogance, and corruption.

Yet when all this is analyzed, it is seen that it was not the kind of practical study that is necessary for the priesthood or any other career which he condemned, but learning for its own sake and the power and pleasure that it can give. "We taught the brethren in regard to books to look to their inwardness and not to their price; to the edification they contained, not to their outward grandeur. He willed that they should be few and held in common and only such as were genuinely needed by the brethren."

Despite the increasing troubles in the order, so long as Peter Catanei lived, Francis could have hoped that his followers would, after all, settle down to a way of life, which, while accidentally different from the flame of utter dedication which had inspired him as he looked at the Crucifix in San Damiano, would nevertheless enable him, as father and conscience of his followers, to protect them from the dangers which had so obviously weakened and even corrupted the official Church and the official organizers within Her. The Pope would understand him, as would also the cardinal protector.

After all, the picture we have to bear in mind at this time is certainly not one of a great body of men, divided into warring factions, one section angrily intent on strictness, another thinking only of laxity, and a third intent on moderation. The sources, we must remember, depend in large measure on the *Zelanti*, who liked to look back on the golden age of the order in Saint Francis's time as a means of expressing their disgust with the evolution of the order into something not sharply to be distinguished from the older orders.

They must not be taken too literally. In spite of the present beginnings of division and the gentle, but strict, way in which Cardinal Ugolino was seeking to protect Francis's work by amendments necessary to enable it to conform with the Church's normal traditions, the picture still remained in 1220 and 1221 a picture of the brethren carrying on with their appointed labors in the spirit of Francis. Probably for the most part, they were hardly aware of more than the fact that the father was studying how the rule could properly be amplified and modified to suit the evident fact that the numbers of the brethren had enormously increased and that the calls upon their service had become much more complex and various.

The point is well illustrated in the story of Anthony. Anthony of Lisbon, who had joined the order because he had been so moved by the account of the Franciscan martyrs of

Morocco, whose remains had been taken to Coimbra, perfectly shared the spirit of Francis. He had attended a chapter general as an unconsidered member of the flock even though he was a priest and had been a canon regular of Coimbra. The lowly job he was given was to say Mass for a few brothers in one of the lonely hermitages. It was near Forli, some forty miles southeast of Bologna.

One day, he went to Forli with other priests to be present at an Ordination, and afterward Franciscans and Dominicans gathered together. Various people present were asked to give a spiritual address to the company, and as everyone else declined, Anthony was ordered to do so. No one expected more than a rough simple sermon — or possibly someone knew better and had engineered the trick. To the amazement of the company, Anthony spoke like a master, and everyone realized that here was a brilliant theologian and a magnificent preacher in the making. Thus, Saint Anthony of Padua (as he is known to history) reconciled in himself the ideal of Francis and the need for learning, properly used according to the spirit of Francis.

At about this time, the affair of the Bologna house which had so infuriated Francis was raised, and Cardinal Ugolino explained that, so far as the poverty question was concerned, Francis need not worry, as the house belonged to the Holy See, the order having only the use of it. Francis was so fully reconciled to the cardinal's plans to institute in Bologna a Franciscan theological school that he himself preached a sermon in the city, a description of which has come down to us in the words of Thomas of Spalato, who was a student at the time.

"When he [Francis] started speaking, he discoursed about angels, men, and devils, and so excellently and neatly did he pursue the argument about his theme, that learned people in the audience were amazed at such eloquence coming from so simple a man. He did not expound so much as stir hearts. The moral which he drew was principally the need to do away with enmities and to foster reconciliation. He stood there in a dirty and torn tunic; his bearing was humble; his appearance disfigured by fasting and penance. But God lent such effectiveness to what he said that the quarreling factions of the nobility whose ferocity had again brought to a head ancient rivalries with so much bloodshed made peace with one another."

Soon Anthony himself, having gained a great reputation for his mystical and penitential preaching, was teaching theology in Bologna, and being charmingly addressed by Francis as "Brother Anthony my Bishop." In other words, Francis was congratulating him for teaching sacred theology to the friars without extinguishing the spirit of prayer laid down by the rule.

It is reasonable, therefore, to think that, had Peter Catanei lived — Peter, who always referred to Francis, technically in subordination to him, as "lord" — it is probable that the last years of Francis's life would have run more smoothly. His own instinctive solution of not dotting *i*s and crossing *t*s, but allowing the spirit loosely to guide him and his brothers, would have ensured a quiet evolution, which would have enabled Francis to insist on utter dedication in the spirit of liberty, while Ugolino tactfully did what was necessary from the ecclesiastical point of view.

Chapter Eighteen

✎

Francis Drafts the Franciscan Rule

Alas, Peter Catanei died on March 10, 1221 — one of the few dates, as already mentioned, exactly known in the story of Saint Francis. We are by now well into the period when Francis's health was giving increasing cause for anxiety. Nor would Francis do anything to help himself.

The *Mirror of Perfection* describes the situation thus: "For a long time and until his dying day, Francis suffered trouble of the stomach, the liver, and the spleen, and ever since he returned from overseas, he suffered great pain in his eyes. But he would do nothing to nurse his ills and cure them. For this, the Bishop of Ostia admonished him. The bishop realized the effects of his constant austerities and was even more troubled by the fact that Francis was losing the sight of his eyes. He knew that Francis would do nothing to obtain cures for these ailments and therefore, with great sympathy, reproved him, saying, "Brother, you are not right not to do anything to improve your health, for your life and health are of very great usefulness to the brothers and to the layfolk and to the whole Church. You do not hesitate to show compassion for your own sick brothers and have always taken care of them with understanding and mercy; you ought not therefore to be hard about yourself, especially in these circumstances. You must therefore look after yourself and allow yourself to be helped.' "

The state of his health, together with Cardinal Ugolino's advice, may well in part account for that exceedingly fateful decision of Francis — namely, to appoint Brother Elias as Peter Catanei's successor and vicar of the order.

Francis's choice of a brother who was in time to become notorious has always been a puzzle to his biographers. How could Francis, the saint, have failed to observe weaknesses in Elias's character which were in time to become a public scandal and injure the reputation of the whole order?

The answer is quite simple. The Elias whom Francis knew was quite a different person from the Elias who, after Francis's death, became the victim of ambitions and flaws in character which were to lead to rebellion against the papacy and to excommunication. The point is vividly illustrated by the two lives of Saint Francis written by Celano. The first of these lives was written very shortly after Francis's death in the odor of sanctity. The second was written nearly twenty years later.

In the first life, Elias is described as the worthy follower of Francis — one fit to be chosen by Francis "in place of another" and to be made the "father of the other brethren." He was a brother admired not only by Francis, but also by Clare. Francis's love of Elias and Elias's consequent hold over Francis enabled Francis to help and encourage Elias, just as Elias succeeded in doing what Ugolino had not been able to do — namely, persuade Francis to nurse his health for the sake of the brethren. In Celano's second life, written when Elias had become an object of scandal, references to him are guarded and his virtues minimized.

Francis Drafts the Franciscan Rule

It was only the first Elias whom Francis had known, the Elias who, like Francis, had given up a position in the world, with all the entanglement that such a position entailed, in order to enjoy the liberation and freedom of spirit which was the special quality of early Franciscanism. But whereas Francis had been converted from a simple life of dissipation and exhibitionism to find in the chivalrous service of God and Lady Poverty an equal but infinitely richer form of simplicity, Elias had been converted from the lure of politics and power by the example of Francis, the romantic, spiritual enchanter.

Francis, who had taken a long time to break away from the entanglements of pleasure-seeking and worldly success, because nothing but the purest and deepest was good enough for him, was certain that if he were not to reject his destiny, he must make this break. But Elias, it would seem, at the call of Francis, suddenly and dramatically liberated himself from the complexities and evils of Assisi's ambitions. He followed Francis and found in the austere life of the cells of Assisi or Cortona a way of penance that he thought would purge the past. Clearly, too, the man who would one day find power and spiritual self-expression in creating the immense basilica of Saint Francis in Assisi as a worthy monument to a saint's life, first found beauty in the grandeur and wildness of nature and the rushing streams near which the Franciscan cells were built.

But the success and worldly glory, which Elias had sought in his unregenerate Assisi days, would come to express itself again. There was, surely, much of the great man of affairs, of the master-builder, of the modern captain of industry or financial juggler about Elias — all ambitions peculiarly repugnant to the spirit of Francis. Such ambitions seemed for a time completely worthless to Elias also, in comparison with Francis's own joy in discovering a way of life which measured on an accurate scale the true value of even artistic, let alone financial, success, as the world understands it.

It is not an uncommon characteristic of men who have a taste for power and a genius for ruling and leading others to appreciate the beauty of the world as God made it. The temptation, however, is to improve that beauty by imposing on it conceptions of one's own creative imagination and peculiar administrative talent. Equally, it is not uncommon for a simple man like Francis to admire in another the administrative and constructive qualities he does not have himself.

Francis had known Elias, not only as a close friend who had shared with him the austerities and simplicities of life with God, but also as the kind of effective administrator who had been his best aid in creating a Franciscan province in the very land where Christ Himself had walked and suffered. The fact that Elias was in Syria at a time when the provincials were attempting to change the nature of the rule shows that Elias at this time had no part in the plans to make the order more effective as Church and world would see it. After Peter's death, and with Francis's own health failing, who better to appoint as vicar than this faithful, close companion with gifts that were not only outstanding, but the very gifts which Francis himself so evidently lacked?

Whatever may be said about the later Elias, the impression one gets of him during the months and years after his appointment and until Francis's death is, on the whole, one of great reverence for Francis and of unwillingness to cross him.

It was not from Peter Catanei or Elias that Francis received the commission to draft a new rule for the Franciscan Order, but from the cardinal protector. Although Francis's legal relation to Elias was the same as his legal relation to Peter Catanei had been — namely, that he was technically subordinate to both in normal government — there was no disputing his far superior rank as the father and founder of the order, who could command their obedience when he wanted it.

Now that circumstances had forced the followers of Saint Francis to diversify their work and especially to imitate the Dominicans in teaching, the drafting of a proper rule had become, in the eyes of Rome, imperative.

Francis had to obey, so, choosing Brother Caesar of Speyer, the learned German whom Brother Elias had recruited into the order, Francis retired to the Portiuncula to obey Cardinal Ugolino's request to rewrite and bring up to date the primitive rule.

But Francis, working at the Portiuncula — the hallowed spot which expressed in its very stones, set among the forest wilderness, the golden days when spontaneous but total dedication reflected the liberty of the true sons of God — could not bring himself to break away from the spirit of that loose grouping of men, whether priests or laymen, in whose hearts dwelt only the spirit of poverty, chastity, and obedience. If there had to be some external discipline in terms of codes and canons and paper regulations, let it be no more than more formal expressions of the vital spirit which had swept like a spiritual rejuvenation over the face of Italy. One may be permitted to imagine that as the weeks of toil went on, Francis's main contribution was that of prayer, while Caesar, with German thoroughness, tried to translate that spirit into chapter and verse.

No wonder the draft of the new rule which he presented to the Pentecost chapter of 1221, the first chapter at which the new minister general Elias presided, was no more than the old rule as evolved during the years, with extra precautions to make sure that the true spirit of the order could not be evaded.

Francis had not forgotten that day in Acre when Brother Stephen had shown him the fasting laws of the usurping vicars, and now he wrote, "The brethren may eat all foods which are placed before them, according to the Gospels. . . . Whensoever necessity shall arise, it is lawful for all the brothers, wherever they may be, to eat of all foods that men do eat."

Despite the fact that houses and schools had come to be built and that many of the brothers, eschewing the old way of living in a hut or a cell, were forming regular communities, Francis not only did not weaken in his hatred of any breach of poverty where the individual was concerned, but also insisted that there could be no common property either. Money itself must be considered as no more than "pebbles." It is not to be carried even when journeying, any more than sack or wallet, bread or staff. Instead, the brothers must live by work and begging, and although work was better than begging, they must not be ashamed of begging, since doing so helped the friars to share life with the most despised of men: lepers, beggars, and the nonpossessors. Francis forbade the assuming of un-Franciscan titles such as "prior," and, recalling what had taken place in his absence, he thundered, "If any of the ministers [provincials] shall command any of the brothers anything contrary to our life or against our soul, the brother is not bound to obey him, because that is not obedience in which a fault or sin is committed."

Recalling, it seemed, the approval of Innocent III, he invoked "the lord Pope" in insisting that "no one take away from these things that are written in this rule or add anything to it over and above. The brethren must have no other rule."

The echo of the reaction on the part of the brothers, already accustomed to interpret the old rule according to the obvious need of the apostolic or teaching work they had undertaken, finds its expression in the pages of the *Mirror of Perfection:* "Although the ministers [vicars] knew that according to the rule, the brothers were bound to the observance of the Gospels, yet they tried to remove from the rule the clause 'Take nothing for your journey . . .' in the belief that, by doing this, they would no longer be held to literal fulfillment of the Gospels. When Francis heard of this, he said in the presence of these brothers, 'The ministers imagine that they can deceive the Lord and myself, although they know very well that all are bound to the observance of the holy Gospel. I insist that both at the beginning and end of the rule, it be written that the brothers are strictly bound to observe the holy Gospels of Jesus Christ. And that they may be forevermore without any excuse, both as regards the past, when I announced what the Lord gave me to speak to them, and now, when I announce it again that they and I may find salvation, I repeat that it is my will that the works they do before God should manifest these things and that, with God's help, so shall they act forever.' That was why he himself observed the holy Gospel to the letter from the very beginnings, when the first brothers followed him, right up to the day of his death."

The same record states, "Others indeed had labored and preached in service of their own wisdom, but it is through your merits that the fruit of salvation has been wrought." In the day of judgment "shall the truth of holy humility and simplicity, of holy prayer and poverty which is our vocation, be exalted and glorified and magnified — such is the truth which they that are puffed up with the wind of knowledge have disparaged in their lives and in the idle service of their own wisdom, saying that truth itself is a lie, and, as though blindness had struck them, cruelly persecuting those who walked in that truth. . . . The barren has borne seven, and she who has many children has grown feeble.[73] The 'barren' is the good religious, simple, humble, poor, despised, bowed, and abject, whose holy prayers and godly works always edify others and bring forth with grievous groaning. This he said again and again and often in the presence of the ministers and other brothers, especially during the chapter general."

Francis's teaching on obedience illustrates in another way the challenge he was now making to the would-be reformers. Obedience to him where the spirit of his rule was concerned must be absolute. "My dearest brothers," he said, "fulfill my injunction, and do not wait for it to be repeated. Do not argue or imagine yourselves judges of the matter. Obedience is never impossible, for even if it seems that in my command to you, I command what is beyond your strength, holy obedience itself will give you the strength you need. . . ."

But his wish was always to avoid having to give orders "under obedience." "The hand," he said, "should not be too ready

[73] 1 Sam. 2:5.

to grasp the sword," and the author of the *Mirror of Perfection* comments, "Nothing can be more true, for what else is the power to command in anyone who gives rash orders but a sword in the hands of a madman? And who is more hopeless than a religious who rejects and despises obedience?"

The highest obedience, he taught, was the obedience in which flesh and blood had no part — the obedience which divinely inspires men to go among the infidels and convert them or through the desire of martyrdom. To ask for such obedience is truly to be acceptable to God.

In the high summer of 1221, the great clearing which by now must have been made around the Portiuncula chapel was yet again filled with the simple wattle huts which housed the friars as, from the four corners of the world, they made their way for the solemn chapter meeting. For the first time, the new vicar general, Brother Elias, would preside, and, to mark the solemnity of the occasion and the protection of the Church, Cardinal Regnierio would make his way down the hill from Assisi to preside. The cardinal protector had not been able to attend, so his brother cardinal had to take his place.

What hierarchical position was the unique Francis to assume? Only he could have written the new rule, and only he could be the real spokesman on such a great occasion. Unfortunately we have no record of the personal part which he played when the new draft rule was being made known to the assembled brothers. Nor do we know what their reaction was. We only possess the picturesque detail that Francis made the new vicar general his spokesman and sat at his feet tugging at his tunic when he wished to interpose his own point of view.

The *Mirror of Perfection*, referring to such a chapter meeting, gives a story which symbolizes the struggle of the suffering Francis with the new men who wished to accommodate the order to circumstances which the founder had never envisaged when he led the early brethren:

> To show you what a lesser brother should be, let me tell you this story. The brothers with great reverence invited me to the great chapter, and moved by their love, I went to the chapter with them. Assembled together, they begged me to announce to them the word of God and to preach among them. So I rose, and I preached to them as the Holy Spirit had taught me. Now, suppose that when I have finished my sermon, they should all cry out against me saying, "We do not want you to rule over us, for you are not eloquent, as a ruler should be; you are too simple and foolish, and, to tell you the truth, we are rather ashamed of having a superior who is so simple and despised. You must not therefore expect to be called our superior." So they cast me out with contumely and disgrace. Now, I would be no true "lesser brother" if I were not glad to find that they held me to be of little account, casting me out with shame, since they could not suffer me to be their superior. I would be fully as glad of this as when they happened to be venerating and honoring me. Both cases indeed, God said, are of equal profit and advantage to those who hear me. For if I am happy since it may profit them and increase their devotion, although indeed it would be dangerous to my soul, how much more should I be glad and happy to the profit and saving of my soul, when they speak evil of me, for this cannot be other than a gain to my soul.

As usual in the Franciscan story, this chapter of 1221 was to be remembered not for the brethren's reaction to the draft of the new rule, but for one of those picturesque incidents which Franciscan history has recorded so much more accurately than the inner developments, strivings, and tensions which were molding the future. The "highest obedience," the obedience that "divinely inspires men to go among the infidels to convert them or through the desire of martyrdom," was put before the brethren by Francis. The first missionary expedition to Germany had, we recall, proved a failure, and apparently had left a sense of horror among many in the order. It was time for a new effort, but as Elias said on Francis's behalf, no one would be ordered to form part of the dreaded mission. It was a case for volunteers who would go forth under "an obedience" more fruitful even than the "obedience to convert the infidels."

Ninety brothers, we are told, stepped forward to offer themselves, as they firmly believed, "to death." The haunting quality of the mission to Germany had impressed itself especially strongly on one man, a man who always regretted not having personally known any of the martyrs of Morocco. Here was his chance, not to volunteer, but to make the personal acquaintance of these brave volunteers who were actually going to risk their lives and come face-to-face with the ferocity of the Germans, which, from his earliest years, he had been taught to dread. A day would come when he would be able to tell the novices how he had actually spoken to the martyrs of Germany! His name was Giordano di Giano, who, in his own chronicles, so valuable to posterity for the history of the order, would tell the story.

Giordano, therefore, went over to the volunteers to chat with them and to find out their names and where they came from. One of them told him that his name was Palmerio and that he came from Apulia. Then, to Giordano's horror, Palmerio took hold of him and said, "Now that you are here, you are one of us. You must go with us." Giordano expostulated and shouted, "No, I am not! I am not one of you; I have no desire whatever to go with you." In despair, he appealed to Elias, who asked him to say whether he really wanted to go or not. Then Giordano began to have scruples, wondering if obedience held him to do the braver thing. In despair, he replied, "I do not want to go, and I do not want *not* to go." In the end, it was decided that Giordano should go.

The mission turned out to be a great success under the leadership of the new German provincial, Caesar of Speyer, who had helped Francis in drafting the rule. Perhaps Elias, who seemed to be in charge of all this, rather than Francis, was not sorry to get rid of Caesar, after he had heard the draft of the new rule.

Among those who went to Germany was Thomas of Celano, and it is curious that Giordano and Celano, both precious sources of Franciscan history and the life of Francis, should have been among the volunteers who were sent on this dangerous mission, as it was believed to be.

That Francis presented the rule, which Ugolino had bade him draw up, at the Pentecost chapter of 1221 is, of course, not certain. It is the date traditionally given, but the occasion might well have been a year later in 1222, when Cardinal Ugolino himself could preside. This chapter is believed by modern writers to be the famous "Chapter of Mats."

The Chapter of Mats stands out in the traditional story of Saint Francis because, it was said, no fewer than five thousand brothers attended it. Even allowing for heavy exaggeration, it is impossible to think of a figure of this order at any period earlier than the 1220s. Cardinal Ugolino was present at that chapter, but we know that he did not attend the chapter of 1221. At Pentecost in 1220, Francis himself was still in the East. This would seem to leave 1222 as the first possible date for the Chapter of Mats.

The English translation *mats* refers to the woven rushes with which temporary shelters for the brethren were made during most of these chapters. The Chapter of Mats is associated with an incident which again illustrates the complexities of Francis's character.

It appears that, at this, the most numerously attended of all chapters in Francis's lifetime, the Commune of Assisi had built up, near the Portiuncula, stone and tile edifices which could house perhaps the older and more infirm brethren. No single house or small number of houses would hold five thousand or anywhere near that number, so presumably the wattle huts were also erected. Francis had evidently come to this chapter from some distance, since the sight of the stone building gave him a tremendous shock. He could hardly believe his eyes. Had he not been fighting all his life against grand houses, corporate possessions, and all creature comforts? His reaction can only be honestly described as a second occasion on which he completely lost his temper.

Despite his weak health, Francis rushed to the building, climbed onto the roof, and began tearing down the tiles with his own fingers. He was ready to continue until the whole building was roofless. But the terrified brothers, realizing well enough the cause of his fury, shouted to him and explained that the building had not been put up by the brethren, but was a gift from the Commune of Assisi. Slowly, we imagine, the fact penetrated, and he realized that the building was not his to destroy. He stopped his destructive work, and climbed down.

Life to Francis during these years had become intolerably painful. He realized that the new forces, supported by the Pope, by Ugolino, and by so many of the newer brethren — although not necessarily by Elias — were threatening finally to break down much of the work for which he had lived and suffered. "They confuse the minds of the best brothers," Celano reports Francis as saying, "through their evil works — and even when they do not sin, they bear responsibility by their bad example."

With Brother Leo and his closest companions, he would speak of evil times. "Brother Leo," he said one day, "the brothers make me feel very sad." And when Leo asked him to explain, he answered, "Because of three things. They refuse to acknowledge the blessings I have conferred upon them in such large measure, as you know very well, and they themselves refuse to sow and reap. They are always grousing and living idly. They quarrel among one another and do not forgive each other the injuries they may receive. The time will come," he continued, "when the religious way which God loves will be the subject of scandal through all this bad example, so much so that it will be ashamed to show itself in public." And he consoled himself by looking forward to the days when he would be justified and when men would be drawn to the order solely by the impulse of the Holy Spirit.

One day, he was told that a bishop had complained that a number of the brothers were growing long beards in order to give the appearance of despising the customs of the world, and the bishop was remarking on the danger of the beauty of religious life being marred by this latest fashion. At this news, Francis burst into a temper, and in an impassioned prayer, he said, "May they be cursed by You, O most holy Lord, by the whole heavenly court, and by me, your poor little one, for by such bad example, they confuse and destroy what in earlier days was built up by the holy men of the order and is still being built up by You."

Never, of course, one to blame others where there might be any grounds for blaming himself still more, he even offered to give up his companions of "the old guard," lest in this love of his closest companions there might be a lack of detachment. "I do not want to seem singular in enjoying a special liberty, namely, in having a special companion. Let the brethren assign me a companion according to the place where I am and as the Lord shall inspire them."

We must remember once more that these sources were written to uphold the views of the *Zelanti*, but we cannot dismiss all this as invention or gross exaggeration, for we know how firm Francis stood in the face of the reformers. While refusing to take open steps to prevent the evolution of the order, since Rome insisted on changes and reforms, he could not change himself. His inspiration from the first had been highly personal, and he felt that he could not change without denying the truths and inspiration which had brought about his conversion and the very existence of the order.

These were certainly the months of deepest darkness, when we cannot even recall the joy of the young Francis, tramping the sunny lanes of Umbria with Brother Giles, as they sang together the praises of the Lord and the evidence of His beauty and His bounty all around them, greeting the townsfolk and villagers with their cheerful "Good morning, good people." Then, the life of mystical contemplation, and practical, light-hearted, yet dedicated life of preaching in the genial sun of Italy with spiritual sunshine in his heart, easily went together. But even now, when the sun's warming rays without and within seemed at times to be a thing of the past, Francis continued to have it, if we may so put it, both ways.

This, it would seem, was the way of perfection in which sorrow and disappointment combined with an increasingly vivid faith and love, to which God was now calling him. This stage of disillusion, trial, and bitterness at seeing the many signs of the seeming ruin of the ideals he had taught was the test of true denudation and the darkness of deepening faith. It was not a time for singing, but Francis would sing again when the dregs of the cup of sorrow were drunk, and his ailing, dying body was given — the first of all men — the mark of the crucified Lord. In this, nature itself was given the privilege of directly reflecting the Divine as Francis, nearly blind, was to sing its praises again.

Francis's refusal to compromise on principle — and he was, of course, the kind of man for whom principles covered everything — was never more severely tested than during these months when the Church's insistence that the order should have a full and proper rule had still to be given effect.

Francis's draft rule of 1221 — the *regula prima* (as distinguished from the *Regula Primitiva*) — had never become legally binding, and therefore it solved nothing. The tension continued. Another new rule had to be made and put into writing, and no one in the order other than Francis, its founder and its father, could conceivably do this.

His feelings were expressed when, lying on a sickbed, he said to a certain brother, "My son, I love the brethren as much as I can, but if only they would follow in my footsteps I would love them much more and feel less isolated from them. Some of the superiors draw them away to other things and set before them the example of the elders, holding my own advice to be of little account. . . . Who are these men who have snatched my order and my brothers from my hands? If I can come to the chapter general, I will let them know what I think." And what Francis thought was always the same: what Christ had revealed to him in San Damiano and what he had learned from the open Gospel in the Portiuncula chapel on the feast of Saint Matthias.

Francis, who had so loved Assisi and the Umbrian plain, the "Galilee of Italy," had also developed a deep affection for a countryside not so very different in appearance from Umbria, namely, the vale of Rieti, near Rome. But there the surrounding mountains were nearer and higher, and the country itself was more diversified and wilder. Perhaps that setting suited Francis's present mood better than the peace of the Umbrian plain. Here, too, as we shall see, he had had land put at his disposal.

It was in the vale of Rieti that Francis's final legislation was to be worked out in prayer and fasting as well as in dramatic form, the precise details of which are very difficult to reconstruct. In order to pray about the rule and to work on its drafting, he took with him two companions, Brother Leo and Brother Bonizzo (once a lawyer) and retired to Fonte Colombo on Monte Rainerio in the wooded highland a few miles south-west of Rieti.

Some people hold that the name derived from the fact that the mountain belonged to a pious widow called Columba, who was a friend of Francis. Others hold that doves were accustomed to fly over the spot near a miraculous spring.[74]

The land falls sharply, yet not precipitously, and vegetation softens the steep gradients. In a cavern or cell, Francis, ready to consult Bonizzo for the best form of words, dictated to Brother Leo. The thought of Francis, cut off from the world in the kind of wild spot where divine inspiration came so naturally to him, was enough to make the practical men of the order fearful of the results.

They knew Francis, and they could have had little hope that this second draft of the old rule would prove very different from the first. Some of them even asked Elias to go to Francis and warn him that they would not be able to accept a rule in effect unchanged from the first. Elias insisted that if he were to go, he should be accompanied, and therefore, all together, they climbed up from the valley to within calling distance of the saint, and Elias expressed the complaints of the brethren.

Francis, we are told, answered by praying to God, and he declared that he had heard Christ telling him that the rule was his and that it was to be kept to the letter and without any gloss. In view of what Francis was to write in that most solemn document of his life, his testament, there is no reason to suppose that this account was invented, even though it may have

[74] The Italian word for dove is *columba*.

been embroidered in order to make Fonte Colombo a Sinai for the Franciscan Order. In his testament, Francis wrote, "In the name of obedience, I forbid anyone, whosoever he may be, clerk or layman, to put glosses on the rule and on this writing, to comment or to indicate how they ought to be understood. But as our Lord has given me the grace to make them clearly and simply, so shall you understand them clearly and simply and observe them even until the end."

In fact, the result of Francis's prayers and studies on the rule which he was drafting to Leo will never be known, although they may well enough be guessed. The reason the contents of this rule will never be known is simply that the manuscript of the rule disappeared entirely. The chroniclers and tradition have blamed this on Elias, suggesting that he destroyed it, pretending that it had become lost, or even accusing Elias of stealing it, before destroying it.

This accusation, directed at Elias personally, who, after all, was the vicar of the order and Francis's friend up to the end of the latter's life, is very difficult to believe; but that, somehow, leading members of the order would have conveniently disposed of the draft, in the hope that, in the end, Francis would accede more readily to their wishes, may well be true.

Whoever was responsible for the misplacing of the precious document cannot have had a very great deal of intelligence, since one thing by this time must have been certain to everyone — namely, that Francis was never going to make any fundamental changes in his own expression of the order's ideal and way of life. If this draft was lost, another would succeed it, and it would not be substantially different from the former. This is, of course, what had to happen.

Once again Francis drew up the rule which *he* wanted. Celano once again gives us a parable which graphically explains what was in Saint Francis's mind and what may well have been a dream, as Celano tells us it was.

Francis dreamed that he was surrounded by famished friars who asked him for something to eat. He tried to gather some crumbs together, crumbs which he saw scattered around him on the ground, but the more he tried, the quicker these crumbs slipped through his fingers. Not knowing what to do or how to distribute them to the brothers, he heard a voice say to him, "From these crumbs, make bread so that thy brethren may be nourished." Francis did so. Some of the brothers ate greedily of this bread, while others refused to touch it. The latter were at once affected with leprosy. Our Lord then explained to Francis the meaning of the parable. The crumbs that were slipping through his fingers were the words of the Gospel. The bread represented the rule which he was drafting. But those who refused to eat of the bread were to be punished, as lepers were punished.

So Francis, instead of acceding to the wishes of his critics, once again climbed the crest of Fonte Colombo and drafted a third version of the rule. Not Francis's rule, but an amendment of it, in which only five verses of the Gospel were quoted, was to be approved by Pope Honorius in Rome on November 29, 1223. The final editing had been done by Cardinal Ugolino.

Yet, in the deepest sense, Francis had never been vanquished. His instinct to have it both ways, which we have so often described, continued even now. This was not just a matter of stubbornness, of digging his heels in. Ill though he was, he knew well what was happening, and it made him unutterably sad. He would never change, and his closest companions would remain with him. So long as he lived, all that he had stood for continued to live. He had incarnated the revolutionary ideal which could not of its nature be applied to all. This, of course, constituted his greatness.

Writers have spoken of the temptation of Saint Francis during this period of conflict and personal anguish. But one wonders whether this could have been so. Francis had really never changed from the earliest days of his conversion. One doubts whether he saw things in rational catalogs. He could only be true to that inspiration which enabled him in the end so startlingly to break with all the conventions of the world. The call of Christ, as he had understood it, remained with him to the end through all problems and anxieties. And he found no difficulty in combining this with the rulings of the Church which he knew to be the Church of Christ. He accepted them with a humility as strong as his own revolutionary faith, yet continued until the end with his own higher message. If it is true to say that, without Ugolino's practical Franciscanism, the Church would have been the worse served, it is also true that, without the unchanging Francis, there would have been no Franciscanism at all.

Chapter Nineteen

※

Francis Brings Christmas Alive

That Francis, in the end, did not allow himself to be so upset by the years of discussion and quarrel over the final form of the rule, as is sometimes made out, is suggested by the events which immediately followed his drafting of the last version. Although he always spoke his mind very plainly and according to his varying moods, the stories and reports of the chroniclers, taken together, may give a somewhat exaggerated and deceptive picture of his quick reactions, his quick joys, and his quick sorrows.

At any rate, one finds it easier to believe that, during this long period of trial, he remained calmly steadfast in his utter conviction that he alone knew what God wanted of him and his followers. Let other people criticize, not least the Pope and the cardinal, for these had the right to do so; let him, however, do what he had to do, and leave the results to God.

Perhaps, too, toward the end of 1223, his health may have somewhat improved. Anyhow, it was his duty to travel to Rome to present his rule to Pope Honorius through the cardinal protector, Ugolino. We have no record of any tension or trouble with the cardinal or the Pope, despite the considerable changes and amendments that were made in the original draft.

Their effect was, in fact, to maintain the spirit of Francis's requirements, while inserting clauses which enabled exemptions from the original severity to be easily obtained. Thus, in one instance "goodwill" was stated to be sufficient in order to dispense from selling all and giving to the poor. And Francis's own words — "When the brothers are going about the world, let them take nothing with them, neither wallet nor bread, nor staff"[75] — words which go back not only to the *Regula Primitiva*, but to the Gospels which Francis had read in the Portiuncula, were now omitted. Also suppressed was the reference to the care of lepers, a reference which must have been instinctive to him, for otherwise he could never have been the Francis we know. But what we know of his last stay in Rome suggests no particular sorrow, but rather gives the impression of a typical and happy sojourn by the old Francis of earlier days.

Thus we have the story of Francis begging for food and meeting Cardinal Ugolino at mealtime. He collected all that had been given to him and took it to the cardinal's table, even though the cardinal was surrounded by official guests. Seating himself next to the cardinal, he offered the food he had collected to the guests. These, it seems, took the holy man's gifts, eating what they had been offered or keeping the food in memory of the holy man. But the poor cardinal did not feel too pleased by this gesture, and he felt ashamed that one of his guests should have given to the others the black bread of poverty rather than the delicate white bread suited to their rank.

After the meal, Cardinal Ugolino remonstrated with Francis for his strange behavior. Francis answered, "Truly, my lord,

[75] Cf. Mark 6:8; Luke 9:3.

I have done you the greatest honor, for when a liege subject does his duty and fulfills his obedience to his lord, he honors that lord. It is right that I should be the pattern of poor men, and when I am your guest, I am not ashamed to beg for alms, for the bread of alms is holy bread that God will bless." If rebuke there was, it was, as usual, courteously expressed.

Another story is told of this visit. Francis, together with Brother Angelo, was asked by Cardinal Roncalleone to visit him in his palace. They agreed, so long as they could stay in a solitary tower in the cardinal's garden. But on the first night, they were both grievously assaulted by devils. Francis told his companion that these devils were probably chastising him through the will of God, because, while the cardinal was giving them hospitality and food, their brothers were suffering hunger and tribulations in different parts of the world, dwelling in hermitages and wretched huts.

"When they hear," said Francis, "that I am staying with the lord cardinal, they might well be tempted to murmur against me and say, 'We endure so much adversity, while he lives in luxury.' It is my duty to give them a good example, and therefore I shall give the brothers more edification if I stay in poor places, for they will bear their tribulations more patiently when they hear that I share them." So they left the tower next day, and, bidding the cardinal goodbye, Francis said to him, "Men believe me to be a holy man, but, see, the devils throw me out of the tower!"

It was the same old sense of humor which somehow managed to express his own deep and genuine humility, as well as an indirect reproach against the laxity, from his point of view, that was seeping through so many of his followers. It was, however, a laxity which, he believed, went with the sad and serious faces of those who wanted to make the order more efficient and more in tune with the superficial needs of the world.

Perhaps we owe this lighter and happier mood of the nearly blind and sick Francis to the love and care which must have been lavished on him in Rome by "Brother Giacoma," as he loved to call her, the great patrician lady of Rome who had first met him a decade earlier. With a feminine intuition, like that of Clare, she had discerned the childlike nature of his saintly genius. As Celano puts it: "Giacoma of Settesoli, celebrated all over Rome through the holiness that paralleled her high nobility, was privileged to be closest to Francis in love."

As we have seen, the story of that "love" has been lost, perhaps because the chroniclers found it difficult to square the stupendous reputation of the saint with a love, however holy, between the founder and a great woman of the world. The little we know is tantalizing. We know that, eating at her great house in Rome, Francis especially enjoyed an almond sweetmeat made by her — a sweetmeat for which he would ask, in a manner so endearing to us today, on his deathbed. In return, Francis gave her a lamb, which followed her even into church, lying down while she prayed. It would even come to her bed in the morning when she overslept and wake her up by gently butting her with its horns. A story like this seems momentarily to draw aside a veil which conceals a whole side of Francis which we may imagine, but cannot describe for lack of records.

Francis had another woman friend in Rome, the recluse Praxedis, who had lived all her life as an anchoress in a narrow prison. For this holy woman Francis had reserved a privilege granted to no other woman — namely, the bestowal on her of the Franciscan habit and cord. Can we doubt that although the Pope and Ugolino had imposed their official will on the final draft of the Franciscan rule, Francis himself had found in the Eternal City friends who were able to give him the personal love and care which restored his gaiety and happiness, even in the growing affliction of his eyes and body? Such, at any rate, was the mood in which he certainly left Rome for the last time, to begin a brief journey which was to give to posterity one of the most celebrated and beautiful of all the stories of the saint's life.

The feast of the Nativity of our Lord was near. And Christmas for Francis was a season of the year when he could not stomach the rigidity and regulation that throughout his life had seemed to him, when done for its own sake, so alien from the spirit of Christian liberty and joy, a joy which bubbled up within him, even as his burning love of Christ and desire to imitate Him prompted the severest austerities and penance. The latter were not for Christmas.

Once, when he was asked whether he should abstain from meat on Christmas Day, Francis answered that the very walls would have the right to eat meat on such a day. Indeed, the walls should be covered with fat, so that they could eat meat in their own way. "All the governors of the towns and all the lords of the castles should be obliged on the feast of the Nativity of our Lord to make men throw wheat and grain along the roads beyond their cities and their towns so that our sisters the larks may have enough to eat, together with all other birds, on a day of such solemnity." In memory of the ox and the ass that lay by the stall in which the infant Christ lay, anyone owning an ox or an ass should be bound to provide special food for them on that day, as well as for all poor people.

In this spirit of anticipated joy, Francis left Rome. He made his way to Rieti and beyond it to the hermitage of Fonte Colombo, where he had written the final drafts of the rule, inspired by Christ his Lord. But it was not at Fonte Colombo that he would spend Christmas itself.

A few miles farther along the hilly range, near the village of Greccio, great pastel-colored, slab-like terrace rocks with their many fissures seem to hang suspended over the flanks of the tree-studded lower slopes. It is a setting for some grandiose play.

The surrounding country belonged to the lord of Greccio, John Velita, one of Francis's many highborn friends. As Christmas was approaching, Francis said to Velita, "If you would like to celebrate the feast of Christmas at Greccio, go there now and do what I tell you. I would like a figure made of the Babe of Bethlehem, so that we can actually see with our own eyes where the Babe lay and in what discomfort for a newborn infant. We must see the manger, and the Babe lying on the hay between an ox and an ass." Here was the classic example of Francis's need to project in concrete, visual, and practical terms his inner perceptions and feelings.

Christmas cribs were not unknown at that time — there was one at Santa Maria in Trastevere in Rome — but it took the imagination of Francis to see the setting of a crib in a rocky cave of a mountainside, from which the people of the country could be present at the mystery enacted before their eyes.

Early on the night of Christmas Eve of 1223, the whole countryside seemed to be astir. The news had gone around that desolate, difficult ridge, overlooking the great plain of Rieti. From far and wide, men, women, and children, carrying torches and candles in the cool, still night, climbed their way up the slopes toward the great rocks. Singing hymns and psalms, appropriate for the feast, they began to gather together in the moonlight, under the dark canopy of stars, while above them an altar was prepared beside the Christmas grotto; and they looked up, wondering at what must have seemed to them a near miracle of Bethlehem come to life in their beloved land.

For the first and only time in his life, if we are to judge from the chronicles, Francis himself decided to officiate at the great solemnity. He chose to be the deacon for the Mass — the only evidence we have, by the way, for the fact that he had been ordained a deacon.

Was Francis, as he looked over the cheerful scene of massed people, lit by their flickering torches, reminded of his early days in Assisi when night so often was made into day? It was all so typically *him* — the festivals of a merry youth with their false pleasures transmuted in his age and infirmity into this religious pageant with its deep joy and symbolism.

"It seemed like midday," Celano relates, "during that midnight so filled with gladness for man and beast; the crowds drawing near, so happy to be present for the renewal of the mystery; the woods themselves filled with voices, and the rocks echoing the sacred hymns."

Francis sang the Gospel with his "strong, sweet, and clear" voice. "Then he preached to the people, and most movingly, about the birth of the poor King in little Bethlehem." And Celano tells the story of how a man watching the figure of the Infant in the manger saw it open its eyes as Francis bent over it.

This Christmas celebration had been without flaw. The brethren in the hermitage close by, the people of Greccio and the surrounding country, and Francis himself had been caught up in this perfect joy, far from the noise of the world; far, too, from the arguments and disputes which, within the order and the chancelleries of Rome, tore his spirit and broke his heart.

Slowly, reluctantly, the people of Greccio and the surrounding villages made their way back to those little squat stone houses, scarcely more than four stone walls and a roof, their keen Italian imaginations having been transported to that other and better world wherein everything, through Francis's imagination and defiant common sense, challenging the hatred, divisions, and false ambitions of the world of men torn by conventions and respectabilities, was to be seen at its true value. This is not a parable, but a fact of history which the world owes to the spiritual vision of the saint. From the pageant of that night has derived the worldwide tradition of the Christmas crib, before which, for a moment, rich and poor, intellectual and peasant, are united in glimpsing the way of sacrifice, peace, and happiness.

But how unpredictable Francis was! A few months later, Easter came. Francis would celebrate it at the Greccio hermitage. Francis, who had once insisted on meat for a Friday Christmas, entered the brothers' humble refectory after the ceremonies of Easter Sunday and saw that a feast, not of joy, but of greed, had been prepared, doubtless with the many gifts of the poor people.

"Francis," Celano says, "did not smile at the smiling table."

Perhaps he had been thinking again of the way the brethren had lost their love of poverty and humility. Certainly he had discerned that the spirit of perfect joy was not being expressed by that overladen table. Having watched for a few moments, he went out in search of a cap and stick, such as beggars use. When the brethren were at table, he knocked at the door and called out, "For the love of God, give alms to this poor, sick pilgrim!"

One account tells us that the brethren did not at first realize who it was that had come to call for alms. "But imagine," says Celano, "the appalling effect which this pilgrim made on these easygoing gentlemen!" And Francis did not let them off. He took a stool and sat apart, saying, "Now I am seated like a friar minor."

The chroniclers suggest that he had been impelled to act thus in order to re-enact the story of the disciples on the way to Emmaus who had sat with the risen Lord and not recognized Him.[76] It may seem to us a harsh lesson for the brothers whose companion he had been for so many weeks. Those poor men had surely earned a good meal after the many weeks of increased austerities and fasting during Lent. But not going far enough and going too far were two evils instinctively recognized by Francis. He disliked austerity for austerity's sake, not for God's sake; he disliked the feast not for God's sake but in order to enjoy an overfull belly, which makes a man forget the needs of others.

Doubtless, too, it was an opportunity of reminding his brethren that, whatever others might say, he at least was

[76] Luke 24:13-16.

determined to take every opportunity of insisting on the rule of absolute poverty, a rule which did not mean that the brothers should not eat and drink and celebrate in proper fashion the great feasts of the year, but that their first responsibility was always to give to the beggars and to the poor.

Francis, now, in this period of serene peace and detachment in the suffering of his body, borne with such patience for the love of his Master, who also had chosen the way of humility and suffering, had evidently resigned all day-to-day control of the order. He was, however, to attend the Pentecost chapter general of 1224 at the Portiuncula. But this was to be the last chapter general at which he would be present, and the two years of life still left to him were to be years of mystical dedication in increasing suffering, yet also years during which we can recall the early days of simplicity, song, and happiness, as though his life had been a life of return to the Crucifix of San Damiano, yet a life intensely enriched and deepened by the years of spiritual joy and pain that lay between the beginnings and the end.

Chapter Twenty

Francis Draws Laymen
to the Franciscan Way

The early months of the year 1224 — from the Greccio Nativity, through Lent, Easter, and the approach to Pentecost —
may well be associated in our minds with two symbols of quiet
joy and fulfillment for Francis.

Those who have traveled in and near Rieti will have seen
from the heights to the north and east of it that little patch of
blue which indicates the lake of Piediluco. In winter, the
heights are covered with snow — snow which never completely retreats until summer approaches. It is a setting of
peace and beauty. There the local fishermen ply their trade, as
though in a world cut off from the traffic and noise of the great
highways of commerce. Evidently, its appeal to Francis at this
time was extremely strong, even though we must presume that
his tired and increasingly defective eyesight allowed him to
see it all only in a haze. Riding, no doubt, on a donkey, for now
he could scarcely walk any distance, or taking a boat with a
fisherman — his mind with Christ in the Sea of Galilee — he
would see in this spot a place of rest and quiet joy.

Piediluco has been particularly associated with Francis's
power over and love of animals. Here it was that one of the

brothers brought to him a hare that had been caught in a trap. Francis took it from the brother and, sharing the fear and trembling of the soft, frightened animal, said, "My sister hare, come closer to me. Why did you let yourself be caught in the trap?" And the hare moved closer to its new friend, nestling and warming itself in his lap. Gently, Francis put it back on the ground, but the hare would not leave him. It tried to follow him like a dog.

Another day, by the lake, a fisherman offered Francis a fish he had just caught. Francis, addressing it as "Brother Fish," put it back in the water. Those around him were furious at the loss of the fish which was to be their dinner. Francis preached to them of the bonds which united all the Lord's creation. To the amazement of everyone, the fish, instead of swimming away, followed the boat in which Francis and his companions were sitting — frisking and jumping around the boat, as though to share in the praise of the Creator. In the end, Francis had to order it to return to its natural fishy life.

That these stories — and there are many others — should be associated with the lake near Greccio and Fonte Colombo at this period of Francis's life signifies, surely, the return of some of the peace and inner happiness that had been broken during the years of stress when the founder struggled to maintain the simplicity and freedom of brethren bound together in protest against the regulations and conventions of Church and world. Like the hare, he himself now felt free, released by his Master from entanglements which, however necessary, were alien to his nature, character, and spiritual vocation.

It was at about this time that an innovation, very typical of Francis's spirit, had begun to establish itself. In some ways, it must have caused more spiritual consolation to him than the immensely rapid growth of his order. The latter had brought about all the anguish of spirit through which he had passed during recent years, whereas there was a simplicity and directness about this new work of his, very much in keeping with early days and the serenity of spirit which Francis had acquired, through tribulation and suffering.

The *Fioretti*, as we have seen, tells us that when Francis, in earlier years, had stilled the twittering of the birds at Cannara and preached to them the praises of the Lord, so that he in his turn might be permitted by the birds to preach to the people, "all the men and women of that town wanted to follow him and leave their homeland." Francis would not allow them to do so. He said, "Do not be in a hurry to go. I will arrange how you should live so that you can save your souls."

We must remember that Francis set no limit on the number of his followers once he was certain that God had called him to bring a new message to the people and renew Christ's teaching, literally interpreted. His words were taken too literally, and the rapid increase in the number of his followers had created a situation which demanded rules and constitutions such as Francis had never dreamed of. The words he had spoken to the people of Cannara, like the Portiuncula Indulgence, must have expressed his desire that the message of Christ and the simplicity of the Gospels should not be arbitrarily limited, but rather should pervade the whole world — all men, women, and children of goodwill.

We do not know exactly when Francis put into practice this idea of somehow incorporating into the ranks of his followers men and women who need not leave their homes and their businesses — men and women, through their work, their homes, their families, and the native genius of their country, witnessing to the fullness of Christianity in the spirit, at least, of the *Regula Primitiva* and the Gospel texts. Perhaps Francis was influenced by the fact that he lived in an age when the special dedication of laypeople to the service of God in the world was a characteristic of those spontaneous reformist movements which too easily drifted into heresy.

He had certainly known such people in Assisi itself, and he may well have heard of the Cistercian abbot Joachim de Flora, whose influence was tremendous and who would later specially influence some of Francis's followers. Joachim preached a renewal of the Christian life and prophesied a new age in the history of the Church, "the Third Kingdom" of the Holy Spirit, which was to follow the Second Kingdom of the Son and the First Kingdom of the Father. In the Third Kingdom, the Church would be completely spiritualized, having transcended the instruments of wealth, coercion, and law.

Francis himself, as we have often seen, possessed a simple, literal mind. He thought of the individual, the person he had known and met, rather than of groups. At Cannara, he had promised to help those men and women who surrounded and encouraged him after he had shown that the hand of God was with him in inspiring the singing of the birds. This lay-following of his would thus be an eminently practical and natural one. Perhaps from Cannara the words spread to others, and little by little, laymen and -women who met the saint during his journeys and preaching, found themselves intimately bound to him and received from him practical advice as to how they could lead their lay lives in harmony with his ideals.

We know, too, that Francis, during his travels, made many friends. These were often men and women of position and responsibility, like the lord of Montefeltro. In Rome itself, as we have seen, he had his close friends. Time and again, he must have found people who showed that they understood him, yet could not literally follow him into his movement.

The story is told of one such, a merchant of Poggibonsi, near Siena, called Lucchesio. He asked Francis to give him a special penitential rule of life, suitable to his condition in the world. Lucchesio's wife, Buona Donna, we are told, was not too pleased, but in the end, the couple devoted themselves together to good works, relying, if need be, on alms to carry out their plans for the poor and sick. Their example spread in the little towns. Those who thus enrolled in a special way within the following of the saint were called "penitential brothers" and "penitential sisters."

Much later, a classification of the different types of followers of Francis became established. The "First Order" referred, of course, to the men who, as priests or lay brothers, took the vows of religion in Francis's company. The "Second Order" referred to the women who, under Saint Clare, lived the same rule (despite Cardinal Ugolino's attempt to make it more in conformity with the traditional rules for women) in the cloister. The "Third Order" naturally became the name of this loose grouping of lay followers in the world, comprising both men and women. This innovation was later to be imitated by other orders.

There was considerable opposition to these penitent groups of layfolk — so much so that ecclesiastical authorities at times had to protect them against persecution by the civic powers.

This suggests that, from early days, Francis had given them positive encouragement and instruction to take steps to avoid the things which he so detested in the organized society of the time. They would not only have to make do with as little money as possible, giving the rest to the poor, not only to dress simply and to avoid the life of what we shall call "society," but also to refuse to bear arms or to take feudal oaths of service. Likewise they were expected to settle their quarrels outside law courts and to appeal to the bishops for protection.

So long as these resolutions were confined to a small minority of eccentrics, they might cause little trouble, but as the Third Order grew, it began to have a profound effect on normal social life in the little towns. However far Francis was from considering himself a revolutionary and however careful he was to avoid rules, instructions, and constitutions, the flame within him inevitably passed to others, and the Third Order was to play a part, in its way, scarcely less annoying to the constituted authorities — in this case, especially of state — than the First Order.

The refusal of feudal oaths, when multiplied over Italy, not only weakened the power of the feudal lords, but liberated the ordinary people from the serfdom of obligatory labor. At the same time, the distribution of the wealth of the many rich people who became "tertiaries," gave a beginning of economic security to the worker and the peasant, while offering some sense of social security also against accident and illness, through the provision of money for the Church, the hospitals, and for works of mercy.

To put it as briefly as possible, a spiritual sociology of love and brotherhood proved to be the answer to the glaring evils of the times. Francis's Gospel teaching, which proved too strong in its primitive Franciscan form to be fitted into the established order of the Church, found, for a period, freer expression in becoming a vital factor in the social revolution which brought to an end the ancient cruel feudal power, and in bringing with it a new degree of liberty and justice, especially within the new towns and communes, in this rapidly changing era of Christendom.

Once again, we can see how, from the very simplest beginnings, the revolutionary genius of Francis's unobscured vision brought about consequences of which he himself could never have dreamed and which he would never have understood.

The date usually given for the establishment of the Third Order was 1221, when Cardinal Ugolino made the first rule on the basis, it seems, of the injunction or rough rules given to his brothers by Francis. But it was not until two years after Francis's death that a rule, the text of which has not come down to us, was written, and we do not know the relation between the rule of 1221 and the so-called Capistrano Rule of 1228, a name due perhaps to modifications and additions by Saint John Capistran[77] many years later.

In any account of Saint Francis, written in the English language, the year 1224 must stand out because of an event, of its nature typical of the whole apostolic work of the saint, but, in this instance, affecting England and those who speak the English tongue. In this year, the followers of Francis crossed the English Channel and brought the message of their founder to the English people. The date is given as September 10, 1224.

---

[77] Saint John Capistran (1386-1456), Franciscan friar.

Nine ragged men, their tattered gray tunics held together with a cord, landed at Dover. It appears that their first request for food and hospitality landed them, as vagabonds, in some kind of lock-up. When these "simple and despicable men" made their way through critical onlookers, someone in the crowd said that they were spies and robbers. At once, one of the friars undid the cord around his waist and, holding it up, said, "Well, if we are robbers, here is a rope with which to hang us." This apparently acted as a passport, and they were allowed to make their way toward Canterbury.

There is no record of any reference to England on the part of Francis, but by now his followers had crossed many frontiers and many seas, and a mission across the English Channel was sooner or later inevitable. The order for sending it may well have been one of the last acts of Francis during a chapter general when he still held the reins of office in important matters.

The story of the mission to England was described thirty-four years after Francis's death by Friar Eccleston, about whom personally we know extremely little. It is nevertheless one of the source books of early Franciscanism.

His chronicle starts with the following sentence: "In the year of our Lord 1224, in the time of the lord Pope Honorius, that is, in the very year in which the rule of Blessed Francis was confirmed by him, in the eighth year of the lord King Henry, son of John, on the Tuesday after the feast of the Blessed Virgin, which that year was upon a Sunday, the Friars Minor first came to England, at Dover."

The party of nine consisted of four clerics and five lay brothers. The minister provincial of the mission was Friar Agnellus of Pisa, an early follower of Francis and, at the time of his appointment, guardian of the Paris friary. Brother Agnellus was to be noted for his holy life and his devotion to poverty and the primitive observance. His saintliness is attested by his beatification.

With him came Brother Richard of Ingworth, said to be a Norfolk man. After the death of Francis, when the Franciscans crossed the Irish Channel, Brother Richard became the Irish minister provincial. Next was Brother Richard of Devon who was to end his days at Romney, suffering for fifteen years of the quartan fever. The third companion of Agnellus was a novice, William of Esseby. He was to be guardian of the Oxford priory and founder of the Cambridge one.

There were no Englishmen among the lay brothers. Brother Henry was a Lombard, and he was to return to his native land after having been guardian of the London friary. Brother Lawrence came from Beauvais, in France, but returned to Italy, very soon to be a personal companion of Francis, who gave him his tunic. This relic he must have brought back to England when he returned to that country. The third, William of Florence, returned to France. And of the last two we know nothing.

From these humble and mean beginnings, the rapid development of the followers of Saint Francis in pre-Reformation England derived. This is not the place to describe that story, but some figures indicate both the pace and ambit of growth that, of course, could be paralleled in Franciscan development in other countries.

The first little band was to establish in the year of its arrival the friaries of Canterbury, Cornhill in London, and Oxford. In the next year, the friaries of Newgate, in London, and

Northampton were started. Of the nine companions, five remained in Canterbury — their first stop after landing at Dover — and the other four went on to London.

Well before the end of the century, Canterbury had about sixty friars. The two friaries in London could boast, within less than twenty years, of eighty friars. There were eighty-four friars at Oxford within the century and thirty-four at Northampton. Some forty friaries were to be established within twenty years, and the numbers of followers of Saint Francis established in England within the century appears to have been something like 1,500.

This record of development, comparable only with the Dominicans, far exceeded the growth of any religious order in the country. It is not surprising, therefore, that it was said that the comings and goings of the friars created an unprecedented traffic across the English Channel.

Multiply this growth by the countries of Europe and beyond, and one begins to get a picture of the way in which the followers of Francis rapidly permeated Christendom with something at least of the revolutionary spirit of this strange, dedicated, Christian revolutionary of Assisi, who sought in all seriousness to challenge Christendom to be literally Christlike.

Perhaps the specific character of the special spirit of Francis was never more happily expressed than in the description of the English friars at Oxford: "The brethren were always so merry and glad together that they could scarcely look upon each other and abstain from laughter." This laughter endured even under scourging and every kind of persecution. It came from the realization that true human joy is only to be found in a sense of freedom, and release from all that pedantry and conformism imply. It was that spiritual joy and freedom which enabled Franciscanism to give to Europe a new poetry and a new art, as well as a renewed religion.

Through the mists of convention, Francis's eye went straight to the reality of men and the world that reflected the mystery and wonder of its Maker. The Franciscan joy was an inner one, springing from the sense of the liberty of the sons of God; consequently it was not affected by the trials of spirit and body which overwhelm and imprison all of us who depend on finding escapes from the prison-house of fear — fear for our lives, for our means of living, for our reputation, for the "right thing to do or what will the neighbors say?" That is why, as we think of the laughter of the English Franciscans, we may also think of the joy in the heart of Francis during these months which followed the terrible trials over the drafting of the rule within an order which was already throwing a bridge between the early days of happiness and the hard days when conformity and officialdom had to be accepted.

In 1224, Francis had, as we have seen, found his joy again, despite the fact that illness, blindness, and weariness of body would otherwise have overcome him. We shall see in the next chapter that this year was to conclude with the great climax of his spiritual life — the transfixing of his very flesh with the piercing happiness of his love of God physically imprinted on that selfsame flesh.

Francis was essentially a literal person for whom ideas and feelings were viewed and felt in dramatic form. He was a poet who saw and understood through imagery, not abstract conceptions. For him, the body and the senses were a natural vehicle of the spirit, for they were the sublimest part of God's creation, and one with his incarnate Master, who worked and suffered in a body like ours. Thus it was, we may believe, that the supreme ecstasy of his life should have been literally a bodily one — expressing in excruciating joy and suffering the joy and suffering of his Master.

Chapter Twenty-One
❀

Francis Receives the Stigmata

The reader will recall the account of the delightful scene when Francis, some years earlier, had accidentally found himself near the knightly celebrations in Count Orlando's castle at Montefeltro. There Francis had sung of a higher chivalry and, with his preaching, had deeply moved the Lord Orlando himself, who surely must have become one of those many great men who joined the Third Order.

In the course of their long conversation, Orlando had offered Francis a part of his great estates near Mount La Verna in the rising Apennines not far from Florence. Francis, in the end, had accepted, attracted no doubt by the silence and solitude that goes with the high places of the world where remoteness from the hurly-burly of life makes a man feel nearer to God. In such places, rocks and caverns were to be found — cells cut out, as it were, by the hand of God for the prayer and recollection which were so dear to Francis's heart and to the hearts of his closest companions.

This love of uninhabited heights contrasted with his other love of lakes, also forming a zone visibly separated from town and village. In one mood, he would seek solitude on a little island in Lake Trasimeno, where everything was lonely joy and fairness; in another, in the wildness of almost inaccessible nature.

La Verna rises some four thousand feet high, a summit in an immense, softly curved range where snow is to be found until late in the spring. La Verna itself is sharply distinguished by its height, its curious formation, and its dark trees. The impression of softness is deceptive, however, for behind the moss and twisted trees, there are great masses of broken limestone that look as though they had been split and contorted by some gigantic earthquake. No wonder there was a tradition that the earthquake took place at the time of the death of Christ on Calvary, thus prefiguring the spiritual wonder that was to take place this year. It is said that Francis had a revelation which made known to him that the tradition was true.

Instead of going to the Michaelmas chapter general, Francis, this year, chose the oldest and closest of his companions to take with him on his pilgrimage to La Verna, as though he already had some foreknowledge of what was to happen to him.

He chose Leo, Angelo, Rufino — the "Three Companions" — Illuminato, his companion in the Holy Land; the faithful Masseo; and Sylvester, who, so many years earlier, had demanded of the strange young church-builder money in return for the stones which Francis had used for the repair of San Damiano, and had received in exchange a fistful of gold from the proceeds of Bernard da Quintavalle's sale when the latter renounced all his possessions.

Francis planned to be at Mount La Verna from the Assumption (August 15) for the feast of the Exaltation of the Holy Cross (September 14) and Michaelmas (September 29). It was therefore in the full heat of the late summer that he and his old guard trudged their way northward along the valley of the Tiber, passing places full of vivid associations, the battle-field of Collestrada, Citta di Castello, Monte Casale, Santo Sepolcro, then, veering west to the valley of the Arno, toward the heights of La Verna itself.

How the little man, scarcely more than skin and bones, managed the arduous journey in the heat of the season, we can scarcely imagine. Indeed, when they drew near to the mountain, he could move no longer, and it was arranged that a *contadino* ("peasant") should lend him his donkey.

That shrewd peasant was not to be taken in by this strange company of beggarly friars. He wanted to make sure that this was truly the holy Francis about whom there was so much gossip. When Francis told him that "the little Frenchman" was his name, the man said, "Well then, let me give you some good advice. It is that you should be as good as your word, for you have a great reputation among us." Francis managed to get off the donkey and onto his knees, kissing the feet of the man and thanking him for his wise advice.

Little by little, they made the long slow climb through the forest of pines, firs, and larch which grew along the slopes. The trees were full of singing birds, which once again seemed to sense the holiness of this man who was able to communicate with them. They followed the travelers, and many were so tame that they settled on Francis's shoulders and arms. Francis took this as a sign that our Lord approved of his pilgrimage and was using his sisters the birds to sing of the joy of the occasion.

Orlando, from his neighboring castle, came to greet his old friend, and promised the party all the provisions they might need. Thus, their prayer and vigils would be undisturbed.

But Francis had no intention of seeking any comfort in a spot chosen by him for austere prayer and recollection. On the high spur of the mountain, there is an enormous fissure plunging deep down and widening a little at a lower level. Determined to live in an absolutely solitary spot for the long period of retreat, Francis chose this fissure, opening into a kind of rough stone cell, to be the boundary between himself and his companions. He allowed Leo to come twice a day and bring him bread and water and to recite with him, as was the Franciscan custom, the Office, with the two choirs — Saint Francis, the one; and Brother Leo, the other. Over the chasm a log of wood was thrown so that Leo could reach the saint and perform the offices which he had been bidden to carry out. But before attempting the crossing, Brother Leo had to say, "Lord, open Thou my lips," and could only cross the fissure when he heard Francis answer, "And my mouth will announce Thy praises."[78]

During those days of solitary prayer and penance high above the world of Italy, Asia, and Africa, into which his followers had spread, Francis saw himself dramatically wrestling with the evil forces led by Satan, to conquer that world for Christ in a kind of supreme journey between Good and Evil.

As with Christ Himself, an angel was to visit him, but an angel so charmingly attuned to the spirit of the saint, that he came with a viol or lute, playing a divine melody so perfect that Francis thought that he would faint under its beauty. "Had the angel played again," Francis explained, "my soul

[78] These are the opening words of the Divine Office.

would have left my body, for my happiness was beyond all bounds and intolerably painful in its keenness."

Another charming tradition is that a falcon lived near him and woke him up when it was time for the recital of the Office. But when the bird thought that Francis was too tired, it did not beat its wings against the little cell, but left Francis to sleep in peace.

Secretary Brother Leo, despite having been ordered by Francis to keep his distance and not pry into these sacred events, possessed all the curiosity of the modern journalist, seeing to it that there was little that happened during these historic days which he did not get to know and write down for the benefit of posterity. Francis caught him out in his curiosity one day when Leo was listening to the saint apparently speaking to God Himself. Leo saw a ball of fire sweep through the heavens in front of the saint. Gently, Francis, who had seen him, reprimanded him and told him that what he had seen was a sign of greater happenings still to come.

It was on the feast of the Exaltation of the Holy Cross, tradition tells us, that the supreme event of this retreat and of the life of Saint Francis took place. At dawn that morning, Francis, kneeling on the advanced spur of rock which fell away below him for thousands of feet and facing the east, where the first light of the sun was breaking, prayed to God for two favors. The first was that before he died, he should feel in his body, as far as might be possible, the actual sufferings of Christ's Passion; and the second was that he might feel the very love that had caused Christ to undergo this sacrifice for mankind.

When this prayer had ended, we are told, a seraph with six flaming wings flew down toward him, and as it approached, the image of a man hanging on a cross appeared between the pairs of wings. It was the figure of Christ Himself, and, as it rested in front of the saint, darts of flame imprinted on Francis's body the wounds of the crucified Christ. His hands and his feet were pierced with the nails, and on his right side was the wound of the lance. His pilgrimage had stretched from the Crucifix of San Damiano to this mystical crucifixion of his own spirit and body.

For the rest of his life, Francis carried on his body the stigmata: the round, blackened nail-head scars on his hands and on his feet, and the lance wound from which at times blood flowed in sufficient quantity in some cases to penetrate through his clothes.

We have Celano's testimony in regard to the nature of these mysterious wounds: "Hands and feet were pierced in the center by nails, the head of which could be seen in the palm of the hand and in the upper side of the feet. The points of these nails came out on the opposite sides; the marks in the palm of the hand were rounded; and, on the back of the hands, they were long, and there appeared a little bit of flesh just like a bent and driven-back point of a nail, coming through beyond the flesh. So also with the feet. The marks of the nails were impressed, and the mark showed up above the rest of the flesh. It was as though the right side had been pierced by a lance, with a long wound which often spouted out blood, which on many an occasion seeped through the tunic and the undergarments.

"Few people indeed were able to see the sacred wounds of the side while the crucified son of the crucified Lord was alive, but how lucky was Elias, who, even during the saint's lifetime, managed to see it. Lucky, too, Rufino, who actually touched it with his own hands. On one occasion, Rufino had to touch the saint's chest in order to rub it, and his hand slipped, as often happens, right over to the right side. In doing so, he touched the precious wound, and the saint, as a result, felt great pain, so much so that he pushed Rufino's hand away, saying, 'May God forgive you.' The fact was that he always did everything he could to hide this prodigy from strangers and kept it as quiet as he possibly could even from his friends. The result was that even the most intimate and fervent of his brothers knew nothing about it for a long time."

There can be no doubt whatever of the essential truth of this whole strange and wonderful episode, at first sight rather uncharacteristic of the Francis of ordinary days who always managed somehow not to seem like a "classic" saint, but rather a most human ascetic, varying greatly in his moods, yet somehow giving out from within him a strength and a force that moved all men around him and caused him to be universally adored and sometimes feared. Those who, because of preconceptions, find themselves unable to accept the very idea of the miraculous, are in fact reduced to explaining the story by the suggestion that Francis, for some unknown reason, inflicted the wounds on himself. This explanation, which would involve our believing that Francis could tell and live a lie through the most solemn period of his life and in the face of death itself, is evidently completely inconsistent with the character of Francis, whom we know from so many and so diverse testimonies.

There would appear to be cases of other stigmatists who, through autosuggestion, managed to produce in their bodies signs of the wounds of Christ, but Francis was the first person in history to make this claim and to have it attested by external wounds, seen and touched by others, whose evidence can hardly be disputed. For a person like Francis, so simple and extroverted in his whole religious life and action, to become the victim of autosuggestion of this degree seems difficult indeed to believe. Either there was conspiracy of lying, in which Francis took part, or the phenomenon (however we explain it) was true.

In a biography, the details and dates of which may be often insecure and the subject of a great apparatus of higher criticism, but which in its main lines is as authentic as any record of history, the mentality of Francis, at the time of this extraordinary spiritual phenomenon and immediately after it, is at least ascertainable by a piece of evidence whose authority may be examined by any tourist who cares to join the crowds that flock to the sacristy of the great basilica of Saint Francis in Assisi. For there before our eyes, we have Francis's own "Words of Praise," written in gratitude for the stigmata, and the moving message which he wrote for Brother Leo on the back, telling him to "take this sheet and keep it carefully to the day of thy death."

This "Praise of the Most High God" reads:

Thou art the holy Lord God;
Thou art God of Gods,
who alone dost marvelous things.
Thou art strong; Thou art great;
Thou art most high.
Thou art almighty, Thou holy Father,
King of Heaven and earth.

Thou art Three in One, and One in Three,
Lord God of Gods.
Thou art good, all good, highest good,
Lord God, living and true.
Thou art love, charity; Thou art wisdom;
Thou art humility; Thou art patience;
Thou art fortitude and prudence; Thou art security;
Thou art quiet; Thou art joy and gladness.
Thou art justice and temperance.
Thou art our wealth and our plenty.
Thou art beauty; Thou art gentleness;
Thou art the protector;
Thou art the guide and defender.
Thou art our refuge and our strength;
Thou art our faith, our hope, and our charity.
Thou art great sweetness to us.
Thou art our eternal life, infinite goodness,
great and wonderful Lord God almighty,
loving and merciful Savior.

This ecstasy of praise could only correspond with the ecstasy on the height of La Verna, the ecstasy that imprinted the marks of the wounds of Christ on the servant who, as so many believe, came nearest to Christ among all born in Original Sin.

Brother Leo, to whom we owe so much of what happened on the mountain peak, even though he saw nothing of the supreme ecstasy, was suddenly afflicted by "spiritual temptations." Perhaps this may have been the result of the secretarial enthusiasm which caused him to disobey Francis's injunctions and to watch as much of Francis's experiences as he could manage. To console him, perhaps, Francis wrote on the back of the manuscript of the "Words of Praise," in his own straggling writing: "May the Lord bless thee and keep thee. May the Lord show thee His face and have mercy on thee. May the Lord lift up the light of His countenance upon thee and give thee peace."[79] And below that, he added a further blessing: "May the Lord bless thee, Brother Leo."

Cutting through Leo's name in the manuscript is the upright stroke of the letter *Thau* which, as we have seen, was of mystic significance to the saint. No one seems to have satisfactorily explained the strange drawing or doodle in which the foot of the letter *Thau* rests. On the other side of the parchment we have, in Brother Leo's own writing, the shortest and most succinct account of the events on La Verna, and as such they may be given here.

"The blessed Francis, two years before his death, kept a forty days' fast in the place called La Verna in honor of the Blessed Virgin Mary, Mother of God, and of the Blessed Archangel Michael, from the feast of the Assumption of the holy Virgin Mary until the feast of Saint Michael in September. And the hand of the Lord was upon him. After the vision and speech which he had of the seraph and the impression of the Stigmata of Christ in his body, he made these praises on the other side of the sheet, and with his own hand, he wrote them out, giving thanks to God for the blessing conferred upon him."

It should be a matter of special interest in Britain that the arrival of the friars at Dover took place just over a fortnight

---

[79] Num. 6:24-26.

before the stigmatization of their father. We may think of the mission to the English-speaking people as the firstfruits of that mystic retreat on La Verna which had begun on August 15, the feast of the Assumption.

Chapter Twenty-Two

Francis Experiences Joy
Even in Suffering

The long retreat and the mystical experiences of La Verna utterly exhausted Francis, who was now, at the end of September, faced with a tiring journey home. It was a journey home in
two senses. It was home to the Portiuncula and San Damiano,
from which his first spiritual commission had derived, and
where the beloved Clare carried on faithfully the essence of
the primitive rule which he would have spread across the
world had he been allowed. But it was home, too, in that he
knew that he had but a few more months to live before welcoming Sister Death with the same spiritual joy as the joy with
which he had welcomed the seraph which had incised in his
body the wounds of the Savior.

The journey home was to be made with Brother Leo. The
saint, hardly able to walk, rode on a donkey lent to him by
Count Orlando. His old guard came with him part of the way,
but the time arrived when they had to return to the hermitage
of La Verna.

"Goodbye, goodbye, goodbye, Brother Masseo," the saint
said. "Goodbye, goodbye, goodbye, Brother Angelo. Goodbye, Brother Sylvester and Brother Illuminato. My dearest

children, remain here in peace. May God bless you all, dearest sons! Goodbye! I leave you in the body, but I also leave you my heart. I go to Santa Maria degli Angeli, and the Brother 'Little Lamb of God' accompanies me. Never shall I come back to this place. I have to leave it. Goodbye, goodbye, goodbye, all of you. Goodbye, goodbye, La Verna. Goodbye, Mount of the Angels. Goodbye, my dearest Brother Falcon; I thank you for the love you have shown me. Goodbye, goodbye, great rock that held me in your arms safe from the Devil. You, too, we shall not see again. Mother of the Eternal Word, I put my children in your care."

Inevitably, rumors of wondrous happenings on the top of the mountain had spread through the countryside, and now, we may say, began the long, strange, sad, but triumphal journey toward the death of a man who, while still alive, was accorded the veneration of a saint. The people of the valley flocked around him, bringing their sick to be cured by him. "Behold the saint! Behold the saint!" was the cry that everywhere greeted him, although he seemed not to hear it.

At length, Francis and Leo reached their Portiuncula home. Nearly blind and desperately tired, Francis felt little happiness at his home, since he saw there the changes from which he had struggled so long, so mournfully, to protect his followers. No longer did he see and live with that simple peace and joy that had characterized the early years.

To many of the brethren, the presence of Francis had already become a living relic of infinite preciousness. Those who had found him most difficult and trying to live with had all the more reason for knowing the quality of his sanctity. The protection of the living saintly relic had become more important than the living father of the order. He had to resign once again the companionship of his old guard and, with a certain bitterness, exclaimed, "Once upon a time, I saw a blind man whose only guide was a little dog. I do not want to be singular in enjoying any special liberty. Let the brothers appoint a companion for me as the Lord shall inspire them. I do not wish to seem better off than that blind man."

In the same mood of reminiscence and sadness, he longed to serve his first friends, the lepers, and to taste again of that scorn with which, as a young man, he had been greeted by the natives of his native town. His mind turned to fresh fancies as he thought of the past. What he said to the brethren suggested that he could dream again of fresh heroic struggles in the service of his Lord.

By now, the winter had set in, and the hills were already covered with snow. In the damp and cold of the Portiuncula, it seemed impossible that he could long survive. Up there, above the great plain, was the church and convent of San Damiano, ruled by Clare, and the thought of this seemed to give Francis new strength. So the brothers arranged that he should be taken there to live in a hut adjoining the hospice, where a priest and two brothers lodged in order to serve the spiritual needs of the community and to obtain the money necessary for their keep.

Francis, it seemed, had come full circle. In that spot, as a young man, he had lived and labored to repair Christ's Church, his young poet's mind filled with the delight of the countryside, singing to him of the wonderful richness of God's creation. Then his young body had been full of energy and the vision of a knight's conquest in the service of God. Now he could only fitfully discern the lights and shadows that told him of the glory of the rising and the setting sun as he had once daily greeted it. Now, too, in the winter, he remained so much of the time in the dark, his tired, burning eyes preventing any proper sleep.

For some mysterious reason, no one, we are told, had taken the trouble to cleanse the hut and free it from rats, ubiquitous in those unhygienic days. So bold were they that they climbed onto the table and even over the resting body of the saint. But, deep in communion with God, the God whom he had always seen in the beauty, force, and diversity of creation, Francis seemed to recall from deep down within him all the joy and love that had filled him when young and forced him to raise his voice in song, as he tramped the valleys and the heights to Gubbio.

It now seemed as though, the greater his tribulations, the more astonishingly he succeeded in recapturing an inner vision and an inner sensitivity which echoed, from within his heart, the sights and wonders of his youth. Now they were purified and linked with the divine in a far closer manner. The Christian paradox of joy in suffering — reward in detachment, finding in losing — had expressed itself much as it might do in the simple mind of a child. Something of a primitive innocence was given to him in a unity of poet and saint, the nature of the mystic and the inner attending to God of the contemplative.

One night in the middle of winter, his sufferings and discomforts had reached the unbearable. In that night, it seems, he suddenly transcended suffering, and early the next morning, he called one of the brothers to explain to him the way in which supernature and nature were so balanced that, for every suffering on earth, every tribulation, and every trouble, there was, through God's grace and blessing, a counterpart of joy. He told the brother that he had heard a voice saying to him, "Be glad and rejoice in your infirmities and tribulations, and for the rest, take no more heed than if you had already entered into my kingdom."

And he went on to explain: "Suppose the emperor gave a whole kingdom to one of his servants. Would not that servant greatly rejoice? Would he not rejoice still more if that emperor could give him his whole empire? That is why it is right that I should be happy in my infirmities and troubles and take comfort in the Lord, giving thanks to God the Father and His own Son, our Lord Jesus Christ, and to the Holy Spirit for having condescended to me, his unworthy servant, still living in the flesh, expressly to assure me of this truth about His kingdom. That is why I feel this morning that I must sing a new song of praise about the creatures of the Lord, the creatures without whom we should not be able to live, and of which we make use every day — creatures, alas, which also cause men so terribly to offend the Creator. For such a wonderful grace and for so many blessings, we only show ourselves ungrateful, refusing to praise the Lord their Creator and the Giver of all good things as we should."

It was in that mood of superb transcendence of suffering and death, corporeal blindness and inner vision, of utter faith despite the long series of moral and physical tribulations with which he had been surrounded in the evolution of his followers, from that first spontaneity and freedom to the conformism to Church and world, that in his native tongue he sang the canticle which Renan described as "the most beautiful spiritual poetry since the Gospels."

> O Most High, most Potent, sweet Lord,
> To you belong the praise, the glory, the honor, and all blessing.
> To you alone, Most High, they look for life,
> And no man may fitly speak Your Name.
> With all Your creatures, Lord, be praised,
> Not least for Sir, our Brother Sun,
> who daily brings us light.
> Beautiful and radiant in his great splendor,
> How well he tells of Thee, Most High.
> Be praised, my Lord, for Sister Moon and stars,
> Carved by You, clear and rich and fair.
> Be praised, my Lord, for Brother Wind,
> For air in every mood and time through
> whom you give your creatures sustenance.
> Be praised, my Lord, for Sister Water,
> So useful, humble, precious, and chaste.
> Be praised, my Lord, for Brother Fire,
> Which lightens us by night,
> fine and gay and healthy and strong.
> Be praised, my Lord, for our sister, Mother Earth,
> Who holds us up and keeps us straight, yielding diverse
> fruits and flowers of different hue, and grass.
> O praise and bless my Lord,
> Thanking Him and serving Him with great humility.

The troubadour of earlier days who would have sung this canticle to the accompaniment of the lute, now strained his eyes, peering into the dark sky with a lined, deeply joyful face as his voice was heard again and again, his sisters in the convent surely echoing the simple, limpid words.

Perhaps there were many other stanzas, unrecorded or unheard by Brother Leo, but the last verses of the canticle, as it has come down to posterity, were occasioned by the return of that old love and fear of his, the strife that leads to battle, yet destroys the heart of men.

It was the old trouble with Perugia once more. Complex treaties led to the intervention of the Commune of Assisi in Perugian quarrels between the nobles and the people. The governor of Assisi, Opportulo di Bernardo, seeking to carry out the terms of the treaty, was excommunicated by Francis's old friend Bishop Guido. The governor replied in kind and called upon his people to cut off all supplies from the bishop.

It was high summer by now, when we may suppose that Francis's infirmities and discomforts were slightly alleviated. News was brought to him of this unhappy strife, led on either side by his own friends: Guido, his early protector, and the governor, or *podestà*, one of his most devoted followers.

With a sudden renewal of strength, Francis asked that both parties should meet him in that very same place where he had renounced his temporal possessions and his father: the court of the episcopal palace. Brother Pacifico, the old "king of song," was with him, and Francis had hoped that Pacifico would sing his canticle, traveling through Christendom. It was a dream, but now Pacifico could be the bearer to the temporal and ecclesiastical authorities of his invitation. The wish of Francis was obeyed, and the men of Church and state, surrounded by the crowds, still hating one another in their hearts, gathered together to listen to the message of the saint.

Instead of an arbitration, the brothers, standing there before the curious crowd, sang the verses of the "Canticle of the Sun." But meanwhile Francis had added new verses — verses intended to lower pride and destroy hate:

> Be praised my Lord, for those who find
> forgiveness in their hearts for Your love's sake,
> And bear with sorrow and affliction.
> Blessed they who bear these in peace
> Because by You, Most High,
> they will be crowned.

Potentates and people, amazed to hear this canticle composed by the already almost legendary Francis, and noting well the meaning of the last two verses, remained silent and disturbed in their hearts. In that silence, we are told, the *podestà*, Opportulo, suddenly stirred and, walking toward the bishop, knelt at his feet. The bishop took his hands and bade him stand. He in his turn asked for pardon, and the two great men embraced one another. It was the kiss of peace.

After all his disappointments and his defeats, the physically broken Francis conquered at last, and, almost miraculously, he conquered just where conquest most mattered to him. To the old soldier of Collestrada who, on the battlefield, had learned his first lesson in the higher ways of God, peace between men — peace externally and peace in the heart — mattered most if this earth and those who lived on it were ever to be worthy of those benefits and graces of God, the beauty of which and gratitude for which he had been singing that year from the garden of San Damiano, as Clare and her sisters echoed his song. For peace between men is something that cannot be attained through negotiation and treaty. It is something that men must embrace in an act of utter faith in God, who created a world of peace and sent His Son to restore it. That it should now have been brought by a dying man, his body broken through endless penance and sacrifice, but his spirit still exultant, taught a lesson of the high cost of any peace worth attaining. Pride, self-will, self-interest: they must all be burned away before peace can come to men, and, with peace, freedom.

Soon after Francis had reached the Portiuncula, Elias, the minister general, shocked by the state of the saint's eyes, told him that he must take steps to see a doctor. But, whether because of the weather or the lack of any suitable doctor in Assisi, the strange decision was taken for him to retire to San Damiano and await the summer, when it was hoped he would be strong enough to travel south and be examined by papal doctors in Rieti, where the pontifical court was temporarily established. This advice had been given by Cardinal Ugolino when he had been told of Francis's growing blindness. He had not realized how ill Francis was and how cruel for him such a journey would be. Now, in the summer of 1225, the time had come for the saint to undertake this journey.[80]

So in that summer, when Francis seemed a little fitter, he said his last goodbye in his life to Clare and, mounted on a

[80] It has been held that Francis did not compose the "Canticle of the Sun" at San Damiano, but at San Fabiano at Rieti. This reconstruction would destroy the tradition of Francis's spending the winter near Clare and, in that hallowed spot, singing the greatest poetic inspiration of his life. The arguments of scholars on both sides leave one uncertain of the truth, as far as texts alone can take one. This should be enough to enable us to feel secure in the belief that the San Damiano tradition is true.

horse, traveled south with his companions along the roads he knew so well — the roads that linked those two spots of central Italy: the placid, fair Umbrian plain at the feet of Assisi and the narrow, stormier valley at the foot of the mountains which Rieti, to the south, guarded. To safeguard his tired eyes on the journey, his companions covered his head with a great cape, which kept his eyes in twilight.

It was already harvest time, and when the travelers reached the little church dedicated to San Fabiano, to the east of Rieti, they were greeted by masses of people who had come to venerate the holy man. The crowds, alas, were so thick and so excited that they trampled down the vineyard of the priest who served the little church. Even the reception of so great a man did not console the priest for the loss of what perhaps was his only revenue. So Francis asked him what the average size of his harvest was. "Fourteen donkey loads," the priest replied. Francis there and then guaranteed that his harvest would be a third greater. And so it turned out.

We can understand why it was that Francis and his advisers were against his moving south to the papal court in the winter. Not only was it a question of cold, but one of the comfort of so sick a man. The story of La Verna had passed from tongue to tongue all over central Italy, and at Rieti, where Ugolino was staying in the episcopal palace, Francis, we may say, was turned into a still-living relic. Crowds flocked around him, seeking to snatch a shred of his clothes and even relics of his body, such as hairs and nail parings. Nor were the cardinals and prelates ashamed to disturb his privacy.

There was no solution but for the saint to retire once again to the less accessible hermitage of Fonte Colombo. There it was decided that the only hope for Francis's eyes and the cure of terrible headaches and pains of the body which seemed to derive from them was in the barbaric surgery of the times. To relieve the general condition, it was felt to be necessary to cauterize the flesh around the worse eye from the eyebrow back to the ear.

Francis, almost certainly a cerebral type with his thin delicate body, the nerves of which were close under the skin, was terrified by the thought of the red-hot iron that would burn his flesh. But with that amazing faith and courage of his, he pulled himself together and, looking at the glowing iron, he broke into song: "O Brother Fire, whose beauty exceeds that of every creature, you were created by the Most High, resplendent and for our benefit. Be piteous to me in this hour; deal gently with me for the love I have always had for you in the Lord. Grant that He may temper the heat so that I may be able to bear it."

Some who were present could bear the sight no longer and tried to leave the room. Francis chided them and told them to have more courage. He promised that if the fire had to be applied twice, he would be ready to bear it.

Making the Sign of the Cross, he bade the doctor approach and do his work. It seemed to the doctor, who, in his visits to the hut, had been greatly edified by the lives of the friars with whom he had more than once shared a frugal meal, that in this scene, the evils and pains of the world had disappeared to be replaced by a primeval innocence.

The remedy, which left terrible wounds in Francis's flesh, naturally proved to be of no effect. Should they perhaps try again? Francis, this time, was taken from the wildness of Fonte

Colombo to the palace of the Bishop of Rieti. There a canon, Theobald the Saracen, gave up his room to the saint. Further medical examinations led to the desperate conclusion that since the first operation had failed, a second had to be attempted. This time, for some unimaginable reason, the cure was to be the perforation of both ears with the red-hot iron.

The dreadful operations inevitably left the saint weaker than ever, and at no time in his life did Francis, who had always found in suffering for Christ's sake the road to joy, suffer more dreadfully. How did he face up to such a test?

We are told that he called one of the brothers and explained to him that the children of this world do not understand divine things. Perhaps it was Brother Pacifico to whom he talked.

"The saintly men of old," Francis said, "used to play musical instruments in praise of God and to solace their spirits." He begged the brother to find a harp so that together they could sing the praises of creatures and other songs to the glory of God, so that his maimed and mauled flesh might be comforted. Thus, he whispered, the pains of his body would be changed into joy and consolation of spirit. The brother hesitated to do Francis's bidding, in case such behavior at such a time might give scandal. "Say no more about it, then," said Francis, resigned as usual to God's will.

But that night, Francis heard in the distance the sound of a harp, as though played below the window of his room. It seemed to be a heavenly serenade. Next morning, he called the brother back again and told him that God had had pity on him and had allowed him to hear a music far lovelier than any made on earth.

Francis Experiences Joy

Francis remained in Rieti throughout the winter. It seemed impossible that he could live through it. All the known medicaments of the time were tried: poultices, ointments, waters — anything and everything that the doctors could think of as possible means of alleviating the pain. When at length the sun of a new spring — the last spring of Francis's life — began to shine and warm the earth, the doctors and the brothers suggested a change of scene. So Francis was taken to Siena.

It was on this journey that, whether in vision or through some inner light, Francis beheld three poor women walking toward him, so like to one another that they might have been three sisters. All were identically dressed. As Francis came closer to them, they greeted him together with the salute "Welcome, Mother Poverty." This salute, echoing perhaps the deepest sentiment in Francis's heart throughout life, filled him with immense joy. The party stopped at Francis's bidding, that he might speak further with the women. But they disappeared as suddenly as they had made themselves visible.

In the early days of April, the party reached Siena and stayed in a convent outside the town. The fatigues of the journey had been too much. It seemed as though the saint would die there and then. One night, he vomited great quantities of blood, and so weak was he that no one expected him to live until the morning. The brothers knelt around his bed like lost children, saying, "Father, how shall we manage without you? You are leaving us orphans. You are our father and our mother who has begotten us and brought us forth in Christ, our captain and our shepherd, our master and our ruler, teaching and correcting us by your example, rather than by any word."

Together, the brothers asked for their father's blessing and for some words of his by which they might remember his last teaching.

A brother was called to take down the saint's last message. "Write," said the saint, "that I give my blessing to all my brothers now and in time to come until the world's end. My weakness and sickness make me unable to speak many words, but in these three words, let my will and intention be made known to all the brothers. Let them, one and all, love one another as I have loved them. Let them ever more love and observe Lady Poverty. Let them ever more be faithful and loyal to the prelates and clergy of Holy Mother the Church."

These were, in fact, the words with which he was accustomed to bring the chapters at Pentecost and Michaelmas to an end.

The worst fears about him were not confirmed, but it seems that the doctors of Siena were unable to do more for him than those of Rieti. The fact was simply that Francis was slowly dying — dying through the nervous and physical exhaustion of an always frail body, submitted through long years to every exposure and every form of physical mortification; dying too, we must believe, of that inner joy and desire of perfect freedom which, he knew, could only reach fulfillment through the death of "Brother Body" and the release of a spirit which could even now burst into song, when, through the beauty of the earth, it seemed already to touch the frontiers of Heaven and eternity. The paradox of his life — joy in suffering; freedom in his terrestrial confinement — was never better illustrated than in these last months, when his wreck of a body, sometimes placed on a horse's back, sometimes carried, was taken on

these tiring, useless journeys or left in the gaunt, austere sur-
roundings of a hut or hermitage.

To the world, it was the illness and death of a man virtually
already canonized — a saint widely reported to be bearing on
his body the wounds of the Savior. To the order and particularly to Brother Elias, the minister general who had been far
away during these anxious months, the living skin and bones
of the founder were the precious burden which tomorrow
would hallow, not only the thousands of disciples scattered
through Europe and across the seas, but the world itself, glori-
fying the Franciscan Order.

Only in Assisi itself could the saint be allowed to die.

Francis's body was now becoming swollen with the weakness of the heart and the consequent dropsy. He could scarcely
eat at all.

It was time for him to go home. They carried him through
Cortona, the wildness of whose hill and valleys had been beloved by both Francis and Elias. Even now, Francis retained
enough spirit and surely enough sense of humor to insist on giving his cloak to a beggar in great want. His companions were
scandalized, doubtless thinking that tomorrow here would be
another famous relic. They tried to snatch the cloak back from
the beggar, but Francis saw to it that if the beggar was forced to
give it back to the brothers, the latter would have to pay well
for it.

The party, it seems, made a detour through Gubbio, perhaps
in order to avoid the Perugians, bellicosely restless as ever and
liable to try to snatch the saint and take him to their city — a
coup which would singularly infuriate their old enemy. But
may it not have been Francis himself who expressed the wish

that, on his way home for the last time, he might see Gubbio once more, the city toward which he had in the first flush of his conversion tramped, praying, laughing, and singing his release from the captivity of his unregenerate days? Once again, he was in mind the happy spiritual troubadour on the eve of gaining the prize of his life.

Now, from Gubbio, he was being carried the reverse way to the city of his birth and fame, his tired, almost-blind eyes scarcely able to distinguish between light and darkness. The wheel had come full circle, and who can doubt that, mysteriously, the present joy in the heart of the physically shattered human being was infinitely greater than the joy of his youth, for in his present spiritual vision, he could see and feel wonders so much deeper and closer to the Lord of all creation than he could have experienced or understood in the early days.

This retracing of his steps, this last return to the Portiuncula seemed to revive his tired being. Now it was summer, and it was thought best to carry the saint into higher country in the hope that the climate of Biagnara, beyond Nocera to the east, would help the recovery. Very soon the terrible swelling of his body increased again, and no one could doubt that the end was approaching.

It seems incredible to us in our time that the approaching death of this holy man, whose fame had been steadily growing among all the people, especially since the story of the stigmatization had passed from mouth to mouth, should, at this supreme moment of his life, have led to obsessional fears that the "prize" — there is no other word — of his dead body might be fought for by the traditional enemies of the Assisians, the neighboring Perugians. But so it was.

Elias, the brothers, the Commune of Assisi: they were all terrified lest somehow the saint's body should be acquired by their old enemies. A deputation from the governor of the commune was sent to Biagnara to make sure that Francis should be in Assisi when the supreme moment came.

Whatever the dying man may have thought of this behavior, he himself could not have wished otherwise.

Even now, the saint's spirit could not be dampened. The *Mirror of Perfection* tells us that "while they were bringing him along, they rested in a certain town [Satriano], and the Blessed Francis lay in the house of a poor man who willingly gave him shelter, while his escort went about town trying to find food. They were unsuccessful. So they came back to Francis and said to him, laughingly, 'Brother, it seems that you must give us your alms, for we can't find anything to eat here.' And Blessed Francis answered, 'I will tell you why you cannot find anything to eat. It is that you put your trust in your flies and your pence [it was his custom to call money "flies"] and not in God. Go back to the places where you were trying to buy food, and instead of buying, ask for alms for the love of God, and you will find that the Holy Spirit will see to it that you get all you need.' "

So once again — and for the last time — Francis passed through that city gate of Assisi, from which he had once sung his way to Gubbio. But this last time, the saint's re-entry was to the accompaniment of thunder and heavy rain, a fierce storm having broken over Assisi.

Elias, believing that the little Portiuncula was an unsuitable and dangerous place for the supreme moments of Francis's life, had arranged that he should be taken to Guido's palace, where guards had been set to prevent his body's being snatched away. Despite the weather, the citizens of Assisi had come to greet him, happy in the certainty that the saint would die among them, and leave his remains to the city of his birth. Down the steep steps and narrow roads, they carried him. As they crossed the Piazza del Commune, the blind saint must surely have turned to his right, remembering the house of his birth and the church of San Niccolo, where he was first schooled. So many memories were enshrined in the hometown which he had once taken by assault through his gaiety and high spirits. Down farther the party went, leaving to the left the church of Saint George — the church which taught him the wonders of chivalry and the way to become a knight of Lady Poverty. There — perhaps he could foresee it — would stand a great basilica, dedicated to his sister, Clare, his spiritual partner whom he would never again see.

They reached the lower city walls, passing through the piazza of Santa Maria Maggiore, leaving behind that ancient church and cathedral. At length they arrived at the episcopal palace, once the scene of that tremendous surrender when Francis, naked before the people, had turned from all that men thought made life worth living.

His old friend Guido, alas, had sometime earlier gone on pilgrimage to the shrine of Saint Michael on Monte Gargano. There the old imperious friend would see Francis again — but in a vision after Francis's death.

The whole city, Celano says, was delighted that Francis had successfully come home, but its desire was that the hour of his death should not be delayed, for every moment counted when it was a question of ensuring that the holy body should belong to Assisi and no one else, especially its old Perugian enemies.

⚜

Chapter Twenty-Three

Francis Dies with a
Song in His Heart

Before watching at the deathbed of Saint Francis, it would be good if we do what we can to penetrate into the mind of the saint during the last period of his life, when he could look back on all his work. Thus we shall know, as best we can, the mind of the man who was dying.

Francis, it is clear, bore little resemblance to the founder and head of an order as we should understand the position today. Similarly, he really bore little resemblance to the conventional picture of a saint, as we nowadays understand that word. It is good to recall again how Brother Jordan, the chronicler, was not so greatly impressed by Francis, and certainly did not think of him as a saint.

Francis never planned and never theorized. He seemed to live from day to day. He was highly emotional and apt to lose his temper. To those who thought in terms of logic and continuity, he seemed inconsistent and arbitrary. He himself seemed to be unable to see things in logical terms. He found no difficulty in holding two points of view that seemed to be inconsistent with each other. But in the whole dedication of his life, he had the inspiration of genius, in that his whole being seemed to follow a piercing light within him, a star outside him about whose revelation he had no doubts and to which he clung with an unshakable tenacity.

The earlier followers, who had shared all with him from the beginning, even if they could not always understand their father, allowed that vision of his to guide them insofar as they could understand it, being content for the rest to do what he bade them. Later, as the number of his followers steadily augmented, the order, instead of remaining within the clear light which Francis saw, drifted inevitably in the penumbra, into the realm of compromise and adaptation to clerical and worldly necessities.

It was in almost blind fighting against this, toward the end of his life, that Francis endured his greatest suffering, a kind of suffering deeper than any of his spiritual and bodily sufferings, because he could not find any exaltation, any spiritual joy and freedom in enduring it. This is why it is good to leave Francis in the mood in which his last words and writings were given to his brethren and to posterity.

The *Mirror of Perfection* tells us that shortly before Francis died, a brother asked him if there was anyone in the order whom Francis could spiritually trust and upon whom the burden of superiorship could be worthily laid.

Francis answered, "Such a man should be serious, discreet, well thought of, without favoritism, one who should hold dear the study of prayer, but leaving time for the care of others. After prayer, let him be at his brothers' disposal, letting himself be plucked and despoiled, so that he can attend to everyone's wants and make provision with charity, patience, and gentleness. He should act toward the simple and foolish as he would act toward the knowing and the wise. If he is learned, let him nevertheless deal with others with piety, simplicity, patience, and humility, and let him cherish godliness in himself and in others. Let him be a blasphemer of money, which is the chief source of corruption to our profession and perfection, and, as head of all and pattern to all, let him not even know what a money box is. It is enough for him to possess his habit and his rule book. Let him not accumulate books or give himself over to reading, since his office is more important than his studies. Let him tenderly console the afflicted, since such consolation, of all things, is the best remedy for suffering. That he may induce them all to tractableness, let him humble himself, and bend more than is his due, thereby, maybe, gaining a soul."

And Francis reminded those to whom he spoke to beware of being severe to the weaker brethren, since the superior "might slide down toward an even steeper precipice."

"It is specially important that he should be able to understand the secrets of conscience and search out truth from its hidden sources. Let him hold all accusations suspect until diligent examination brings out the truth. Let him not listen to tale-bearers. Lastly, let him not forget equity and justice through the temptation of personal ambitions. By excess of vigor let none be lost, nor by excess of mildness let lukewarmness be born, and let not too-easy pardon destroy discipline. Let him be feared by others, but only in such a way that he is loved by those who fear. Let him always think of his office as a burden rather than an honor."

More dramatic, authentic, and final were the words of Francis's testament, the document in which, above all, the secret of

307

Francis of Assisi

Francis is told. It must have represented the mind of the dying Francis:

> The Lord gave me, Brother Francis, the grace to begin to do penance thus: when I was in sin, it seemed to me very bitter to look upon lepers, but the Lord led me to them, and on them I had pity. And when I left them, that which seemed so bitter to me was converted into consolation of mind and body. Then, after a little while, I came out of the world.
>
> And the Lord gave me such faith in His Church that I adored Him in all simplicity, and said, "We adore Thee, most holy Lord Jesus Christ, who art in all the churches of the world, and we bless Thee because Thy holy Cross has redeemed the world."
>
> Furthermore, the Lord gave me and gives me such faith in the priests who live according to the form of the holy Roman Church, in respect of their orders, that even if they should persecute me, I would have recourse to them. And were I to have as much wisdom as Solomon, I would not preach in their parishes against their wills. I will fear them and love and honor them as my masters. I will not see any sin in them, because I see in them the Son of God, and I look upon them as my masters. This I do, because I can see nothing else with my bodily eyes in this world than the most high Son of God, save His most holy Body and Blood, which they consecrate and they alone administer to others. And I wish that these most holy mysteries be honored above all other things and venerated and placed in precious places.
>
> After the Lord had given me the care of the brethren and when there was none to show me what to do, He revealed to me that I must live according to the rule of the holy Gospels. This I have written down in few and simple words, and the lord Pope confirmed it for me. And those who came to

embrace this way of life divided among the poor all they possessed, and they were content with a single tunic, patched inside and out (those who wanted it) and a cord and a pair of breeches, and they did not desire to have anything more.

Those of us who were clerics said the Office like other clerics, and the laymen said the Our Father. And very happily we stayed in poor and abandoned churches, and we were ignorant and subject to all men. And I worked with my hands and still so wish to work. It is my firm will that all the other brothers should do some manual work which belongs to an honest way of life. And those who do not know how to work should learn; not out of greed to receive the price of their labor, but in order to give a good example and to banish idleness. And if we should not be given a reward of our labor, then let us have recourse to the bounty of the Lord and beg our bread from door to door. The Lord has revealed to me that we should employ this salutation: "The Lord give you peace."

Let the brethren beware that they do not accept, in any manner whatever, any church, habitation, or other thing constructed for them, unless it conforms to the observance of holy poverty which we have vowed in our rule, ever taking shelter like wanderers and strangers.

I strictly commend by holy obedience that all brothers, wherever they may be, should beware of asking for any letters of privilege from the court of Rome, either themselves or through another person, neither for a church nor for any other place, neither under the pretext that it is needed for preaching or to escape the persecution of their person. But if they should not be received in any place, let them flee elsewhere and do penance with the blessing of God.

And I will strictly obey the minister general of this brotherhood and the guardian he pleases to assign to me; but I desire to be placed into his hands in such a manner that I am not to go anywhere or do anything against his will.

Do not let the brothers say, "This is another rule," because this is a reminder, an admonition and exhortation, and my last will and testament, which I, your lowly little brother, Francis, make for you, my blessed brothers, that we should in true Catholic fashion better observe the rule which we have promised to observe before the Lord.

And the minister general and all the other ministers and custodians shall be held by holy obedience to add nothing to these words nor to take anything away from them. And let them always carry this writing with them, together with the rule, and, in all the chapters they will hold, let them read these words as well when they read the rule.

And to all my brethren, clerics and laymen, I strictly command by holy obedience that they shall make no gloss to the rule or to these words saying, "Thus we want them to be understood." But as the Lord has given me the grace to write the rule and these words purely and simply, you are to understand them just as purely and simply without any gloss, and observe them by saintly deeds until the end.

And whosoever shall observe these things will be filled with the blessing of the highest heavenly Father in Heaven, and on earth with the blessing of His beloved Son and the most holy Paraclete, with all the virtues of Heaven and all the saints.

And I, Brother Francis, your most lowly servant of the Lord, as far as I can, confirm you inwardly and outwardly in this most holy blessing. So be it.

Francis, as he lay in Bishop Guido's palace, his mind turned toward God and recalling the ideals, enshrined in this last document of his, must surely have been ready to give up all the fame and growth of his order, in exchange for the certainty that all his companions would remain faithful to the spirit of the *Regula Primitiva* and the ideals prescribed in his testament. His consolation must have been in those near him who had always remained faithful to him — "those of us who were with him," as they were proudly to describe themselves.

What of Brother Elias, in whose charge everything was — and also one of those who were with him? Could the saint have failed entirely to see how far he was to wander, not merely from the spirit of Francis and his order, but from the Church Herself? Yet there is no reason to believe that Elias, in Francis's lifetime, manifested the pride and self-indulgence which were later to become so strong. Elias loved Francis and stood by him, but after the early days, he seemed to imitate, not Francis's fervor and spirit of sacrifice, but Francis's free spirit and, as the world would call it, irresponsibility. Without the dedication which, with Francis, expressed itself in spiritual freedom and joy, Elias drifted, and was later far more quickly to drift, into the pursuit of a self-interest and a corporate interest that could only have revolted the saint. So easy it is for the corruption of the best to turn out to be the worst. But the dying man, it seems, was spared any realization or premonition of what would happen to one of his closest friends and companions.

One wonders, too, why Francis's old friend and critic Cardinal Ugolino, was not present sometime during these solemn days. Francis, with that inconsistency that was so much part of his apparent character, loved him even though he must have known how much the change of spirit in his followers was due to that prelate. But no one seems to have missed him, either at the deathbed or among the biographers.

The question soon arose as to whether Francis should actually be allowed to die at the Portiuncula, for this was certainly his own wish. The authorities and citizens of Assisi feared this, in case once again the precious relic of his body might be endangered through resting in that unguarded spot. For the moment nothing was done.

Although Francis confessed that the cruelest martyrdom would be less difficult to bear than these days of suffering, he could still sing, and when he felt too weak to sing, he turned to the brothers around him and asked them to sing for him. Together they sang again the "Canticle of the Sun," in which all creatures of God were again and again named in praise of the Lord. This extraordinary and unique deathbed was more than some of the brothers could stand — among them, Elias himself, who reported the scandal being caused in the city. Elias, perhaps, already had his mind on that site to the west of the city where one day a sumptuous church would be built to bring home to the world once and for all the glory not only of Francis, but of the Franciscan Order. "Should you not," Elias said to the saint, "keep recollected and silent?"

"O let me rejoice in God," Francis said, "and in praising Him in all my sufferings, since by a wonderful grace, I feel myself so close to my Lord that, in the knowledge of His mercy, I can sing again."

It seemed to those present that somehow the saint's spirit had already in some degree been separated from that poor flesh and bones which tomorrow would be so universally venerated. In these hours of weakness, Francis's mind seemed to go back to the past, picking out, not the great things of life, but the little ones, the little things he enjoyed and loved, the little self-indulgences which made him the most charming of saints, despite his fierce dedication and mortification. Once during the night, he asked the cook to go out and pick him some parsley. The cook could not imagine how he could find parsley in the middle of the night, but, doing his best, he went out and picked some grass. When he returned, he found he had picked some parsley with the grass, and he gave it to the saint, who took it with joy.

On another occasion, Francis asked for some eels. Eels? Where could they find eels? But shortly after, we are told, a man knocked at the door and brought a basket of eels and crayfish.

Nor was the dying Francis above making puns, for when a doctor called Bongiovanni, an old friend of his, came to see him, Francis, always unwilling to use the name Bonus ("good") of any human being, since God alone was good, called him by the name of his uncle, Benvegnate ("well-come"). "What do you think of my illness, Benvegnate [*Bene venias*]?" "*Bene erit* ['It will go well'], Brother, through the grace of God." But when the saint assured him that he was not afraid of death, but was ready to accept life or death equally according to the will of God, the doctor answered, "So far as our knowledge goes, your illness is incurable. I think you will die toward the end of September or the beginning of October." Francis answered, "*Bene veniat* ['Death comes timely']. Sister Death will be well-come."

This news that he must certainly die very soon was indeed welcomed by Francis as the right setting for his last manifestation of a joy so great that he must sing once again the praise of his Lord and finish his "Canticle of the Sun" with its final

verses. He called on Leo and Angelo to come and sing his famous canticle once again with him. And when they had finished the verses known to them, the saint alone continued
singing:

Praised be my Lord, for our Sister Mortal Death,
From whom no man alive will escape.
Woe to those who die in mortal sin
Blessed those who are found
walking in Your most holy ways
For the second death will bring them no evil.

A living canticle himself, he had to end as a dying canticle.

Everyone, in fact, thought that he was now at the point of
death, and Francis called the brethren around his bed. As he
lay there, now completely blind, his hand tremblingly sought
the head of the brother nearest to him. He asked who it was,
and was told, "Brother Elias."

"Be blessed, my son," he said, "and since the Most High has
multiplied my sons and brothers under your rule, I bless them
all in you and over you. In Heaven and in earth may the Lord,
King of the universe, bless you. I bless you as I can and more
than I can. And where I cannot bless you, pay heed to Him for
whom all things are possible. Bless you. May God remember
your labors and your work, and may destiny grant you the prize
of the just. Whatever blessing you desire, may you find it. And
may you obtain all that you have a right to demand."

And then he went on speaking to all the gathering. "Goodbye in Christ, goodbye to all, my sons. In Him remain firm, for
the day will come when all will be put to the greatest proof,
and trouble will already be near. Blessed are they who will

persevere when others will flee. Now I hurry to the Lord; in faith, I turn toward my God, who in my spirit I have sought every day devotedly to serve."

Then he bade the brothers never to abandon the mother house, the Portiuncula. It was truly a holy place, and every grace and blessing that had fallen upon his brethren had fallen in that spot.

This last moving request that never should the Portiuncula be abandoned expressed his own sorrow at finding himself dying in the unsuitable apartment of a great bishop. So, with the consent of the magistrates of Assisi and the help of an armed escort, the dying man was moved for the last time, and carried to the Portiuncula.

The litter was carried down the hill into the valley and when the sad company reached the crossroads of the so-called Strada Francesca and the Strada della Portiuncula, Francis asked that the litter should be laid down, his face turned back toward his native city.

Then, trying to raise himself from the litter, he held up his hand in blessing over the city, saying, "Lord, whereas this city was in olden times a place inhabited by wicked men, I see now that through Your great mercy in Your own good time, You have been merciful to it even more than to other cities. You have chosen it to be the home of those who in truth acknowledge and give glory to Your holy Name. It is giving the world an example of good report, saintly life, full and pure teaching and of evangelical perfection. I ask You then, my Lord Jesus Christ, Father of all mercy, to overlook our ingratitude, and always to bear in mind Your great pity, that the city should forever be the home and habitation of those who truly know

Thee and glorify Thy blessed and most glorious Name forever and ever. Amen."

When speaking, Francis must have tried to turn his head from side to side and, through his blind eyes, picture again that unforgettable view of the spur of mountain on which the little city stood. From its soft, green heights, he had set out so often: there to his left, along the way to the battlefield of Collestrada, and then to the right, on that frustrated way to fight with the knights for the Holy Land. There he had repaired the churches, including the Portiuncula itself, where he was ready to meet Sister Death. There to the right, so much nearer to him, was San Damiano, where Christ on the Cross had spoken to him, and where his beloved Clare now lay, as had been reported to him, sick in body and in mind because of her terrible anxiety about him. He told a brother to tell her to forget her grief at being unable to see him again. "Let her know that before she leaves this life, she will see me again and be greatly comforted in regard to me." High above was Monte Subasio with its Benedictine monastery, which once had rented to him the land and chapel of Santa Maria degli Angeli, where he was now to die. Hidden in the woods over there was that first of those spots torn and twisted by nature, so that the rocks formed prison cells, as it were, within which he and his brothers could enclose themselves to be alone with God in prayer and sacrifice.

All this he would never see again, but in his mind he could visualize every detail. Yet he had never been a man to dwell unnecessarily on the past. He lived in the present — the present which God chose for him at the different stages of his life and the All-Present, God Himself, with whom his being was saturated. It was time now to make his final appointment with Sister Death, and this last appointment was no more a mournful one than had been that varied story of his dedicated life. He must hasten onward, so with a gentle nod he indicated that the company should move on through the forest of the Portiuncula to stop outside the church and enter the little hut where his last days would be spent.

With Francis, life was always a series of surprises, and not the least surprise for posterity was left to the end. His closest followers were around him, and across the face of Italy, Europe, and beyond the seas in England and in Syria, his immense family in religion was scattered, the great majority unaware that their father was dying. But who, at this moment, should come to his deathbed?

It was none of these, nor any of the great men of the Church, nor any of the vast throng of men of all classes and stations whose lives had been changed by meeting him. Of all people, it was a woman — that woman of Rome, of whom we hear so little in his life because it was not thought to be edifying that the chroniclers should give in detail an account of this particular friendship.

How deeply the Lady Giacoma dei Settisoli — "Brother Giacoma," as Francis liked to call her — was in his mind and thoughts is shown by the fact that now he dictated to her a letter with the inscription: "To the Madonna Giacoma, Servant of God, Brother Francis, the poor little man, sends his salute in Christ Jesus." And he went on to tell her that he was on the point of death and that if she wished to see him before he journeyed to his heavenly country, she should come to him without delay. And he asked her to bring with her a shroud of the color of ashes and also some of those sweetmeats which she used to give him in Rome.

To the very end, Francis remained the same: that strange mixture of fierce ascetic and simple, childlike humanity, a man who could always find freedom and joy and the delight in the simplest things of life. Scarcely had the letter been written when the noise of travelers making their way through the wood was heard. The silence of the solitude was broken by voices and the rattle of harnesses as the horses were brought to a halt. To their amazement, the brothers saw the Lady Giacoma dismounting and hurrying toward them. "What is the news? Is Father Francis still alive?" No one could understand how the great lady had managed to arrive so soon. She told them that she had heard a mysterious voice in her Roman palace bidding her hurry to Assisi if she wished to see her old friend again before he died. The voice also bade her bring the sheet, the sweetmeats which he loved, and the wax and the incense for the funeral rites.

When Francis was told, he exclaimed, "God be praised!" He asked that Brother Giacoma should at once be brought in, since the rule forbidding women to enter into a religious enclosure was not for her. What these two old friends said to one another we do not know, any more than we possess more than a hint of the relations between them during Francis's life. This is a tragedy, for Giacoma's arrival at this supreme hour, drawn by an inner spiritual sense, makes it certain that here had been a friendship, as spiritually pure and deep as that of any of the saintly loves between dedicated men and women which Christian history has recorded. Different from, shorter and less continuous than Francis's love for Clare, his love for

Giacoma must be matched with it, Giacoma's reward being her presence at this supreme moment. Clare, the religious companion and disciple of Francis, had to bear for years the terrible sacrifice of being but a few hundred yards away, yet canonically unable to be by his side.

Kneeling by the bedside, Giacoma, we know, tried to coax the dying saint into eating a little of the almond sweetmeats which she had brought. With a smile of happiness, Francis did his best to enjoy them, the more so in that the appearance of Giacoma seemed to have given him new life and a momentary flush of recovered health. But he was too weak and sick to do more than taste a piece.

The presence of this great noblewoman, accustomed to deal with critical situations, seems to have created something of a panic. She was clearly shocked at the measures taken by the Assisians to keep guard on the Portiuncula lest, at the last moment, the body of the saint might be secreted away by the Perugians. She hoped to remain to nurse him in reasonable conditions, and to send her people away. Francis gently broke the news to her that it was not worth bothering about all this, since he would die the coming Saturday.

The dying man wanted a different death rite. Just as he had started his religious life by a physical nakedness, symbolic of his renunciation of parents, money, and all the ties which he believed to make for servitude, unhappiness, anxieties, and war among men, so he now wished to die in that same symbolic nakedness. He instructed the brothers to remove his tunic and let him lie naked on the bare floor. Covering with his hand the wound on his side, to those around him he said, "My work is finished. May Christ teach you to carry out yours."

As soon as the symbolic denudation had been accomplished, the superior brought back his clothes and said, "In the spirit of holy obedience, take this tunic and this cowl. I lend them to you, and I forbid you, since they are not your property, to give them to any other person."

Happy in the thought of this last acceptance of the spirit of poverty, Francis smiled and allowed himself to be reclothed. And so he continued as one day followed another, consoled, we may be sure, by his old guard, which was also a choir ready to sing to him again and again the praises of the Lord, while he tried so hard, despite his utter weakness, to join in the singing.

His end was now only a few hours away, and, turning to his brothers, he said, "When you see that the end has come, put me naked on the bare earth again as you did the day before yesterday; and leave me there after death for the time it takes to cover a mile walking." This was probably on Thursday, October 1.

Next morning, Friday, he gathered his brothers around him in that more solemn fashion when he had blessed and kissed Brother Elias. Standing around their father, one by one, they moved in turn to his right hand and knelt by him. Francis laid his hand on each one's head and blessed him. This time, he was particularly affected when it was the turn of Bernard — Bernard da Quintavalle, his first companion, the first rich man to realize all the common sense and all the blessings that derived from the renunciation of status, career, honor, and wealth.

Speaking to all the brothers, he said, "The first brother that the Lord gave me was Brother Bernard. The first, he fulfilled most perfectly the wish of the Holy Spirit by giving his goods to the poor. That is why I am bound to love him better than any brother in the order. Therefore, insofar as I may, I direct that whosoever shall be minister general shall love and honor him as myself. Let the ministers and the brothers of the whole order look to him as they would look to me."

So it was that, at this supreme moment, Francis in the most solemn way possible remembered the tie of friendship and loyalty to the second Franciscan, even though the chroniclers leave us to think that he found in other brothers a greater spiritual and personal intimacy, the brothers of the old guard and especially the "Three Companions."

With that faith and simplicity which always encouraged him to imitate the example of Christ in the most literal fashion, he asked that bread be brought to him. Too weak to break it himself, he asked that it should be broken for him and then gave a piece to each of those present.

Next morning, Saturday, October 3, Francis asked that the Passion according to Saint John be read to him. He was now very near his end, but neither his mind nor his spirits seemed to droop. He called two of his brothers to come closer to him, for his voice was now weakening. He asked them to sing for him once again the verses of his canticle, including the last in praise of Sister Death. We may be sure that as they sang, Francis tried with almost silent lips to join in the hymn, so that it may truly be said that Francis, who began his life singing and dancing in the streets of Assisi, the leader of earthly festivities, died literally singing with spiritual joy his release from all the beauty and all the sorrow of life on earth. His passage toward that eternal joy and eternal liberty, which he had in that deep, pure, untutored intuition of his, perhaps more deeply understood than any man born with the taint of Original Sin, was being made, not in conventional prayer, but with a hymn — that first poem in a common tongue which shapes into words and rhythm the love and praise of God in the words of the common man.

He had one more call to make — one more debt to pay. In life, he had promised that Clare would see him again and, as the next day, Sunday, dawned, with all solemnity, the brothers carried the open bier back to his native city, the skylarks singing above as they had sung at the hour of his death. But they stopped outside the convent of San Damiano so that Clare and her sisters from behind the grille could look for the last time at the transfigured mortal remains of Francis, who had reacquired in death that look of peace and beauty which seems even in the earthly body to proclaim eternal rest.

The little opening through which the sisters received Communion was unlocked and through it, Clare, the tears flooding down her face, cried out, "Father, father, what shall we do? Why do you desert us in our misery? Why do you leave us lost? Why did you not let us go before you in joy, rather than leave us here in sorrow? What can we do here, enclosed behind these bars, now that never more, as in former times, will you come to visit us? Now that you have gone, all our consolation goes, too, and buried to the world, we can have no further comfort. Who now will comfort us in such poverty, poverty both spiritual and temporal? O father of the poor, O lover of poverty, who will now help us in the hour of temptation, now that you, so wise and experienced in matters of the spirit, have gone? Who now will help the suffering in their suffering, now that you, our help in the sufferings that overcome us, have left us?"

Francis Dies with a Song in His Heart

The desolation of Clare and her sisters was not only shared by those who were present at the end, but by all the people of Assisi, worried though they still might be lest the Perugians might yet succeed in stealing the relic of the body of the holy man. But there were no untoward happenings.

The solemn funeral cortège proceeded on its way between the crowds of mourning citizens through the gate on the Foligno road and into the Piazza of Saint George.

So Francis, the knight of Christ and Lady Poverty, found for a time his earthly resting place in that church of chivalry, where, as a small boy, he had heard the legendary story of Saint George and the dragon, of Saint George, who had slain the dragon of worldly pretensions and ambitions in order to free the maiden who one summer evening had confused and dazzled the master of the revels by her beauty, simplicity, and purity — the maiden who would finally be revealed to him as the Lady Poverty.

Biographical Note
⚜

Michael de la Bedoyere
(1900-1973)

Michael de la Bedoyere was educated at the Jesuit Stonyhurst College and at Oxford University, where he received first-class honors in Modern Greats. After teaching philosophy at the University of Minnesota for a short time, he became the assistant editor of the *Dublin Review* and, in 1934, became the editor of *The Catholic Herald*, the London weekly whose modest circulation rose significantly under his editorship. Later, with his wife, Charlotte, he founded and launched the independent newsletter *Search*, which he published from 1962-1968. He became known as one of the foremost scholars and journalists of his time.

During his journalistic career, he wrote more than thirty books — many of them biographies of both religious and secular subjects, including Saint Francis de Sales (published by Sophia Institute Press in 1998 as *SaintMaker: The Remarkable Life of Francis de Sales, Shepherd of Kings and Commoners, Sinners and Saints*), Saint Catherine of Siena, Baron von Hügel, Lafayette, and Washington. Skillfully weaving together historical events, personal accounts, eyewitness testimony, and writings by and about his subjects, de la Bedoyere brings these religious and historical figures alive for today's readers. His popular biographies of the saints offer practical, real-life examples of how Catholics can be active as Catholics in all aspects of their lives — a matter of great importance to de la Bedoyere and in today's largely secular world.

❧

Sophia Institute Press®

Sophia Institute is a nonprofit institution that seeks to restore man's knowledge of eternal truth, including man's knowledge of his own nature, his relation to other persons, and his relation to God. Sophia Institute Press® serves this end in numerous ways: by publishing translations of foreign works to make them accessible for the first time to English-speaking readers; bringing out-of-print books back into print; and publishing important new books that fulfill the ideals of Sophia Institute. These books afford readers a rich source of the enduring wisdom of mankind.

Sophia Institute Press® makes these high-quality books available to the general public by using advanced technology and by soliciting donations to subsidize its general publishing costs. Your generosity can help Sophia Institute Press® to provide the public with editions of works containing the enduring wisdom of the ages. Please send your tax-deductible contribution to the address below. We also welcome your questions, comments, and suggestions.

For your free catalog, call:
Toll-free: 1-800-888-9344
or write:
Sophia Institute Press®
Box 5284, Manchester, NH 03108
www.sophiainstitute.com

Sophia Institute is a tax-exempt institution as defined by the Internal Revenue Code, Section 501(c)(3). Tax I.D. 22-2548708.